THE COMPLETE GUIDE TO INVESTING IN REAL ESTATE TAX LIENS & DEEDS

How to Earn High Rates of Return — Safely

By

Jamaine Burrell

THE COMPLETE GUIDE TO INVESTING IN REAL ESTATE TAX LIENS & DEEDS: How to Earn High Rates of Return – Safely

ISBN-13: 978-0-910627-73-3   ISBN-10: 0-910627-73-8

Library of Congress Cataloging-in-Publication Data

Burrell, Jamaine, 1958-
  The complete guide to investing in real estate tax liens & deeds : how to earn high rates of return-safely / Jamaine Burrell.
    p. cm.
  Includes index.
  ISBN-13: 978-0-910627-73-3 (alk. paper)
  ISBN-10: 0-910627-73-8
  1. Real estate investment--United States. 2. Real estate investment--Law and legislation--United States. 3. Tax liens--United States. I. Title.

  HD255.B875 2006
  332.63'24--dc22
                                        2006013806

                    10 9 8 7 6 5 4 3

EDITORS: Jackie Ness • jackie_ness@charter.net • C. L. Hogan • wordwerks@msn.com
ART DIRECTION, FRONT COVER & INTERIOR DESIGN: Lisa Peterson, Michael Meister • info@6sense.net
GLOSSARY COMPILED BY: Christina Mohammed

Printed in the United States

Contents

Chapter 4: Bidding on Tax Lien Certificates   53

Chapter 5: Income and Growth Potential   69

Chapter 6: Investing in Tax Lien Certificates   77

Chapter 7: Obtaining Investment Dollars   89

Chapter 8: Return on Investment Dollars   109

Foreword

According to the SANCO Business Group, less than 1 percent of the population knows about tax lien certificates and tax deeds. Why? Because local governments usually are not the best marketers. It isn't their specialty. If you've ever glanced at legal notices in the newspaper, you've probably noticed that they weren't too inviting.

Another reason that many investors do not know about tax sales is because many financial advisors don't offer them as a viable option! There's a common misconception that tax sale auctions are too complicated to understand or they are too risky. Like all things in life, always seek a second opinion.

The truth is, tax sale auctions are one of the best investment vehicles created by the government. Tax lien certificates have fixed returns as mandated by state statutes. They're also secured by real property. Plus, all sales are open to the public and regulated by the state; hence, your investment will not likely experience an Enron or WorldCom-like collapse.

After reading *The Complete Guide to Investing in Real Estate Tax Liens &*

Deeds, you'll have a comprehensive introduction to the world of tax sale auctions. You'll learn bidding strategies of real estate gurus and how to find auctions in your own area. You'll also learn how to avoid new investors' common pitfalls. Whether you've been investing in real estate for a while or this is your first time, you'll refer to this book for years as your guide to public tax sale auctions.

Happy Reading!
Don Sausa
Vice President, LandTrades.com
Author of *Investing Without Losing*

Dedication

My writing is dedicated to both my biological family and my street family. A special dedication is reserved for my single mother, who lost the battle with cancer, the many, many neighborhood youths of Baltimore City who were murdered before we were ever privileged to see their adult faces and those who had their adulthood abruptly shortened. R.I.P.

chapter one

What Is a Tax Lien Certificate?

When property owners fail to pay the required property tax assessed on real property, the property may be auctioned and sold at a real property tax sale, though real property is not always sold at tax sales. Some states engage in the sale of deeds to real property to recoup losses from delinquent property taxes. Other states engage in the sale of liens against real property to recoup the losses.

The purchase of a tax deed is significantly different from the purchase of a tax lien. States that engage in the sale of tax deeds are considered tax deed states. The winning bidder bids for immediate possession of deed and title to a property. A tax deed is issued or assigned in return for the payment of unpaid real property taxes as well as associated penalties, interest, and costs of the tax sale. States that engage in the sale of tax liens are considered tax lien states. The tax sale initiates a process or system by which an investor pays the delinquent tax on behalf of the property owner. The property owner is then given an opportunity to repay the investor or be forced to relinquish title and deed to the property in the future. A certificate that indicates payment of the tax lien is issued or assigned in return for the payment of unpaid real property taxes as well as associated penalties, interest, and costs of the tax sale.

Tax Deed States

In tax deed states, the winning bidder at a tax sale purchases ownership to a property, as specified by a tax deed. The bidder becomes the property owner upon payment of the delinquent tax amount and any other costs and fees assessed against the property. In some tax deed states, the previous property owner is given an opportunity to redeem the property from the newly established owner. The redemption period varies among the states, but generally ranges from six months to two years. These states are considered hybrid tax deed states. **Hybrid tax deed states** include ten states and the territory of Guam, as follows: (Ref. 5)

- Connecticut
- Delaware
- Georgia
- Guam
- Hawaii
- Louisiana
- Massachusetts
- Pennsylvania*
- Rhode Island
- Tennessee
- Texas

*Pennsylvania engages in a hybrid tax sale system for improved properties that are legally occupied at least 90 days prior to the tax sale. Otherwise, Pennsylvania does not provide an opportunity for the previous property owner to redeem the property from the new owner. In hybrid tax deed states, even though the sale of a tax deed transfers ownership to the tax deed purchaser, the purchaser has no right of possession to the property. Hybrid tax deed states allow property owners to retain all rights of possession.

Other tax deed states do not provide the previous property owner with an opportunity to redeem a property and regain ownership. Because property owners are not allowed an opportunity to redeem their properties, there is no redemption period or interest rates and penalties applied to redemption amounts. These states are considered to be **"pure" tax deed states** and are listed below. (Ref. 5)

- Alaska[2]
- Arkansas[2]
- California[1]
- Idaho
- Kansas
- Maine
- Michigan[2]
- Minnesota
- Nevada[2]
- New Hampshire[1]
- New Mexico
- New York[1]
- North Carolina
- Ohio[1]
- Oregon
- Virginia
- Washington
- Wisconsin[2]

[1]Some tax deed states have statutes that allow for the sale of tax certificates rather than or in addition to tax deeds. These states are considered to be tax deed states, because they are inconsistent in engaging in the sale of tax lien certificates across the entire state.

[2]Some tax deed states engage in peculiarities that should be noted.

- **California** is relatively new to tax sales and has never sold a tax lien certificate, even though state legislation includes statutes authorizing each of its 58 counties to do so.

- **New Hampshire** statutes are rarely exercised.

- **New York** statutes have been exercised only in certain cities and counties.

- **Ohio** statutes allow for the sale of tax liens in municipalities with populations greater than 200,000.

- **Alaska** offers tax deeds for sale only to the municipality in which the property is located. If the property owner fails to redeem the property from the municipality within one year, the municipality offers the property for sale, usually at the fair market value.

- **Arkansas** allows property owners to redeem their properties within 30 days of the tax sale.

- **Michigan** and **Wisconsin** offer properties for sale after they have been foreclosed by judgment.

- **Nevada** uses tax lien certificates to foreclose special assessments or improvements, such as repairs to sidewalks, curbs, gutters, and the like.

Tax Lien States

In tax lien states, no deed or title transfers are executed as a direct result of a tax sale. The winning bidder purchases a tax lien certificate, and a parcel of property is used to secure the lien. The delinquent property owner retains ownership of the property and is allowed an opportunity to redeem the tax lien held against the property. Some states consistently rely upon the sale of tax lien certificates to recoup losses due to delinquent property taxes. These states are considered to be **"pure"** tax lien

states. Twenty-two states are pure tax lien states as well as the District of Columbia and the commonwealth of Puerto Rico, as follows: (Ref. 8)

- Alabama
- Arizona
- Colorado
- District of Columbia
- Florida
- Illinois
- Indiana
- Iowa
- Kentucky
- Maryland
- Michigan
- Mississippi
- Missouri
- Montana
- Nebraska
- New Jersey
- North Dakota
- Oklahoma
- Puerto Rico
- South Carolina
- South Dakota
- Vermont
- West Virginia
- Wyoming

Different tax lien states have differing systems for recouping delinquent real estate tax. Florida is a tax lien state, but the established tax sale system does not allow a tax lien holder to foreclose the property owner's right of redemption. The sale of tax lien certificates is strictly an offer to investors to collect interest on the cost of a tax lien certificate in return for paying the delinquent property tax. If the property owner fails to redeem a tax lien certificate during the redemption period, the deed to the property is offered for sale at a second auction. During this phase of the Florida tax sale system, Florida converts to a tax deed state.

Tax Lien Certificates

A **tax lien certificate** is a real estate document that serves as evidence of indebtedness against a parcel of real estate. When tax lien certificates are sold, the parcel of real estate serves as collateral to secure the purchase of the tax lien certificate. Tax lien certificates are sold by tax lien states and in specific jurisdictions of some tax deed states. Different states refer to the document by various names that include the following:

- Tax Lien Certificate
- Certificate of Purchase

- Tax Sale Certificate
- Certificate of Purchase

- Tax Sale Receipt
- Certificate of Sale

- Tax Lien
- Certificate of Delinquency

- Tax Claim
- Receipt Showing the Amount Paid

- Tax Certificate
- Receipt for the Purchase Money

Form 1 (see page 22) shows a sample of a tax lien certificate purchased in Iowa during a 2001 tax sale. In Iowa, a tax lien certificate is issued as a certificate of purchase.

When an individual purchases a tax lien certificate, that individual is, in effect, making a loan to the property owner for the payment of delinquent property taxes. The tax lien certificate indicates the particular individual making the loan and assigns the specified property as security against the loan. The particular parcel of property may serve as collateral in part or as a whole. The property owner must repay the loan in an amount equal to the delinquent tax and associated penalties, interest, and costs of the sale to maintain ownership of the property. As long as a tax lien is outstanding, the property owner may not borrow against the property; nor may the property owner trade, sell, or otherwise dispose of the property. If the property owner fails to repay the loan within a predetermined period of time, the tax lien certificate holder is entitled to foreclose the property owner's right to redeem the property or the property owner's right to redeem the portion of the property held and assigned as collateral. Foreclosure permits the transfer of title to the deed from the property owner to either the tax lien certificate holder or both the lien holder and property owner. When a tax lien certificate is secured by less than 100 percent of the real property, foreclosure transfers the title of the property to both the lien certificate holder and property owner as **tenants-in-common**.

CERTIFICATE OF PURCHASE AT TAX SALE NUMBER 01-1772
TREASURER'S OFFICE, SHELBY COUNTY, STATE OF IOWA

I,   , TREASURER, DO HEREBY CERTIFY THAT ON THE 18 DAY
OF JUNE,   2001, AT THE REGULAR   TAX SALE PUBLICLY HELD ON THAT DATE,
THE FOLLOWING PROPERTY SITUATED IN SHELBY COUNTY WAS SOLD TO:

FOR THE AMOUNT OF TAXES, INTEREST AND COSTS DUE AND REMAINING UNPAID.

DIST SH-CP   TAXED TO:
ASSHC PARCEL 832916000003

LEGAL DESCRIPTION: 33-78-40   PT NW SW

YEAR TYPE RECEIPT	AMOUNT	INTEREST	COSTS	TOTAL
1999 RE 90998.0	838.00	76.00	4.00	918.00
		SUBTOTAL		918.00
		CERTIFICATE FEE		10.00
		GRAND TOTAL		928.00

****
THIS BID WAS FOR A 100% INTEREST IN THE PROPERTY.
****

WITNESS MY HAND:
DATE JUNE 18, 2001
                        TREASURER OF SHELBY COUNTY,

****
ASSIGNMENT: FOR THE PAYMENT OF $_____, AS PER AGREEMENT, I HEREBY
ASSIGN ALL RIGHTS, TITLE, AND INTEREST IN THIS CERTIFICATE TO:
_____ SS _____
DATE _____
01-1772   ASSIGNOR

Form 1: Sample Tax Lien Certificate (5, p. 15)

The sale of tax lien certificates benefits the taxing municipality, the property owner, and the purchaser. The taxing municipality benefits from the sale process by collecting the delinquent tax amount needed to fund government services. The timeliness of payments from investors not only allows the government to fund services, but also allows the government to provide uninterrupted services to the taxpaying community. The property owner who is delinquent in paying taxes benefits from the tax sale process because he or she is given an extended opportunity to pay delinquent property taxes. However, the inclusion of penalties, interest, and costs increases the amount that must be repaid to the lien certificate holder. The investor benefits by receiving, in most cases, either a high return on investment dollars used to acquire the tax lien certificate or ownership of the property if the loan is not repaid. The return on investment dollars is realized from the interest, penalty, or both that is required for redemption of the tax lien certificate.

Ownership is realized once the investor engages in specific procedures to foreclose the right of redemption and obtain the deed and right of possession to the property.

Different states have different methods of enforcing the laws pertaining to delinquent real estate taxes and tax lien certificates. State laws dictate the particular processes for conducting the annual tax sale. State laws, for example, may allow for the tax sale to take place at any given time, on a specific date, or within some specified period of time. The particular city or county treasurer is responsible for determining where and when the tax sale is held, though the treasurer may allow an outside entity to host the sale on his or her behalf.

Tax Lien Certificate Costs

Most states are governed by statute that dictates the process for delinquent property tax sales, the assignment of tax lien certificates, the redemption of tax lien certificates, and the foreclosure process. In states that do not have statutes governing the annual tax sale, a reputable governing body is responsible for defining the process and entities responsible for the sale. The treasurer of each municipality usually makes a determination of the cost to be applied to tax lien certificates. The cost may include any of the following:

- Delinquent property tax amount

- Other delinquent fees assessed against the securing real property

- Penalties

- Interest

- Administrative fees

- Cost of the tax sale

- Cost of issuing the tax certificate

The delinquent property tax amount is always included in the cost of a tax lien certificate. Other delinquent fees may include unpaid costs assessed for water and services provided by the governing body. Either state statute or a governing body of the particular jurisdiction establishes penalties, interest, administrative fees, and the cost of auctioning tax lien certificates at the tax sale. Each municipality's determination of the combination of costs is the advertised opening bid amount offered when tax lien certificates are auctioned at the delinquent property tax sale. The opening bid amount usually represents the minimum amount that must be bid.

Right of Redemption

The sale of a tax lien certificate does not indicate a transfer of ownership to the tax lien certificate holder; nor does it allow the certificate holder any right of possession to the property that secures the tax lien certificate. States allow property owners to hold title to their property during the redemption period. This is inclusive of the property owner, mortgage lenders, and other lenders that may hold a deed of trust against the property. The delinquent property owner owns the property and has all rights of possession to the property until the lien certificate holder is able to foreclose the property owner's right of redemption. Even then, the owner may still hold partial ownership if the tax lien certificate was purchased by competitively bidding down ownership in the property.

Anyone can pay the redemption amount on behalf of the property owner, but only the bidder at the tax sale or the over-the-counter purchaser is able to purchase a tax lien certificate. The tax lien certificate holder, however, may assign his or her interest in the tax lien certificate to another party by entering into a contractual agreement with the other party or assignee. Contractual assignments are common among institutional investors that send hired representatives to tax sales. A representative bids on behalf of the company, using his or her own identity and transfers interest in any lien certificates acquired to his or her employer. The assignment is recorded with the taxing authority, and upon redemption, the last recorded assignee is paid the redemption amount.

The treasurer or tax collector is responsible for handling the redemption of tax lien certificates. He or she collects the redemption amounts and notifies the last assigned and recorded certificate holder of the redemption. Upon receipt of such notice, the tax lien certificate holder is required to return the tax lien certificate to the treasurer or tax collector. The treasurer or tax collector is then responsible for paying the redemption proceeds to the party to which the certificate is assigned.

Redemption Period

The delinquent property owner has a responsibility to redeem the tax lien certificate from the tax lien certificate holder by paying the delinquent tax assessed against the property plus interest, penalties, fees, and costs of the sale within a specified period of time. This period of time is known as the redemption period, and it may range from 60 days to 4 years, depending upon the particular state's statutes. The start of the redemption period is usually established as the day of the tax sale and may be applicable to tax lien certificates sold over-the-counter or auctioned at a later date.

Interest and penalties may be applied to the redemption amount. Annual interest rates generally range between 6 percent and 24 percent of the tax lien plus associated costs, as established by state statute or a governing body. Penalty amounts are also established by state statute or a governing body and are usually set at a fixed percentage of the tax lien amount. Estimates indicate that property owners will redeem between 95 percent and 98 percent of all tax lien certificates offered for sale during the redemption period.

No Right of Redemption

In all states except Florida and Kentucky, if no one redeems a tax certificate within the specified redemption period, the certificate holder may follow prescribed procedures to foreclose the right of redemption and obtain title to the deed and right of possession to the property. Both Florida and Kentucky have processes in place to prevent a transfer of deed due solely to delinquent property taxes.

Florida state laws prohibit individuals from taking deed to property as a result of delinquent property taxes by including an additional step in the tax sale process. When a tax certificate is not redeemed during the redemption period, the property is auctioned again at a public oral bid foreclosure auction. The sale of tax lien certificates is really an offer to investors to profit from the redemption amount in return for paying delinquent taxes that are needed to fund government services. With this particular type of auction, the actual real estate is sold to the highest bidder, who may or may not be the tax lien certificate holder.

In Kentucky, if a tax lien certificate is not redeemed within one year of the tax sale, the tax lien holder is required to take legal action against the property owner for the amount paid to secure the tax lien certificate, the right to foreclose the right of redemption, or both. If the tax lien holder seeks to foreclose the right of redemption, the property must first be appraised and offered for sale at a public oral bid foreclosure auction. If there is no purchaser at the auction, the state commissioner may make deed to the tax certificate holder. If the tax lien certificate specifies a percentage of ownership, the winning bidder is deeded the applicable percentage of the tenancy-in-common. Kentucky laws further stipulate the following:

- If the foreclosure auction does not result in proceeds equal to two-thirds of the appraised value of the property, the property owner is given an additional year to redeem the property at the original purchase price of the tax lien certificate plus 10 percent of that purchase price.

- During the new redemption period, the property owner receives a writ of possession and a deed with a lien in favor of the owner.

- Upon paying the newly established redemption amount to the court that ordered the judgment, the state commissioner may make deed to the property owner.

chapter two

The Annual Tax Sale

Most tax deed states hold periodic delinquent property tax sales. Depending upon the taxing jurisdiction of the state, sales may be held as often as weekly, or the range of sales may extend to monthly, quarterly, or biannually. Most tax lien states, on the other hand, hold annual property tax sales. The annual sale is a process of auctioning available tax lien certificates to the public. In order to participate and bid on properties offered for auction, individuals must register and obtain a bidder number and bidder card. Auctions are held throughout a time frame predetermined and set by the taxing authority to complete the offering of tax lien certificates. Some smaller jurisdictions are capable of completing the tax sale in a single day. Larger jurisdictions usually set aside a period of days for the annual tax sale.

Tax Sale Listings

A listing of properties with delinquent property taxes precedes the annual tax sale. Most municipalities publish the listing in a local newspaper weeks before the tax sale takes place.

Municipalities that do not have a local newspaper may publish the listing in some other form of print media, or they may be required to post it at some public location. In recent years, some municipalities have published tax sale listings on the Internet. The city or county treasurer is usually responsible for the tax sale and serves as the primary point of contact for information regarding the publication of a municipality's tax sale listing. Newspaper listings are most likely to be published in the legal section of the newspaper, along with other public and legal notices. Most listings include a parcel number, a legal description, and the amount of delinquent taxes. The listing may also contain the name and address of the property owner. Some advertised properties might also have designations that indicate specific characteristics of the property. Some tax assessors have Web sites that may provide the investor with general characteristics of a property, such as zoning information, square footage, the year in which structures were built, and the property's appraised value. Investors should understand that an assessor's appraised valuation is not necessarily the same as the property's market value.

Registration

Bidders are required to register before participating in an annual tax sale auction. Registration involves requiring participants to provide their Social Security or tax identification number (TIN), together with other identifying information, to the taxing municipality. Different municipalities have differing rules and procedures with respect to registration, but most require a Social Security number or TIN. States may require bidders to complete Internal Revenue Service (IRS) Form W-9, "Request for Taxpayer Identification Number and Certification." The identifying

Social Security number or TIN is necessary so the municipality can meet its legal obligation to report interest received from redemptions to the IRS. Interest received from the redemption of a tax lien certificate is income to a certificate holder. Registrants may also be required to pay a registration fee before bidding, or they may be required to make a minimum deposit. When a deposit is required, it is applied to the total dollar amount of lien certificates purchased by a particular bidder. If a bidder does not purchase any tax lien certificates, the deposit is refunded to him or her. Some taxing authorities require participants to register for the tax sale as much as a month in advance of the auction. Others allow participants to register in advance of the sale or on the day of auction. While a tax sale may be held at a town hall or convention center, it is usually situated so that the actual auction is held in a different area than the registration. Registered bidders are assigned a bidder number and given a bidder card to be used at the auction, which is usually an oral bid-type auction in which bidders must orally convey their bid amounts to the auctioneer.

Some municipalities allow bidders to acquire multiple bidder numbers and bid for multiple tax lien certificates. In Los Angeles, for example, the registration process allows an individual to register on behalf of another person as long as a notarized copy of the power of attorney, as granted to the bidder, is provided along with a valid photo ID. A sample of the bidder registration form used in Los Angeles is shown in Form 2 (see page 32). Los Angeles also allows individuals to register on behalf of a company, corporation, public agency, or partnership as long as notarized copies of the documents granting the bidder authority to register and bid on behalf of the particular entity are provided along with a valid photo ID. Such documentation may include a power of attorney, a resolution showing the corporate seal, a partnership agreement, or corporate minutes showing the corporate seal. The form of a document used to authorize an individual to act on behalf of another entity is shown in Form 3 (see page 33). Bidders must be clear in indicating the manner in which they are bidding on behalf of another entity. Should a property owner fail to redeem a tax lien certificate, the deed conveying title to the property will be vested in the same manner as the registration was vested to purchase the certificate.

Los Angeles County
TREASURER AND TAX COLLECTOR

BIDDER REGISTRATION FORM

Attention Bidders: Persons wishing to bid at the tax sale must pre-register **in-person**. A deposit of $1,000 in the form of a Cashier's Check or bank issued Money Order payable to the Los Angeles County Tax Collector is required at the time of registration. A Bidder Registration Form must be completed and submitted in-person with your deposit. Valid picture identification (driver's license, military identification or state identification card) is required for all registering parties. If you register or request vesting for someone else, you must provide a notarized copy of the power of attorney for each person you represent, along with your valid picture identification. If you register or request vesting for a public agency, company, corporation, or partnership, you will need to provide <u>notarized copies</u> of the document that gives you the authority to register and bid on their behalf, along with your valid picture identification.

BIDDER'S NAME: _____
signature(s) required below   REQUIRED FIELD (PLEASE PRINT CLEARLY)

8:00 AM TO 5:00 PM PHONE NUMBER (___)_____
                                    REQUIRED FIELD

VESTING NAME: _____
signature(s) required below

ADDRESS: _____
_____
                CITY   STATE   ZIP

PLEASE SHOW HOW TITLE IS TO BE VESTED

____ HUSBAND AND WIFE AS JOINT TENANTS (REQUIRES BOTH SIGNATURES)	____ A SINGLE MAN
____ AS TENANTS IN COMMON (REQUIRES SIGNATURES OF ALL PARTIES)	____ A SINGLE WOMAN
____ A MARRIED MAN AS HIS SOLE & SEPARATE PROPERTY	____ AN UNMARRIED MAN
____ A MARRIED WOMAN AS HER SOLE & SEPARATE PROPERTY	____ AN UNMARRIED WOMAN
____ A MARRIED MAN	____ A CORPORATION (REQUIRES ARTICLES OF INCORPORATION AND ORDER BY AUTHORIZED MEMBER OF THE BOARD OF DIRECTORS GIVING YOU AUTHORITY TO BID & VEST PROPERTY.)
____ A MARRIED WOMAN	
____ A WIDOWER (MAN)	____ A PUBLIC AGENCY (REQUIRES CERTIFIED ORDER FROM THE GOVERNING BOARD GIVING YOU AUTHORITY TO BID & VEST PROPERTY)
____ A WIDOW (WOMAN)	
____ OTHER	

BIDDER'S SIGNATURE _____

OTHER SIGNATURES _____

DATE _____

PLEASE NOTE THAT THE PURCHASE OF TAX-DEFAULTED PROPERTY MADE IS AT YOUR OWN RISK. VESTING INFORMATION CANNOT BE CHANGED AFTER THE REGISTRATION PERIOD HAS CLOSED.

Form 2: Bidder Registration Form (5, p. 186)

To: Treasurer Name
Jurisdiction County Treasurer
123 Municipal Avenue
Anytown, USA 123456

AUTHORIZATION TO REPRESENT BIDDER

I / we, (please print) _____

(Bidder's name, as it appears on the registration form)

authorize (please print) _____

to act as my / our personal representative at the Harrison County Tax Sale held on _____

_____

(Signature)

_____

(Address)

_____

(City, State, Zip Code)

Subscribed and sworn before me this _____ day of _____, 20___.

_____

(Signature of Notary)

Form 3: Authorization to Represent Bidder

Meeting the Schedule

Municipalities have established times and schedules for completing the tax sale process and are either mandated or courteous in publishing the schedule to be followed for the tax sale as well as the listing of properties with delinquent taxes. However, tax sale auctioneers and officials have a tendency to fall behind schedule, particularly in those municipalities that engage in competitive bidding and those that are mandated to sell their tax lien certificates during the tax sale. When the auctioning gets behind schedule, modifications to the schedule are either announced during the tax sale or distributed to the participants, but not formally published in the newspaper. Likewise, new listings may be generated, but not formally published and distributed to the public. The published tax sale schedule usually allows for breaks to enable bidders and officials ample time to handle administrative and other issues during the tax sale process. However, tax sale officials often rotate auctioneers to keep the process flowing during breaks or extend the tax sale day beyond the published and advertised hours to meet their schedule. Thus, tax sales may continue throughout the day with no breaks, or the sales may extend until 7 or 8 p.m. — well beyond the published and documented end of the tax sale day.

The sale may also continue until all available and scheduled certificates are offered for sale. In many instances, tax sale officials may switch the bidding system being used in an attempt to meet their schedules. Florida, for example, allows competitive bidding on the percentage of interest to be paid upon redemption. When they are behind schedule, however, officials have been known to resort to random methods of choosing winning bidders. This switch in bidding systems usually occurs at or near the end of the tax sale day and on the final day of the tax sale. When this happens, the auctioneers and tax sale officials have some indication as to whether they will be capable of meeting the goal of offering a certain number of tax liens for sale. If they perceive that the day's "quota" cannot be met using established procedures, they may, without notice, switch to a quicker method of bidding.

Keeping Pace

Auctioneers, like bidders, are human and must deal with the fast, repetitive process inherent in oral bid auctions. Most auctions follow some sort of tempo, but generally auctions move at a fast pace, particularly when the auctioneers have several hundred or several thousand tax lien certificates to sell within a matter of days. As with most auctions, once a property is introduced and an opening bid is announced, bidders must be prepared to offer their bids because, in most instances, a pause in the bidding ends the bidding for a particular tax lien certificate. Once a winner has been announced, the auctioneer will not go back.

Bidders must be both patient and alert to avoid becoming distracted. A distracted bidder may not realize that the bidding for a particular property has ended. He or she then jumps back into the process, but ends up bidding on the wrong property. In some states, if a bidder realizes his or her mistake and makes the auctioneer or official aware of it before the bidding ends for the day, he or she may be relieved of the obligation to pay for the tax lien certificate. In most instances, however, bids are final. They may not be exchanged or refunded. In some states, failure to pay the bid amount and associated fees can lead to a penalty, imprisonment, or both. The county of Marion, Indiana, for example, stipulates that bidders who fail to pay the bid price in acceptable funds will be charged a penalty equal to 25 percent of the bid amount and may be subject to prosecution. The city of Los Angeles stipulates that all sales are final and that payment must be made immediately upon winning the bid. Bidders and any co-registered bidders who fail to pay the bid amount on bids less than $5,000 simply have their bidder cards confiscated and voided and forfeit their right to further participate in the sale. Bids over $5,000 require a minimum deposit equal to the greater of $5,000 or 10 percent of the bid amount. The balance must be paid within 30 days of the tax sale day. If the balance of the bid is not paid within the 30-day time frame, the bidder forfeits his or her total deposit.

Restrictions on Bids

States may impose restrictions on the number of bids that a
bidder can make at auction by requiring one or more of the
following:

1. A deposit for each bid opportunity.

2. A different Social Security number or tax identification
    number for each bidder number.

3. One bid per bidder number.

The most restrictive auctions implement all three. Only
investors who are capable of bringing associates to the auction
may overcome such restrictions, and even then, he or she would
need to have an associate for each bid to acquire multiple tax
lien certificates. As an alternative, the investor and his or her
associates may register and bid at auction, leave the auction
area, and reregister to bid with a different bidder number. This
process would continue until all lien certificates of interest
had been bid. This is particularly useful for investors who are
restricted by a municipality that insists on one bid per bidder
number. Even when a municipality requires a different Social
Security or tax identification number for each bidder number,
an investor can use his or her own Social Security number to
represent himself or herself, a tax identification number to
represent a corporate interest, and the Social Security numbers
of children, relatives, or associates to overcome such restrictions.
The acquired tax lien certificates may then be assigned to the
investor for a nominal charge.

Opportunities to Invest

One of the disadvantages of tax sales for investors is that most are held annually. In addition, many states hold their annual tax sales on the same day, making it impossible for investors to be present at multiple auctions. This limits the number of opportunities that investors have to invest in tax lien certificates. Investors are able to maximize their investment dollars if they can reinvest funds received from redemption amounts in new tax liens. But, since most tax sales are only offered annually, the opportunity to reinvest in a particular municipality's lien certificates is lost unless that municipality offers over-the-counter sales of unsold lien certificates. In municipalities that offer attractive interest rates, it is highly unlikely that any such tax lien certificates will be available for offer after the tax sale has ended.

Public Oral Bid

Most states still engage in the traditional method of offering tax lien certificates at auction using a public oral bid system. This type of system requires that bidders be present at the sale during the time in which properties of interest are offered. Tax lien certificates are usually offered in the order in which they are publicized in the tax sale listing. Listings may be ordered by block and lot number, street address, or some other classification established by the treasurer of the municipality. If an investor is interested in multiple properties located in different areas of the municipality, the properties of interest are likely to be distributed throughout the tax sale listing. In larger municipalities, the investor may have to attend the tax sale for multiple days in order to bid personally on properties of interest. Larger municipalities may have so many tax lien certificates for sale that their auctions may take days to complete. In smaller municipalities, the tax sale may be completed within hours or within a day. Adequate research will uncover the smaller municipalities with fewer lien certificates for sale. The very organized and mobile investor may be capable of attending multiple auctions in a single state during the state's auctioning period. In all public oral bid auctions, the investor is limited to the choice of lien certificates available during his or her attendance.

Over-the-Counter Sales

In most states, when tax lien certificates are not sold at the annual tax sale, those certificates are offered for sale over-the-counter after the tax sale. When tax lien certificates are offered over-the-counter, there are no competitive bidders to bid against one another. Tax lien certificates are purchased for the minimum amount, which includes the delinquent tax amount and incurred penalties, interest, and costs. There is no premium amount added to the cost of tax lien certificates. The interest and penalty rates to be applied to redemption amounts are usually the same as those applied to tax lien certificates sold at the annual tax sale for all states except those states that engage in the competitive bidding down of interest rates. Since there is no competitive bidding, the interest and penalty rates applied to redemption amounts are set at the maximum rates established by state statute or the maximum rate established by the governing body of the municipality. Some municipalities even allow investors to purchase over-the-counter lien certificates through the mail, eliminating the need for investors to be physically present for the sale. This creates additional opportunities for an investor to invest in tax lien certificates and also reduces an investor's traveling expenses.

In some municipalities, the demand for over-the-counter certificates is more intense than the demand for lien certificates offered for sale at the annual tax sale. In the tax deed state of Michigan, for example, a tax lien certificate is assigned to the winning bidder at auction. The property owner is given one year to redeem the tax lien certificate, or the lien certificate holder may surrender the certificate for a tax deed. The interest rate for tax lien certificates is 15 percent annually and increases to 50 percent annually in the second year of delinquency. The bidding system used at tax sales provides for bidders to bid down the percentage of ownership in a property. The investor becomes a tenant-in-common with the property owner if no redemption takes place. If, however, lien certificates are offered over-the-counter after the tax sale, the investor is entitled to purchase the certificates without bidding down ownership. Should the property owner fail to redeem the certificate, the investor may foreclose the right of redemption and follow procedures to gain 100 percent ownership of the property. Even more attractive to investors are over-the-counter certificates secured by properties that are in the second year of delinquency, when the interest rate applied to redemption amounts is maximized to 50 percent.

Online Auctions

As an alternative to traditional oral bid auctions that require bidders to be physically present, some municipalities are engaging in online Internet auctions. This type of auction is relatively new, and the investor must rely upon his or her ability to research the systems used in municipalities of interest to understand the system. Florida, for example, has implemented online auctioning for many of its larger jurisdictions.

Orange County, (Orlando) is one of the larger municipalities in Florida where the traditional oral bid auction has been replaced by an online system. The online system is now used to handle the bid down auctioning system used by Orange County. The process is as follows: (Ref. 5)

1. Bidders register online at the specified Web site.

2. Advance payment of $1,000 per bidder number is paid to Orange County.

3. Registrants search tax liens that are published with the particular lien amount and parcel identification number.

4. Bidders enter a bid percentage for a desired property.

5. At the specified time during the auction, a computer algorithm chooses the winning bid and bidder.

6. In a tie, the computer algorithm makes a random pick of the winner.

Online auctions promise to increase the efficiency of auctioning systems. Investors accustomed to the interaction of traditional oral bid auctions will have to adjust to the convenience of bidding online rather than traveling to various locations to participate in the auction process. The Internet also promises to provide more efficiency and accuracy in listing properties for sale and eliminating properties from the listing when redemption occurs soon before the tax sale.

Payment

Each taxing municipality establishes and publishes rules and guidelines to be followed during the auction process. When tax lien certificates are purchased, payment is made to the taxing jurisdiction responsible for the tax sale. The rules and guidelines dictate how payments for the certificates are to be made to the particular taxing municipality.

Most tax collectors request that payments be made with certified funds during the tax sale auction. Some municipalities require that deposits be made with certified funds, prior to the tax sale auction. All municipalities require either full or partial payment for tax lien certificate amounts on the day on which they are auctioned. Some municipalities may accept personal checks, and most will accept cash payments. However, investors, particularly those who bid on multiple properties, are not always capable of determining the amount that will be needed to secure the tax lien certificates purchased at a particular tax sale. Investors may attend the tax sale with a select list of potential lien certificates to purchase, but during the bidding process, the desired certificates may be awarded to someone else. Investors may also invest in more or fewer lien certificates than anticipated, depending upon the bidding competition. Under such circumstances, the amount that the investor had anticipated spending changes. Municipalities often provide investors with some time frame for obtaining the necessary funds to cover the cost of purchases required at the tax sale. This may range from a couple of hours to one day or some other time frame established by the taxing authority.

Indiana, for example, does not require investors to make a deposit to register for the tax sale. The jurisdictions of Indianapolis require that the full amount of a tax lien certificate be paid upon winning the bid. Investors have been known to make a large deposit to a municipality to cover the anticipated costs of bidding during the auction. Form 4 shows a receipt provided to a bidder in return for the deposit of funds to be used during the bidding process. Any unused balance is refunded to the bidder once an accounting of all bids is made. Likewise, Iowa does not require bidders to make a deposit for registration. However, some jurisdictions are allowed to charge a fee in the range of $75 to $100 for bidder cards. Payment for tax lien certificate purchases is then required in certified funds by the end of the day of auction.

TREASURER OF MARION COUNTY, INDIANA
RECEIPT TO BIDDER FOR FUNDS DEPOSITED WITH TREASURER FOR USE
AS AN OPEN ACCOUNT FOR PURCHASE OF TAX SALE PROPERTY

BIDDER NO. _189_

BIDDER NAME: _The Loftis Companies_

TAX ID #: _____ PHONE: _____ CONTACT: _____

ADDRESS: _____

CITY: _____ STATE: _____ ZIP: _____

THE TREASURER ACKNOWLEDGES RECEIPT FOR DEPOSIT TO BIDDER
ACCOUNT FOR PURCHASES DURING TAX SALE FOR THIS AMOUNT . ➔ $2,000⁰⁰

[ ] CURRENCY
[ ] CERTIFIED CHECK
RECEIVED BY MARION   [X] CASHIER'S CHECK
COUNTY TREASURER _B.A____ DATE: 8/6/01 [ ] EFT

PLEASE NOTE: ALL REFUNDS FROM YOUR BIDDER DEPOSIT ACCOUNT FOR MONEY NOT
                USED DURING AUCTION WILL BE MADE BY COUNTY TREASURER CHECK.

White - Bidder/Agent
Yellow - Accounting
Pink - Bidder Envelope

MCT-711 7/01

Form 4: Receipt for Bidding Deposit (5, p. 201)

In Washington, D.C., bidders must make a minimum deposit of 10 percent of the tax lien certificates purchased. If an investor attempts to purchase tax lien certificates in an amount for which the deposit does not account for 10 percent of the purchase amount, he or she is required to make an additional deposit before continuing with the purchase of lien certificates. The full amount for all bids is required by the end of the tax sale day.

Some large jurisdictions in Florida require a $1,000 deposit. Some jurisdictions invoice the bidder for the balance of lien certificates purchased and provide the bidder with a two-week period to make payment in full. Other jurisdictions require full payment for all lien certificates purchased within one to two days. Some jurisdictions, particularly the smaller jurisdictions, may allow the bidder to pay using a personal check.

Obtaining Deed

When a property owner fails to redeem a tax lien certificate, an investor may foreclose the property owner's right of redemption. However, the investor must follow very specific procedures to obtain the deed before engaging in the process of foreclosure on the property. Some states issue the investor what is termed a grant deed. Other states issue a warranty deed, and some states issue both. A grant deed uses the term grant in the language of the deed. A grant deed transfers title from the property owner to the investor with two implied warranties. The first warranty implies that the property owner has not previously transferred title to another party. The second warranty implies that the title is free from encumbrances. A grant deed also transfers any title acquired by the property owner subsequent to delivery of the grant deed. A warranty deed transfers title from the property owner to the investor. A warranty deed differs from a grant in that a warranty deed guarantees the title to be in the condition specified and documented in the warranty deed. The property owner agrees to protect the investor from all claims to the property. All tax lien states and tax deed states, with the exception of the commonwealth of Puerto Rico and the territory of Guam, issue a grant deed, a warranty deed, or both. Puerto Rico and Guam issue special deeds peculiar to their tax sale system. The language of the deed used in Puerto Rico is likely to be written in Spanish. Table 1 shows the types of deeds that are used in each state:

Table 1

TYPES OF TAX DEEDS LISTED BY STATE		
State	**Classification**	**Type of Deed**
Alabama	Tax Lien	Warranty Deed
Alaska	Tax Deed	Warranty Deed
Arizona	Tax Lien	Grant Deed
California	Tax Deed	Grant Deed
Colorado	Tax Lien	Warranty Deed
Connecticut	Hybrid Tax Deed	Warranty Deed
Delaware	Hybrid Tax Deed	Grant Deed
District of Columbia	Tax Lien	Grant Deed
Florida	Tax Lien	Warranty Deed
Georgia	Hybrid Tax Deed	Warranty Deed
Guam	Hybrid Tax Deed	Special Deed
Hawaii	Hybrid Tax Deed	Warranty Deed
Idaho	Tax Deed	Warranty Deed
Illinois	Tax Lien	Grant Deed, Warranty Deed
Indiana	Tax Lien	Warranty Deed
Iowa	Tax Lien	Warranty Deed
Kansas	Tax Deed	Warranty Deed
Kentucky	Tax Lien	Warranty Deed
Louisiana	Hybrid Tax Deed	Warranty Deed
Maine	Tax Deed	Warranty Deed
Maryland	Tax Lien	Warranty Deed
Massachusetts	Hybrid Tax Deed	Warranty Deed
Michigan	Tax Deed	Warranty Deed
Minnesota	Tax Deed	Warranty Deed
Mississippi	Tax Lien	Warranty Deed
Missouri	Tax Lien	Warranty Deed

TYPES OF TAX DEEDS LISTED BY STATE		
State	**Classification**	**Type of Deed**
Montana	Tax Lien	Grant Deed
Nebraska	Tax Lien	Warranty Deed
Nevada	Tax Deed	Grant Deed
New Hampshire		
New Jersey	Tax Lien	Grant Deed, Warranty Deed
New Mexico	Tax Deed	Warranty Deed
New York	Tax Deed	Grant Deed
North Carolina	Tax Deed	Warranty Deed
North Dakota	Tax Lien	Grant Deed, Warranty Deed
Ohio	Tax Deed	Warranty Deed
Oklahoma	Tax Lien	Grant Deed, Warranty Deed
Oregon	Tax Lien	Grant Deed
Pennsylvania	Hybrid Tax Deed	Grant Deed
Puerto Rico	Tax Lien	Grant Deed, Warranty Deed
South Dakota	Tax Lien	Warranty Deed
Tennessee	Hybrid Tax Deed	Warranty Deed
Texas	Hybrid Tax Deed	Grant Deed
Utah	Tax Deed	Warranty Deed
Vermont	Tax Lien	Warranty Deed
Washington	Tax Deed	Warranty Deed
West Virginia	Tax Lien	Grant Deed
Wisconsin	Tax lien	Warranty Deed
Wyoming	Tax Lien	Warranty Deed

chapter three

Delinquent Properties

Each state requires real property owners to pay
real property taxes for each parcel of improved or
unimproved property owned. Property taxes are ad
valorem taxes, which means that the tax is based on the value
of the property. Each state and each municipality within the
state has its own method of calculating the value of property
and the associated tax amount required from its taxpayers.
Real property taxes are assessed against residential homes,
rental homes, vacant lots, commercial properties, and industrial
properties. The state and taxing municipalities that provide
services and functionality to the various jurisdictions use these
taxes to maintain and provide services to the community. Real
property taxes are assessed by the governing municipality and
billed to the property owner for payment. Payment is required
within a specified time frame each year. When real property
taxes are not paid within the specified time frame, the tax on the
property becomes delinquent. Delinquent property taxes create
a shortfall for the governing municipality, interrupting its ability
to provide needed and vital services. To encourage property
owners to pay the necessary property taxes, municipalities

assess penalties, interest, and costs against the delinquent property when the tax is not paid on time. Furthermore, governing bodies may offer the property or a lien against the property for sale at the particular municipality's real property tax sale.

Single-Family Housing Units

Single-family units continue to make up the largest percentage of properties with tax lien certificates offered for sale. Single-family housing units provide living space for a single-family. These properties offer profit potential when the assessed property taxes become delinquent, because individuals are likely to redeem the tax lien held against a property that they own. Single-family homes that are also owner-occupied offer the greatest chance of being redeemed by the owner-occupants. Homeowners are not likely to allow the loss of their investment and living space for the relatively small cost of property taxes. When a single-family unit is also a rental unit, the property is used to generate income for the property owner. To continue receiving income from the property, the property owner is likely to redeem the tax lien certificate. Since the delinquent tax amount represents the tax for a single property, the property tax lien is often more affordable than tax liens for multiple family units. Property owners are not only likely to redeem such small debts against the property, but they are also more likely to redeem the tax lien quickly.

Multiple-Family Housing Units

Companies, as opposed to individuals, usually own multiple-family housing units, such as duplexes and apartment buildings. This type of property is usually held as an income-producing investment, and any tax lien held against the property is likely to be redeemed to maintain the investment. Multiple-family housing units that are composed of one to four family units offer the most profit potential, since the tax liens held against properties of this magnitude are far more affordable than those of larger housing units that provide living space for many more family units.

Homestead Properties

A homestead property is an occupied property for which the occupants have filed an exemption to pay property taxes. If the occupants qualify for the exemption, the municipality deducts a fixed amount from the appraised value of the property and uses the newly established value in determining the real property tax to be paid on the property. A homestead property indicates that a property serves as a principal residence. Homestead properties offer profit potential, since the property is likely to be the only residence of the property owner and he or she is not interested in losing such accommodations, particularly at the reduced property tax amount. Homestead property owners are very likely to redeem any tax liens held against the property as quickly as possible, offering a high rate of return on investment dollars.

Mortgaged Properties

Mortgaged properties are almost guaranteed to be redeemed by the mortgage lender. Mortgaged properties provide security for the mortgage loan held by the property owner. When the property owner fails to pay required property taxes and allows the property to go to tax sale, the mortgage company risks having the mortgage wiped out should the tax lien certificate holder foreclose the property owner's right to redeem the tax lien certificate. Since tax liens are senior to mortgage and other lender liens held against a parcel of property, a foreclosure by the tax lien certificate holder wipes out any lender liens. Mortgage companies have a vested interest in redeeming tax lien certificates so they, not the tax lien certificate holder, are in the position of being able to foreclose the property owner's right to the property. A mortgage company is not going to have its loan erased for the relatively small cost associated with delinquent taxes unless it is upside down in the property, which implies that the loan amount exceeds the property value by a significant amount. Otherwise, the mortgage company will redeem the tax lien certificate and exercise its right to foreclose the property owner's right to the mortgage loan due to failure to pay property taxes. The property owner would then be put in the position of having to pay the delinquent property taxes and any arrearages to reinstate the mortgage loan. If the property owner is not capable of paying, the mortgage company will foreclose the property and resell it. To prevent property owners from defaulting on property tax payments, mortgage lenders generally require that property owners pay into a tax and insurance escrow account as part of their monthly mortgage payments. The mortgage company, not the individual, is then responsible for withdrawing funds from the escrow account to pay any real property taxes when they become due. Many states allow property taxes to be paid semiannually. In such instances, the mortgage company will disburse funds from the escrow account on a semiannual basis in line with the state's payment schedule.

Trust Deed

Rather than a traditional mortgage, some states allow lenders to engage property owners with a trust deed against the property. A trust deed is a contract that is used as security for a loan. The property owner, by engaging in a trust deed, transfers legal title to his or her property to a trustee for the duration of the loan. The trust deed gives the trustee the power to sell the property if the property owner does not live up to the terms of the trust deed agreement. Even though the property owner transfers legal title to the property, he or she retains possession of it for the duration of the loan.

Worthless Properties

Without making a visual inspection of properties offered for sale at the annual tax sale, the investor has no way of knowing whether a lien certificate is secured by a valuable piece of property, a vacant lot, or an abandoned and dilapidated property. The objective of investing in tax lien certificates is to profit from high redemption amounts or to gain property ownership. When a worthless parcel of property secures a tax lien certificate, the certificate is also worthless. That is why investors are encouraged to research properties to determine the suitability of a property for investment purposes. A given in investing in tax lien certificates is that raw land or vacant lots require more research and investigation than improved properties. In most instances, it is safe to assume that an improved property provides some use even if its current use is not the best use of the property. A vacant lot, on the other hand, may not prove to be of much use.

Vacant Lots

Vacant lots may be valuable to investors seeking to develop land, but they must be suitable for a development effort and must not be landlocked, which means that a parcel of property has no method of entry or departure, except through someone else's property. Landlocked and vacant lots may also be positioned so they are not served by utilities and are far out of the path of any utility-servicing entities, such as those that provide gas and electricity. For the investor seeking to profit from redemption amounts or the investor seeking to gain ownership of a useful or valuable property, a vacant lot may prove to be a worthless investment. A truly worthless property that serves no use or no longer supports its intended use is not likely to be redeemed by the property owner. Such a property will be just as worthless to the investor who foreclosures and obtains ownership. This is common with properties that are situated in the desert, on mountainous terrain, or in flood plains. Vacant lots are usually sold at the low end of bid prices. Some tax collectors attempt to prevent the sale of worthless properties by not selling liens on properties with delinquent tax amounts under a certain threshold, say $100. Most tax collectors, on the other hand, put the responsibility for researching properties on the investor and sell tax lien certificates on worthless and landlocked properties.

The responsibility to research the zoning regulations that apply to a particular parcel of land falls on the investor. The investor should also research any proposed or contingent plans of the municipality to determine what will be done with the land in the near future. If the municipality is in the process of zoning a potential parcel of land for industrial use or it is planning to zone the areas surrounding the parcel for industrial use, the investor needs to know that before acquiring the land for the development of residential homes.

An investor must determine whether the land has any access to water or a sewage disposal system. In many urban areas, a developer simply hooks into the existing systems. However, some areas are not in the vicinity of such systems. The owner may need to provide water for the land if the land has no usable ground water or install a leach field for the property when access to a public sewage disposal system is not attainable. These could be expensive and time-consuming processes if the local municipality does not service the land. Trying to make use of a watershed that is owned by someone or installing a leach field on land that cannot accommodate the system could complicate the investment strategy by creating additional legal and environmental issues.

An investor must also determine if the property lies in a flood plain or is in the path of any historical mudslides. Properties affected by these and other types of natural occurrences may not show any visible signs of damage. Events such as flooding may only occur during specific times of the year. If flooding is excessive during summer, it may not be obvious to the investor during the winter months. A check of the records held by the local planning department may indicate any special designations, such as flood plains, that are recorded. Also, the library or other sources of reference materials may indicate any historical events that may have affected the area.

Abandoned Properties

Tax lien certificates may be sold when they are secured by worthless properties with vacant and dilapidated structures. Some of these properties may be identified by the small amount of delinquent taxes assessed against them, which assumes that advertised properties are in their first year of delinquency. That is not always the case. Some states allow property taxes to accrue on abandoned properties for years, even if the property has been partially or completely destroyed. The delinquent tax amount advertised for tax sale purposes may have accrued over years and can be misleading to the investor who is not familiar with the community. Proper research of advertised properties will indicate whether the delinquent tax amount represents a fair amount or an amount in excess of the property's worth. Assessments may not be accurate, as assessors are not immune from making mistakes or recording the wrong information for their valuations. Proper assessments are also not made as frequently as jurisdictions claim they are. It is not uncommon for properties to undergo major renovations, restructurings, or damages that are not considered in valuation assessments.

Commercial Properties

Commercial properties can also be worthless for the investor who is not skilled in commercial real estate. These properties may include structures that indicate a useful business purpose. However, the structures and property may prove to be inadequate for establishing a business operation. The property may be in violation of zoning and other regulations, and environmental, health, and building codes. It may have served its previous owners well until new laws and regulations were enacted, and it may be too expensive to bring it into compliance with new codes and standards. Institutional investors usually invest in these types of properties because they have the capital to maintain the properties or revitalize those that have deteriorated or are in violation of codes.

chapter four

Bidding on Tax Lien Certificates

G enerally, tax lien certificates are made available to the public via an annual delinquent property tax sale. The public is allowed to participate in the auction and bid on all properties in a jurisdiction that have been identified as having delinquent property taxes. The minimum bid for a tax lien certificate offered for sale is termed the opening bid. Usually the opening bid is an amount equal to the delinquent taxes, penalties and interest on the delinquent tax amount, and fees and costs associated with offering and issuing the tax lien certificate. The bidding process is different in every jurisdiction, but involves some form of competitive or noncompetitive bidding.

Competitive Bidding

In states such as Wyoming, tax liens may be assigned based on a competitive bidding process. In competitive bidding, the bidder may engage in either a process of bidding up the cost or bidding down the return of a tax lien certificate. Bidding up the cost is also known as **premium bidding**. It is a simple process of auctioning a tax lien certificate and assigning it to the bidder who is willing to pay the highest amount above the opening bid amount. A process known as **late-entry bidding** is also used to bid up the cost of tax lien certificates by taking advantage of the bidding process. **Bidding down** the return on tax lien certificates allows bidders to bid down the percentage of ownership in the property held as security for the tax lien certificate or to bid down the percentage of interest to be paid upon redemption.

Bidding Up the Premium

Bidding up the premium is a process that involves bidding up the cost of the tax certificate. The cost of acquiring a tax lien certificate is a bid beyond the minimum cost necessary to satisfy the tax lien amount or opening bid amount. The amount of the bid that is in excess of the opening bid amount is considered the premium bid amount. The bidder willing to pay the highest premium amount is the winning bidder. States that allow bidding up of the premium amount on tax lien certificates may use the following methods of applying interest to the redemption amount to be paid to the investor:

- Applying the same rate to both the opening bid amount and the premium bid amount.

- Applying different rates to the different amounts.

- Applying interest to the opening bid amount, but not the premium amount.

- Applying interest to the premium bid amount, but not the opening bid amount.

- Not refunding the premium amount as part of the redemption amount.

The premium amount is held by some states to help defray the cost of providing government services to the taxpaying community. Other states provide for the premium amount to be refunded to the tax lien certificate holder upon redemption or to the property owner upon foreclosure.

Indiana engages in premium bidding. The redemption of a tax lien certificate does not require the property owner to pay interest as a part of the redemption amount. Instead, a penalty is assessed against the opening bid amount; no penalty is assessed against the premium amount. The penalty varies depending upon when the tax lien certificate is redeemed. If it is redeemed within the first six months following the tax sale, the penalty is 10 percent of the opening bid amount. If it is redeemed after six months, but before one year has elapsed, the penalty is 15 percent of the opening bid amount. If it is redeemed after one year, the penalty is 25 percent of the opening bid amount. The premium amount is refunded to the tax lien certificate holder upon redemption. Subsequent taxes and assessments that may accrue during the redemption period have interest applied upon redemption at 12 percent annually. If the property owner fails to redeem the certificate, the certificate holder may file a claim for premium amount that was paid to acquire the certificate. If the premium amount is not claimed within five years of the foreclosure, it is forfeited to the municipality's general fund.

Mississippi also engages in premium bidding of tax lien certificates. Redemption requires a 12 percent interest rate to be applied to the opening bid amount. A one-time penalty of 5 percent of the opening bid amount is also required for redemption. No interest is applied to the premium amount, and it is retained by the taxing municipality. It is not refunded to the tax lien certificate holder or the property owner.

Bidding Down Ownership

In the process of bidding down ownership, tax lien certificates are sold and assigned to the bidder wishing to pay the lesser percentage of interest in the property. The bidder who bids to purchase a 95 percent interest in a property used to secure a tax lien certificate is chosen over the bidder who bids to purchase 100 percent interest in the property. Bidders compete until one bidder reaches a minimum percentage that no other bidder will drop beneath.

If a property owner fails to redeem a tax lien certificate during the predetermined redemption period, the bidder may foreclose the property with a transfer of title to a treasurer's deed. A treasurer's deed allows both the bidder and original owner to hold tenancy-in-common interest in the property. The bidder holds interest at the percentage that he or she bid at auction. The original owner holds the remaining percentage of interest in the property. For example, a winning bidder purchases a tax lien certificate for 85 percent interest in the securing property. Upon foreclosure, the tax lien certificate holder owns 85 percent of the property, and the original property owner owns 15 percent. The two parties become tenants-in-common. Competitive bidding down for tenancy-in-common ownership provides an opportunity for the original property owner to retain partial ownership in the property and also to control the disposition of the property. The original property owner's percentage of the tenancy-in-common, however small, restricts the new partial owner from selling or financing the property. For either party of the tenancy-in-common to sell or secure financing against the property, both parties must agree to the action or initiate a partition action, which is a request to the courts to sell the property and split the proceeds from the sale in proportion to each party's percentage of interest. For example, a bidder acquires a property tax lien certificate for 97 percent interest in the property value. The property owner retains the remaining 3 percent interest. A completed partition action allows the bidder to secure 97 percent of the net proceeds from the sale of the property and the owner to secure 3 percent of the net proceeds.

Missouri provides for bidders to bid down ownership in a property. Missouri's tax sale is limited to residents of the particular municipality. For persons residing outside the municipality to participate in the bidding, the outsider must designate a resident agent to act on his or her behalf. The resident agent, like all other bidders, must be a resident of the taxing municipality.

New Hampshire also engages in a tax sale system that provides for bidders to bid down ownership in a property. The winning bidder is required by state law to notify the mortgage lenders of record of the purchase within 30 days of making the purchase. The notification is necessary for the sale of the tax lien certificate to be valid. Part property owners are allowed to redeem their share of the tax lien certificate to retain their share of tenancy-in-common ownership should foreclosure occur. All property owners are allowed to make partial payments of the redemption amount during the two-year redemption period.

Bidding Down Interest

Some states also allow bidders to bid down the percentage of interest to be paid upon redemption of the tax lien certificate by the property owner. A bidder may purchase a tax lien certificate with the stipulation that the property owner may redeem the tax certificate by paying less than the amount established by state statute for redemption.

Arizona, for example, has state statutes that specify the redemption interest amount to be paid by the property owner as 16 percent annually. In competitive bidding down, the bidder who bids to purchase a tax lien certificate with a 12 percent redemption interest is chosen over the bidder who bids to purchase it at 14 percent redemption interest. In Arizona, property owners are allowed to redeem tax lien certificates after the established redemption period has ended and foreclosure has been initiated. The property owner's right to foreclose does not end until a foreclosure judgment has been made and recorded by the courts. When the property owner redeems after the redemption period has ended, but before a foreclosure judgment is made, the property owner is required to pay additional costs. Property owners are also required to pay reasonable attorney's fees, in addition to the 16 percent interest applied to the cost of the tax lien and subsequent taxes as well as fees and costs associated with the sale of the certificate. Municipalities of Arizona calculate interest so that any fraction of a month is counted as a whole month.

New Jersey also allows bidders to bid down the interest to be paid upon redemption. The statutory redemption interest is 18 percent, but the bidder may bid the percentage down to as low as 1 percent. When the bidding reduces the interest to 1 percent, the state engages in a system of competitively bidding a premium amount. To the benefit of investors, the state also imposes a penalty on the redemption that varies depending upon when the redemption takes place. If the redemption occurs within 10 days of the tax sale, no penalty is assessed. If the redemption occurs after 10 days, the property owner is required to pay the cost of the tax lien, the bid interest, any subsequent taxes, and municipal liens and penalties based on the amount of the redemption amount. If the redemption amount is in excess of $200, the assessed penalty is 2 percent of the redemption amount. If the redemption amount is in excess of $5,000, the assessed penalty is 4 percent of the redemption amount. If the redemption amount is in excess of $10,000, the assessed penalty is 6 percent of the redemption amount.

Late-Entry Bidding

Late-entry bidding is more of a psychological technique than an established bidding process. A late-entry bidder is usually a very seasoned bidder who takes advantage of the bidding frenzy that builds during auctions. He or she allows bidders to compete for bid amounts. When the frenzy has subsided and the final frenzy bidder has made his or her offer, the late-entry bidder makes an offer at a large increase above that of the highest previous bidder. By the time bidders involved in the frenzy are able to readjust their thinking and consider whether they want to top the offer made by the late-entry bidder, the auctioneer recognizes the relatively long pause as the end of bidding. The late-entry bidder takes advantage of the fast pace with which bids are awarded and essentially shocks the last frenzied bidder who was psyched into believing that his or her bid had won. Late-entry bidding is possible in almost every tax sale auctioning system.

Noncompetitive Bidding

In states such as Oklahoma and Wyoming, the bidding is noncompetitive and the bid amount remains constant. Tax lien certificates are offered on a first-come, first-served basis. When more than one bidder offers to pay for the same tax lien certificate, the treasurer is responsible for implementing his or her own fair and impartial method of choosing a winning bidder. In Wyoming, treasurers have established four noncompetitive methods for selling tax certificates. These methods are not unique to Wyoming and are used in other states that engage in noncompetitive bidding.

First-Come, First-Served Methods

1. A first-come, first-served method means that bidders form a line outside the location where the tax sale is held and wait their turn to make bids. Individuals are allowed to purchase all available tax lien certificates that have not been sold until all are sold. Alternatively, bidders register for the tax sale, are assigned bidder numbers, and indicate the properties for which he or she wishes to purchase tax lien certificates. If more than one bidder wishes to purchase a tax lien certificate secured by the same property, the earliest registered bidder wins the bid.

2. Another first-come, first-served method is unique to the county of Johnson, Wyoming. Each bidder is assigned a bidder number upon registration for the tax sale. The auctioneer assigns tax lien certificates according to the sequential order of the bidder number. Bidder number 1 gets first pick of a single tax lien certificate of his or her choice. Bidder number 2 gets to choose one of the

remaining tax lien certificates and so on until either all bidders' numbers have been exhausted or all tax lien certificates have been sold. If the number of available tax lien certificates exceeds the number of bidders, the assignment of tax lien certificates begins again, starting with bidder number 1. If there is a second round, bidders get an opportunity to purchase a second tax lien certificate, and this process continues until all possible tax lien certificates have been sold.

Lottery-Type Methods

1. A lottery-type or random method provides for each bidder to be assigned a bidder number. A bingo machine, hat, or other container is used to select a bidder number for each available tax lien certificate. The selected bidder may accept or refuse the draw of his or her bidder number for a particular tax lien certificate. If the bidder accepts the draw, he or she wins the bid. If he or she rejects the draw, additional bidder numbers are randomly drawn until a bidder number is drawn that corresponds to a bidder who wishes to purchase the certificate. After a certificate is sold, all bidder numbers are put back into the "pot" to be randomly drawn for the next available tax lien certificate.

2. Another lottery-type method that is used when more than one bidder wishes to purchase an available tax lien certificate is to collect bidder numbers for all parties interested in a particular certificate. A winning bidder is then randomly selected from the pool of bidders interested in the certificate.

The complications associated with bidding down percentages of ownership in a property make investors reluctant to participate in the process. Most taxing authorities are also partial to the complicated bid-down scheme. To avoid this competition in selling tax lien certificates, city and county treasurers have resorted to various first-come, first-served and lottery-type methods of selecting bidders. State statutes regarding tax lien certificates in Wyoming provide for competitive bidding for a percentage of ownership in a property. However, the effect of implementing one of the above methods is the same as if the state did not engage in competitive bidding or the selling of percentages of ownership in property. It should be noted that this type of bidding is not applicable to the sale of irrigation assessments. State statutes allow for the noncompetitive bidding of 100 percent interest in the sale of irrigation assessments in Wyoming. The bid is awarded to the first bidder offering an amount sufficient to cover the assessment as well as associated penalties, interest, and costs—not to the bidder offering to purchase the lowest percentage of ownership in the property.

The established bidding methods used by tax lien states are shown in Table 2 which also shows the bidding method used by those tax deed states that allow property owners an opportunity to redeem tax deeds held against their property. Interest rates, penalties, and redemption periods are also shown.

Table 2

	BIDDING METHODS FOR TAX LIEN STATES AND TAX DEED STATES WITH REDEMPTION PERIODS					
	Bid Method	State	Classification	Interest Rate	Penalty	Redemption Period
1	Bid Down Interest	Arizona	Tax Lien	16%		3 years
2	Bid Down Interest	Florida[1]	Tax Lien	18% (tax liens & deeds)		2 years
3	Bid Down Interest	Illinois	Tax Lien	24% Scavenger Sale	18% Tax Sale	2–3 years
4	Bid Down Interest	Louisiana	Hybrid Tax Deed	12%	5%	3 years
5	Bid Down Interest or Premium	New Jersey	Tax Lien	18%	2%–6%	2 years
6	Bid Down Interest	North Dakota	Tax Lien	9%–12%		3 years
7	Bid Down Interest or Premium	Rhode Island	Hybrid Tax Deed		10%	1 year
8	Bid Down Ownership	Massachusetts	Hybrid Tax Deed	16%		6 months
9	Bid Down Ownership	Michigan	Tax Deed	15% 1st year	50% 2nd year	1 year
10	Bid Down Ownership	Missouri	Tax Lien	10%		2 years
11	Bid Down Ownership or Random	Nebraska	Tax Lien	14%		3 years
12	Bid Down Ownership	New Hampshire	Tax Deed	18%		2 years
13	Premium	Alabama	Tax Lien	12%		3 years

BIDDING METHODS FOR TAX LIEN STATES AND TAX DEED STATES WITH REDEMPTION PERIODS

	Bid Method	State	Classification	Interest Rate	Penalty	Redemption Period
14	Premium	California[1]	Tax Deed	18% (tax liens)		2 years (tax liens)
15	Premium	Colorado[2]	Tax Lien	9% plus FDR		3 years
16	Premium	Connecticut	Hybrid Tax Deed	18%		1 year
17	Premium	District of Columbia	Tax Lien	18%		6 months
18	Premium	Delaware	Hybrid Tax Deed		15%	60 days
19	Premium	Georgia	Hybrid Tax Deed		10–20%	1 year
20	Premium	Guam	Hybrid Tax Deed	12%		6 months
21	Premium	Hawaii	Hybrid Tax Deed	12%		1 year
22	Premium	Indiana	Tax Lien		10–15%	1 year
23	Premium	Kentucky	Tax Lien	12%		1 year
24	Premium	Maryland	Tax Lien	6%–24%		6 months
25	Premium	Mississippi	Tax Lien	12%	5%	2 years
26	Premium	New York	Tax Deed	14%		1 year
27	Premium	Ohio[1]	Tax Deed	18% (tax liens)		15 days (tax deeds) 1 year (tax liens)
28	Premium	Pennsylvania	Hybrid Tax Deed	10%		1 year
29	Premium	Puerto Rico	Tax Lien		20%	3 years
30	Premium	South Carolina	Tax Lien	3%–12%		1 3/4 years

	Bid Method	State	Classification	Interest Rate	Penalty	Redemption Period
					BIDDING METHODS FOR TAX LIEN STATES AND TAX DEED STATES WITH REDEMPTION PERIODS	
31	Premium	South Dakota	Tax Lien	12%		3–4 years
32	Premium	Tennessee	Hybrid Tax Deed	10%		1 year
33	Premium	Texas	Hybrid Tax Deed		25%	6 months–2 years
34	Premium	Vermont	Tax Lien	12%		1 year
35	Premium	West Virginia	Tax Lien	12%		18 months
36	Premium	Wisconsin	Tax Lien	18%		2 years
37	Random	Iowa	Tax Lien	24%		1 $3/4$ years
38	Random	Montana	Tax Lien	10%	2%	3 years
39	Random	Oklahoma	Tax Lien	8%		2 years
40	Random or Bid Down Ownership	Wyoming	Tax Lien	18%	3%	4 years

[1] States that sell both tax deeds and tax lien certificates regardless of the classification.

[2] Interest rates are based on the Federal Discount Rate (FDR).

The remaining 13 tax deed states include Alaska, Arkansas, Idaho, Kansas, Maine, Minnesota, Nevada, New Mexico, North Carolina, Oregon, Utah, Virginia, and Washington. These states offer no redemption period for property owners to regain ownership of their properties. Tax deeds are offered for sale by bidding up the premium cost of tax deeds.

Over-the-Counter Tax Certificates

Many state municipalities hold tax sales on the same date making it impossible to acquire tax lien certificates for multiple properties, in multiple jurisdictions. In most states, if a tax certificate is not sold at the tax sale, the certificate is bought and held by the city, county, or state responsible for the sale. In some states, tax lien certificates are offered for resale at public auction at a later date. In most other states, the unsold tax lien certificates are made available for resale, over-the-counter, to the general public on a first-come, first-served or other basis. Tax lien certificates sold over-the-counter are not subject to the bidding process, so they are bid neither up nor down. They are sold for 100 percent interest in the securing real estate. Investors often choose to purchase tax lien certificates over-the-counter after the tax sale has ended as an alternative to buying them at tax sales. Purchasing tax lien certificates over-the-counter offers many other advantages, as outlined below:

- Personnel at the treasurer's or tax collector's office have more time to assist with property issues than they do in days preceding and during the annual tax sale.

- In states that engage in competitive bidding down during the tax sale, purchasers may only be capable of securing a percentage of ownership in properties. Likewise, in states that engage in premium bidding during the tax sale, purchasers are likely to purchase tax lien certificates above cost. Certificates sold over-the-counter after the tax sale, however, are sold at the opening bid amount for 100 percent ownership in the property.

• Certificates that are not sold at tax sale may be purchased at any time of year. In most states, no matter when the tax lien certificate is purchased, the redemption period begins on the day of the annual tax sale. Thus, when a tax lien certificate is purchased at a later date, the redemption period is shortened. The shortened redemption period offers the benefit of reducing the time before foreclosure can be initiated to obtain the deed to the securing property. If a property owner redeems the certificate, the reduced waiting time reduces the time necessary to receive a return on investment, thereby increasing the investor's rate of return.

chapter five

Income and Growth Potential

An investment in tax lien certificates is considered to be safe because it is is secured by real estate. Tax lien certificates offer income and growth potential that is more consistent than that of other investment opportunities such as real estate, stocks, bonds, certificates of deposit, and money market funds. The risks are also relatively small compared to other investments. When investors invest in residential real estate by purchasing the property on the real estate market, for example, the property has no income potential unless it is used as a rental property. That parcel of residential real estate, on the other hand, offers profit potential as either a personal residence or rental property. The growth in profit, however, depends upon an expected increase in the property's value over the years of ownership. Overall residential property values have a history of steady increases, but there is no guarantee that increases will take place for a particular parcel of property securing a tax lien certificate. It is hoped and expected that foreclosing a property owner's right to redeem a tax lien certificate will leave the investor with a residential property that increases in value during ownership. The investor would then be capable of selling the property at a profit over the amount invested. When investors invest in tax lien certificates that are secured by residential properties, the tax lien certificates guarantee both income potential and growth potential. Income potential is realized when a property owner redeems a tax lien certificate. The property owner has to pay, at a minimum, the delinquent tax amount plus any assessed interest and penalties. The tax lien certificate purchaser is guaranteed to collect the investment amount with interest at the established rate. The interest continues to accrue throughout the redemption period, offering growth potential throughout this period. Even if the property owner should fail to redeem the tax lien certificate, the investor may foreclose the right of redemption and gain ownership of the property at a fraction of the property's value. The newly owned property offers the investor both income and growth potential, since the property may either be sold at market value for an amount in excess of the amount spent to acquire the property, or it may be rented to produce income over time.

Risk Factors

In all investments, including investments in tax lien certificates, there are risks. Since there is no way to avoid all investment risk, the smart investor must develop strategies to manage and minimize risk. Following good investment practices by consulting with or hiring an experienced accountant and attorney is the first step in eliminating and minimizing investment risk. Another successful method of minimizing risk is to engage in practices of risk management. At first thought, it would seem that the only way to avoid investment risk is to avoid making investments. After all, accumulated monies that are left "under the mattress" are safe from loss and taxation. The money incurs no tax obligations, because there is no income from the money, no gain for the owner, and no amount to tax. However, taxes are just one aspect of an investment. The money will never be lost unless, of course, someone steals it from under the mattress. Notwithstanding any type of theft, the same amount of money put under the mattress will be available when the money is taken from under the mattress. However, the value of money kept under the mattress will decrease over time due to inflation. So, rather than avoiding risk, money left under the mattress really generates a loss. Even if such funds were deposited into a bank savings account, the low interest rates applied to savings would also create a loss over time. The interest rate paid by banks is usually not sufficient to keep up with inflation, and it certainly does not compare to the high interest rates applied to the redemption of tax lien certificates.

An investor must weigh all options that are responsible for creating the various types of risk and determine the level of risk that is appropriate for the particular type of investment opportunity. An investor must also consider the effect that investing will have on employment, assets, and other life factors. A young investor, for example, may want to invest huge sums of money in investment opportunities with the expectation of huge returns in the future. The theory behind this type of investment strategy is that the young investor will be vested for many years and thus is guaranteed to profit on those investments in later years. There is one problem with this type of strategy: longevity is not guaranteed. The young investor, by engaging in this type of strategy, may incur other losses during his or her young life and not benefit from the profits promised for the future. The young investor, for example, may accumulate huge lines of credit during the investment years that will consume the profits made from investing in later years. Even worse, the investor may not live long enough to collect on the profit. The smart investor must use techniques of risk management that will reduce the likelihood of all losses. These techniques must include methods of diversification and dollar cost averaging, but one of the most important techniques involves choosing quality markets to invest in. Some markets are more capable of protecting investors against loss than others. The investor should dedicate time and resources to finding the appropriate, quality markets and understand when he or she is allowed to enter them and when he or she should or is able to get rid of them. Investments in tax lien certificates are protected against loss, because the investment dollars are secured by real estate, which if properly chosen, provides more worth than the dollars invested.

Market Risk

Market risk means that an investment may sell in the marketplace for less than the amount that was invested to acquire it. Using the stock market as an example, an investor may purchase stock in a company that offers unlimited growth potential. The investor makes the purchase when the stock is at its high point and later discovers that the value of the stock is on a constant decline. The investor then sells the stock at a much lower amount than its purchase price and accepts the resulting loss. Market risks may be caused by a number of factors that are internal and external to a business entity. The decline in the value of stocks is such a risk. Tax lien certificates, on the other hand, offer no market risk, because established laws require the property owner to pay the interest and other costs required for redemption or risk losing their property. The tax lien certificate holder is guaranteed to receive a return on the investment through either the interest-bearing redemption amount paid by the property owner or the right to foreclose and take ownership of the property itself.

Safety Risk

Safety risk is the risk of investing in an investment that is not secured. Certificates of deposit, for example, may be backed by a federal insurance agency, which seems to indicate a safe and secure investment opportunity. However, such agencies have been known to have internal issues that deplete the agency of its funds. If the federal government chooses not to replenish the fund, the security of the investment is lost. Tax lien certificates, on the other hand, are secured by real estate. In particular, the parcel of real estate for which a tax lien certificate is assigned acts as the security for the tax lien certificate. In addition, the cost of a tax lien certificate is rarely in excess of the value of the property. With the inclusion of penalties, interest, fees, and other costs that are added to the cost of a lien certificate, the certificate usually represents only a fraction of the property's market value. As such, the amount invested in tax lien certificates is safe whether the tax lien certificate is redeemed or the right of redemption is foreclosed. In the case of foreclosure, the investor may incur additional expenses to complete the foreclosure process, but the total costs are almost always much less than the fair market value of the property that would be received if the property were sold. Many investors are likely to sell the property to recover the costs and also to make a profit. Properties are often sold at less than fair market value, and the investor is still able to recover, at a minimum, the total investment amount. Other investors may rent the property to recover the cost and also profit from the investment.

Liquidity Risk

Liquidity risk is the risk that the investment is not capable of being quickly converted to cash. Some markets are structured so it is not easy to convert the investment to cash when needed. Certificates of deposit, for example, must be held until maturity or the investor is required to pay penalties for early withdrawals. The penalty amount along with the tax consequences may wipe out any profit from the investment, and in the worst case, an early withdrawal could create an investment loss. As another example, the income generated from investments such as money market accounts is dependent upon interest rates. When interest rates fall, investment dollars may be transferable to other types of investments, but the investment dollars may not be liquidated without paying a penalty for the withdrawal of funds. If the money is withdrawn rather than transferred, not only is a penalty applied, but the investor is also obligated to pay taxes on the amount withdrawn. Tax lien certificates, on the other hand, offer limited liquidity, since the return on investment dollars cannot be realized until the property owner redeems the tax lien certificate, a foreclosure takes place and the foreclosed property is sold, or the tax lien certificate holder assigns the certificate to another party for a fee. No matter how long the investor waits for redemption, the established interest rate remains constant and will not fluctuate as stock prices do. The return is guaranteed to exceed the cost of acquiring the tax lien certificate. When certificates are assigned to another party, the assignee pays an amount in excess of the amount spent to acquire the tax lien certificate. The proceeds from both redemption and assignment of a tax lien certificate are totally liquid. Likewise, when a foreclosure takes place, the property may be sold or rented for amounts that exceed the amount spent to acquire the certificate and to foreclose. The proceeds from a foreclosure sale or from renting a foreclosed property are liquid.

Overhead

Overhead risk is the risk of taking a loss in the operation of a business entity. In some business ventures, the amount of overhead expenses consumes any profits that are made, and the cost is never recovered. Labor, travel, research, and investigation are necessary overhead expenses that accrue regardless of the outcome of the investment opportunity. In most businesses, these types of overhead expenses are deductible. The laws pertaining to tax lien investment opportunities are not so clearly defined. The consensus is that the expenses associated with traveling to various tax sales in search of tax lien certificates and the cost of researching and investigating properties that secure tax lien certificates are not considered to be overhead expense, but part of the cost of investing. Only after a tax lien certificate is purchased and assigned are such expenses considered deductible overhead expenses. The investor should consult with his or her accountant or lawyer for the specifics of the tax law.

Tax lien certificates offer minimal risks compared to other investment opportunities. Table 3 below outlines a comparison of tax lien certificates versus other forms of investment.

Table 3

COMPARISON OF INVESTMENT OPPORTUNITIES						
Investment	Income Potential	Growth Potential	Market Risk	Safety	Liquidity	Overhead
Tax Lien Certificates	Yes	Yes	Minimal	Yes	No[1]	High
Residential Real Estate	No	Inconsistent	High	Yes	No[2]	High
Rental Real Estate	Inconsistent	Inconsistent	High	Yes	No[2]	High
Stocks	Inconsistent	Inconsistent	High	Inconsistent	Yes	Minimal
Bonds	Yes	Inconsistent	High	Yes	Yes	Minimal
Certificates of Deposit	Yes	No	Minimal	Yes	No[1]	Minimal
Money Market Funds	Yes	No	High	Yes	Yes	Minimal

[1] Liquidity requires redemption.

[2] Liquidity requires the sale of the investment.

chapter six

Investing in Tax Lien Certificates

A nnual tax sales are open to the public, but the tax sale process is considered complex and is not understood by the general population. As such, attendees at tax sales are usually limited to apprehensive citizens and investors. Apprehensive citizens include those individuals with a vested interest in particular properties and those citizens who are curious about the sale process. The majority of attendees, however, are those involved in the investment opportunity presented by tax lien certificates. Investors invest in the purchase of tax lien certificates for one of two reasons. They either attempt to use tax lien certificates as a method of gaining ownership of valuable property for pennies on the dollar, or they attempt to profit from the high rate of return realized by redemption amounts.

Ownership as the Objective

Tax lien certificates offer investors a relatively safe and reliable investment opportunity. They are administered and controlled by state governments, secured by real estate, and in most instances, offer a fixed rate of interest on the investment amount. One of the investment objectives is to take ownership of valuable property for pennies on the dollar. To maximize the return on investment dollars, the investor attempts to invest in lien certificates that are secured by valuable property and to purchase those certificates that are least likely to be redeemed by the property owner. One of the biggest obstacles in investing in tax lien certificates is in determining those tax lien certificates that are least likely to be redeemed. Most cities and counties offer far more tax lien certificates for sale than any one individual or group of individuals could possibly investigate. Since it is impossible for investors to determine, with accuracy, the probability that the property owner will redeem a tax lien certificate, they are encouraged to rely on the law of averages and invest in certificates that have as little as a ten percent chance of not being redeemed. The law of averages suggests that if an investor invests in 10 tax lien certificates with a 10 percent chance of not being redeemed (10 x 10% = 100%), then there is a 100 percent chance that the investor will successfully invest in at least one tax lien certificate that the owner will fail to redeem.

The law of averages, however, is more theoretical than practical. Property owners redeem most tax lien certificates that are offered for sale during some point of the redemption period. Even when a tax lien certificate is redeemed, the investor's only loss is access to the money used in the investment during the redemption period. In most states, the investor, at a minimum, has his or her investment dollars returned with interest, as determined by the particular state.

Ownership Before the Tax Sale

Though tax lien certificates are usually acquired at tax sales or over-the-counter after a tax sale, opportunities exist to invest in the sale of certificates before the sale begins. An investor is free to contact the owners of properties listed in the tax sale listing. If the property owner is in agreement, the investor can offer one of three opportunities for settling the delinquent tax amount, as follows:

Buying Equity

The investor may offer to buy the owner's equity in the property and take ownership of the property. In exchange for a mutually agreed-upon price, the property owner provides the investor with ownership by issuing the investor a quitclaim deed to the property. This option works best for property owners who are seeking to rid themselves of a property or are seeking a buy out of a property. The investor usually agrees to pay or assume any debt or liens against the property and negotiates with the property owner for a selling price that is less than the property's fair market value. As an example, a property owner may have an $80,000 outstanding mortgage on a property valued at $200,000. The property owner is also delinquent in paying $4,200 in property taxes. In exchange for the owner's equity of $115,800, the investor may offer to pay the delinquent tax amount, the loan balance, and $50,000 cash to the property owner. In return, the property owner provides the investor a quitclaim deed to the property. The investor becomes the new property owner for an amount equal to the following:

Equity Offer:	$ 50,000
Loan Balance:	80,000
Delinquent Property Tax:	4,200
TOTAL	**134,200**

The investor owns the property free and clear and has about one-third equity in the property.

Investor's Equity

$65,800 = $200,000 ÷ $134,200

33% = $65,800 + $200,000

Sharing Equity

Rather than offering a property owner with an option that relieves him or her of home ownership, the investor may offer to share equity with the property owner. Using the terms of the previous example, the investor offers to pay the delinquent tax amount for a 50 percent equity position in the property. Since the property owner has $115,800 equity in the property, the investor would pay the $4,200 delinquent property tax, which increases the shared equity to $120,000. Since the shared equity is 50-50, both the investor and the property owner would hold $60,000 equity in the property. Both parties of the shared equity would pay an equal share of the $80,000 outstanding loan balance. The investor would pay 50 percent of the remaining balance, and the property owner would pay the other 50 percent. Though the example presented here represents a 50-50 equity-sharing agreement, it does not have to be 50-50. Shared equity can be 25-75 or any division agreed upon and specified in the terms of an equity-sharing agreement.

The percentage of sharing and other terms of the equity-sharing plan must be clearly spelled out in a contract agreement. In most instances, property owners are allowed to maintain possession of the property. The most common equity-sharing agreements provide for the property owner to pay fair market rent to the investor in return for having the investor pay the debts held against the property. The investor is, in effect, renting the property to the property owner, but instead of engaging a typical landlord-tenant type of arrangement, the tenant is part owner. An advantage to this type of arrangement is that the tenant-owner is more likely to maintain the property than a tenant in a typical tenant-landlord relationship. The expenses of the property, including the outstanding mortgage, are split according to the equity percentage. In a 50-50 arrangement, the expenses are evenly divided between both parties. If the arrangement were such that the investor held 75 percent equity and the property owner held 25 percent, the expenses would be divided 75-25 accordingly. The owner-occupants are usually able to deduct their share of the interest on any loan amounts as well as the property tax. The investor deducts his or her share of any interest on loan amounts, property taxes, and any other expenses of the property. The investor also depreciates his or her share of ownership in the property and deducts one-half of the rents received.

Reverse Lease Option

The investor may also offer to purchase the property and lease it back to the property owner with an option allowing the property owner to repurchase the property at a future date. This option is similar to lease options offered for rental properties where the tenant agrees to pay rent to the landlord with an option to buy the rental unit in the future. A portion of the monthly rents is reserved and applied to the down payment when the purchase takes place. The specifications of a reverse lease option must be clearly defined by contractual agreement. A legal instrument must define the terms of the payment and time frame for purchase of the property.

Ownership After the Tax Sale

For a tax lien investor to gain ownership of a property that secures a tax lien certificate, the property owner must fail to redeem the tax lien certificate during the redemption period. But even when the property owner fails to redeem, ownership is not automatic. The investor must follow prescribed procedures to foreclose the property owner's right to redemption and acquire deed and title to the property. Various states and individual municipalities require different procedures. Some municipalities will allow the investor to engage in a rather simplistic administrative filing of foreclosure. Other states require the investor to engage in a lengthy and complicated judicial method of foreclosure. Judicial foreclosures involve the time, use, and expense of legal counsel and the courts.

Return as the Objective

When tax lien certificates do not lead to ownership, another reward for investing in them is the high rate of return offered by redemption. When property owners redeem tax lien certificates, the property owner must reimburse the certificate holder for paying the delinquent tax amount that created the tax lien. In addition to the delinquent tax amount, the property owner may be required to pay interest, penalties, and fees as well as costs associated with the establishment and offering of the tax lien certificate.

Different states have differing methods of determining the additional penalty, interest, fees, and costs to be added to the delinquent tax amount. In some states, a penalty may be imposed as a flat amount to be applied annually during the redemption period. States also include interest on the delinquent tax amount, the penalty amount, or both. The interest rates may range from 6 percent to 24 percent, and they are usually applied annually. The redemption period also varies by state but usually ranges from six months to four years. It is the combination of penalties and interest that accrue over the redemption period that draws investors to tax lien certificates. Other fees and costs that are reimbursed as part of the redemption amount are an added benefit. Some of the costs include legal fees that may be pricey in some jurisdictions.

Illinois, for example, is a favorable state for tax lien certificate investing. The typical redemption period for tax lien certificates is two years; however, the tax lien certificate holder may file notice with the particular municipality to extend the redemption period to three years. The state requires redeeming property owners to pay interest and penalties in addition to the delinquent tax amount upon redemption. The statutory interest rate is 18 percent for six months, but state statutes provide for bidders to bid down the interest rate to be applied to redemption amounts. Penalties are applied as a percentage of the bid amount and are staggered throughout the redemption period.

- If a tax lien certificate is redeemed within the first two months, the penalty amount is 3 percent of the cost of the certificate.

- If a tax lien certificate is redeemed after the expiration of two months, but before six months, the penalty amount is equal to the percentage of interest that was bid. For example, if a winning bid is bid down to 2 percent interest upon redemption, the penalty would also be 2 percent during this period. If the winning bid is bid down to 10 percent interest, the penalty amount would also be 10 percent.

- If a tax lien certificate is redeemed after the expiration of six months, but before one year, the penalty amount is double the bid down interest rate. That is, if the winning bid is bid down to 10 percent interest upon redemption, the penalty would be 20 percent during this period.

- If a tax lien certificate is redeemed after the expiration of one year, but before 18 months, the penalty is triple the bid down interest rate. So, if the winning bid is bid down to 10 percent interest upon redemption, the penalty would be 30 percent during this period.

- If a tax lien certificate is redeemed after the expiration of 18 months, but before two years, the penalty is four times the bid down interest rate. If the winning bid is bid down to 10 percent interest upon redemption, the penalty would be 40 percent during this period.

- If a tax lien certificate is redeemed after the expiration of two years, but before the requested and approved three-year redemption period has expired, the penalty increases 6 percent per year. If the winning bid is bid down to 10 percent interest upon redemption, the penalty would be 16 percent during this period.

The preceding rates apply to tax lien certificates purchased at the annual tax sale. When the certificates are not purchased at the tax sale, the unsold certificates are offered for sale at a scavenger sale. The bidding method used at scavenger sales is premium bidding to the highest bidder. The bidder is not reimbursed for the premium amount used to win the bid, and interest is not applied to the premium amount. Nevertheless, the redemption interest rate still offers a favorable return. The interest rate for tax lien certificates purchased at the scavenger sale is 12 percent for six months (24 percent annually) for the first four years. An additional 6 percent per year is added after the expiration of four years.

Investors

There are two primary types of investors: independent investors and institutional investors. Independent investors are small investors with limited funds to invest. Institutional investors are large corporate investors with millions of investment dollars.

Independent Investors

Independent investors are individuals or groups of individuals who purchase tax lien certificates as an investment opportunity. They usually do not have millions of dollars to invest, but may have hundreds, thousands, or more to invest. They usually invest on behalf of themselves and are very selective with the limited funds they have to invest.

Institutional Investors

Institutional investors consist of banks, mortgage companies, brokerage houses, and other large institutions with millions of dollars available for investment purposes. Institutional investors are usually composed of several individuals acting on behalf of the institution. Their research is usually replete with detailed notes specifying which available properties to bid and the optimal range of bidding to maximize yield. Institutional investors are skilled in the bidding process and may be identified at tax sales by some or all of the following characteristics:

- Arrive at the tax sale on time.

- Sit at the front of the auction room.

- Favor tax sales in large municipalities with many thousands of tax lien certificates available for sale.

- Bid on tax lien certificates that are secured by more valuable properties. Property taxes are usually assessed between 1 percent and 2 percent of the fair market value of a property. Institutional investors are more focused on lien certificates above certain thresholds, generally $1,000 to $1,500. These thresholds are used to identify properties that are likely to have market values in excess of $100,000 and $150,000, respectively.

- Bid down the interest on redemption amounts. The goal of institutional investors is to raise the overall yield on investments and continue to invest in more properties, which further increases their yield. Institutional investors are willing to accept the lower interest on redemption in exchange for the higher yield from properties that are likely to redeem quickly and properties that have penalties attached to the redemption amount.

- Seek properties that are homestead properties. Homestead properties are likely to be redeemed, because the designation indicates that the property serves as a personal residence and the property is not a vacant lot.

- Employ staff to do the bidding on behalf of the

institution. Staff persons typically work a nine to five workday and may not be present to increase the competition during lunch hours or extended bidding hours.

chapter seven

Obtaining Investment Dollars

Unless an investor is independently wealthy with excess funds to invest in real estate tax liens, he or she will need to find ways of obtaining the necessary investment funds. One of the most widely used methods of obtaining money to fund tax lien certificate investments is to form a partnership or investment group. Partners work together to research and bid on valuable investment properties and then split the profits returned by the investment. Another good source of investment dollars is an individual's retirement plan. In the same manner as money held in a retirement plan is sheltered from taxation, investments made in the name of a retirement plan are also sheltered from taxation. Taxes play a vital role in the investment of tax lien certificates, since the return on investment is increased when the investor is capable of engaging methods of decreasing federal, state, and local income taxes.

Tax Considerations

A partnership or investment group needs to understand the tax laws applicable to tax liens and business operations. The best way to bring this type of knowledge to the partnership is to include an accountant or an attorney who is knowledgeable in tax liens and business taxes. An accountant is able to analyze business transactions and provides advice on how to shelter income from taxes. As with any business entity that involves real estate, the tax lien investor needs the assistance of an accountant or attorney who is experienced in the specifics of real estate taxes and laws. The advertised returns on tax lien certificate investments may never be fully realized by a partnership, because investment income is taxable income to the business entity and the individual partners thereof. The true return on tax lien certificate investments or any type of investment is the amount of money that the investor or investment group is allowed to keep after satisfying any tax obligations. To assist in the planning and continuity of tax lien certificate investments, investors need expert knowledge and advice, not only in the laws that pertain to real estate taxes, but also in the laws that pertain to investments, investment groups, business taxes, accounting, and contracts.

Attorneys and accountants need to have similar knowledge and skills to assist an investment partnership in making decisions that are in the best interests of the business entity. Though there are attorneys who are also competent accountants and accountants who are competent attorneys, the partnership is best served by having two separate and distinct individuals in the roles of attorney and accountant, though it is not absolutely necessary. An accountant takes a more personable approach to the everyday aspects of the business functions. He or she will document and distribute a financial history of the business entity on a quarterly basis and will periodically perform checks and balances of the business entity to ensure that business practices are being followed and that documentation is being distributed to necessary parties, both internal and external to the business entity. Attorneys are overseers of the partners, since they engage in various contracts and agreements relative to real estate transactions and partnerships. The attorney ensures that all rules, regulations, and transactions are being followed as dictated by contract and defends such actions in legal proceedings. Unless there is some dispute relative to business practices, an attorney does not need to be involved in the everyday aspects of the business in the same manner as the accountant. However, the attorney should be competent to analyze and interpret the financial descriptions of the business, as provided by the accountant.

An investor, for example, who is establishing a new investment venture, needs to consult with an accountant who understands the tax obligations of starting a new business. The IRS allows a $50,000 deduction on the startup costs associated with establishing a new business. However, the first $5,000 dollars may be deducted in the first year, and the remaining startup costs must be amortized over 15 years. Suppose an investor establishes a business for the purpose of investing in tax lien certificates. He or she spends $11,000 to establish the business and in the first year of operation, he or she receives a profit from redemptions that equals $6,500. The IRS allows the business to take an initial $5,000 deduction and an additional $400 deduction for the first year of amortization. A $400 deduction is also allowed over the next 14 years to account for the remaining startup cost of $5,600.

Startup Cost:	$11,000	
First-Year Startup Deduction:	+ 5,000	
Remaining Startup Amount:	6,000	($11,000 - $ 5,000)
First-Year Amortized Deduction:	400	($6,000 ÷ 15)
Total First-Year Deductions	$5,400	($5,000 + $400)

The $6,500 profit realized in the first-year of business is partially offset by $5,400 (first year startup deduction plus first year amortized deduction) that is also allowed in the first year of the business operation. The investor has to be knowledgeable of such deductions in order to offset profits in such a manner. An accountant ensures that the business entity makes such deductions, and a lawyer defends the right to make such deductions. If the same investor realizes a loss in the first year, the loss may be carried forward to offset gains that may be realized in future years. If, on the other hand, the business had been in existence for years and suffered a loss, the loss may be carried back, up to three years, to offset gains in those previous years. An amended tax return must be filed for the business, in this situation, in order to claim the loss.

To acquire lien certificates, investors are required by most states to travel to the taxing municipality to make a physical appearance at the tax sale or at the appropriate tax collector's office for the sale of over-the-counter tax lien certificates. Business tax laws allow individuals engaged in business to deduct business expenses, such as travel. However, an investor is not allowed to deduct travel expenses for the investigation of investment opportunities. Investors are generally not considered to be in the business of the entity in which they are investing. If an investor, for example, travels from Maryland to Chicago to investigate a restaurant for which he or she is considering purchasing a tax lien certificate, he or she is not considered to be in the restaurant business. Investors who hold substantial investments in tax lien certificates may make the argument that their profession is purchasing tax lien certificates, but generally, an investor who invests in lien certificates is not considered to be in the business of purchasing certificates. For tax purposes, the expenses of purchasing tax lien certificates are included in the cost of the tax lien certificate as the cost basis of the investment. However, once tax lien certificates are purchased and paid for, the expenses required to manage the certificates, such as travel expenses necessary to make court appearances to foreclose a property, are deductible. Such travel expenses must exceed 2 percent of the investor's adjusted gross income to qualify for a deduction, and the deduction may be reduced for high-income taxpayers.

Once foreclosure has taken place, the tax consequences of acquiring ownership to the property are not clearly defined. The IRS established policy for mortgaged or pledged properties makes the gain realized by foreclosure taxable when the property is acquired for an amount less than the fair market value. However, foreclosed tax lien certificates do not fall into the category of mortgaged or pledged properties. The ambiguity stems from the lack of statutes from the IRS. The IRS has not established whether a gain is realized when an investor completes the foreclosure of a tax lien certificate or when and if the foreclosed property is sold.

The tax law specifies mortgaged and pledged properties, because mortgage companies are allowed to deduct a debt if a property is sold for less than the mortgage amount. As the complement, mortgage companies are required to report a gain if a property is sold for more than the mortgage amount. When the right to redeem a tax lien certificate is foreclosed, it is not likely that a property will ever sell for less than the cost of foreclosure. Unlike with mortgages, there is rarely a loss that needs to be deducted for foreclosing a tax lien certificate. As such, the IRS's position of requiring mortgage lenders to report gains to offset losses does not apply to tax lien certificates. Investors are encouraged to consult with their accountants to determine how to apply the law to their particular situations. An interesting analogy: If an investor sells a vehicle valued at $25,000 for $15,000, does the new owner have a gain of $10,000 as a result of the sale? More important, is it a taxable event, such that the new owner should be required to pay tax on the gain? In most states the answer is no. A taxable event does not occur unless a vehicle owner sells a vehicle for more than it is worth, not less than it is worth. The seller is taxed on the gain, and the buyer has no tax obligation to report.

To avoid the uncertainty in tax laws with regard to the foreclosing of tax lien certificates, investors are encouraged to take advantage of their ability to schedule a foreclosure to occur at the beginning of the year. Doing so gives the investor an opportunity to sell the property before the year ends. In such a case, the investor realizes a gain upon selling the property, and if any taxes are due, the investor has converted the investment to cash and is able to pay the tax. Investors are also encouraged to market the foreclosed property early and sell the property as quickly as possible. Given the relatively small amount invested in the foreclosure, the investor is in a position to offer a buyer a bargain in return for a quick sale. Quickly converting a foreclosed property to cash offers the benefit of allowing the proceeds to continue to be invested in buying tax lien certificates or other investments as well as avoiding the uncertainties of the tax law.

Retirement Programs

Investing money contributed to retirement programs in tax lien certificates may offer the benefit of increasing the amount of funds in the plan without incurring any additional tax obligations. Tax lien certificates are an investment that qualifies for inclusion in an Individual Retirement Arrangement (IRA). However, the IRA must be a true self-directed IRA. A true self-directed IRA allows an individual to have control of the investments to include investments outside those established by the retirement program. Some mutual funds, for example, advertise that they offer self-directed IRAs. However, these types of IRAs are self-directed only in the sense that the individual may control investments between Fund A and Fund B, as predetermined by the plan. An individual may not include outside investments, such as tax lien certificates.

Retirement programs are commonplace in today's society, and caps on the amounts that may be contributed by individuals are steadily on the increase, providing individuals with more dollars to invest. Table 4 below shows the caps that have been established for some of the most common retirement programs.

Table 4

CAPS FOR RETIREMENT PLANS		
Plan	Caps for Contributions	
	Individuals born before 1954	Individuals born after 1954
401(k)	$18,000	$14,000
403(b)	$18,000	$14,000
457	$18,000	$14,000
SIMPLE IRA	$12,000	$10,000
Keoghs		$42,000
Profit Sharing		$42,000
Pension Plans		$170,000

Investors are allowed to use money secured by a retirement program to buy tax lien certificates in the name of the retirement program. When a property owner fails to redeem a lien certificate that is named in a retirement program, the retirement program may foreclose the right of redemption and obtain title and ownership of the property. Investing in tax lien certificates in the name of a retirement program protects the investment should the investor foreclose the property owner's right of redemption and then sell the property. When a property is titled to a retirement program and then sold in the name of the retirement program, the retirement program, not the individual enrolled in the program, secures the proceeds from the sale of the property. This shields all proceeds of the sale from tax obligations in the same manner as the retirement plan itself. The anomaly is that investments made through retirement programs cannot be converted to cash, without penalty and additional tax consequences, until the age requirement of the retirement program is met. The funds may, however, be used as a line of credit; though borrowing against funds held in a retirement program incurs interest. For these reasons, it would not be wise for an investor to make all of his or her investments within a retirement program. Retirement programs limit the investor's ability to liquidate the investment when cash is needed. Also, if an investor is successful in foreclosing a property and the property is used to generate income under the retirement program, none of the tax benefits of business ownership are offered to the retirement program, because it is already sheltered from taxes. The investor may find it more cost-effective to assign the property to himself or herself and take advantage of the tax benefits offered by business ownership, such as depreciation and deductions.

As a business entity, either as an individual investor or investment group, an investment in tax lien certificates that profits from redemption amounts also incurs tax obligations. Proceeds from redemption are profit to the business entity and, as such, they are taxable. If the investment is a capital investment, profits may be taxed at the rate established for capital gains, 15 percent. The IRS has established guidelines for determining when income may be classified as a capital gain. If the investment is not a capital investment, the profit is taxed as ordinary income. The IRS taxes ordinary income at a maximum of 36 percent. Again, consultation with an accountant will assist investors in determining the types of income that the investment business receives and the tax rate that is applicable to their redemption amounts.

Partnerships

A partnership among individuals provides a source of investment dollars that may be used to invest in tax lien certificates. The partnerships should include not only a collaboration of the money, but also a collaboration of knowledge, talent, skills, resources, and economic clout. Individual partners must be responsible for bringing one or more of these assets to the partnership. Partners may collaborate to create the following types of investment groups:

Corporations

Corporations have been in existence for more than a century and are incorporated business units with limits placed on the personal liability of the incorporated partners. Corporations are established as documented business entities that offer shares of the business unit to the public. The corporate partnership design is meant to limit lawsuits against the corporation to the assets of the corporation, not the personal assets of the incorporated members. However, some very skilled attorneys have been successful in taking personal assets of partners under special circumstances. Another caveat of a corporate partnership is that its profits are taxed twice. When a corporation offers shares on the stock market, its shareholders are paid dividends on dollars invested in the corporation. The shareholders are personally taxed on the dividends distributed by the corporation. The corporation itself is also taxed on its income at the corporate rate. When a sole proprietor establishes him or herself as an S corporation, no double taxation is assessed against the corporation. The individual proprietor is taxed only on the profits of the corporation.

Limited Liability Company

Two or more individuals may form a limited liability partnership. Unlike a corporation, no shares are offered for sale to investors and no double taxation is imposed on the partnership. Limited liability partnerships offer the protection of personal assets that is inherent in corporations, but the partners do not have the responsibility of recordkeeping and bookkeeping associated with selling shares like that of a corporate business structure.

General Partnership

A general partnership is a contractual agreement formed between individuals, with each individual having an equal role in the business relationship. The parties to a general partnership have unlimited liability. A legal suit against one of the partners extends to all of the partners. The general partnership must file taxes as a general partnership.

Real Estate Investment Trust

A real estate investment trust is a trust that is offered for investment to the general public. The trust produces income, of which 90 percent is distributed to its shareholders. A real estate investment trust is free of double taxation because the trust itself is not taxed. Only the investors who receive distributions from the trust are taxed. The partners have the responsibility of record keeping and bookkeeping associated with selling shares in the same manner as a corporation

Limited Partnership

A limited partnership must have at least two partners, of which one must be a general partner, who is responsible for the decision making of the business. A general partner is responsible for the decision making of the business. He or she decides when, where, and how to invest the money of the partnership and receives a fee for his or her services as the general partner. In addition, any expenses incurred to perform the duties of the general partner are paid by the partnership.

In a limited partnership, there must be at least one limited partner, who has limited liability equal to the amount he or she has invested in the partnership and has no say in how the partnership's money is invested. The limited partnership agreement should spell out the specific terms of the partnership, but in general, the limited partners are entitled to a return on their investment and a share of any profit. As stated above, the general partner is usually entitled to receive a fee or bonus for his or her services before any profit is divided among the remaining partners and is also entitled to a return on dollars invested and a share of the profits.

Partnership Agreements

A partnership agreement should clearly specify a beginning and ending date of the partnership. Investors are encouraged to draft separate agreements for tax lien investment opportunities in different areas and also for different investment years. A partnership agreement, at a minimum, should last throughout the redemption period of all tax lien certificates purchased by the partnership or until the partnership is otherwise dissolved. Other information that should be included in the partnership agreement includes the following:

Purpose

The partnership agreement should clearly indicate that the purpose of the partnership is to make money investing in tax lien certificates. The purpose should be direct and to the point. In the event of a dispute, the purpose of entering into the contractual agreement should not be vague or ambiguous to the person arbitrating or judging the circumstances.

Goal

The business goals of the partnership should be clearly defined, and each partner must be in agreement with the overall goals of the partnership. Individual goals may be different based on the specific expertise of the individual, the amount of funds contributed to the partnership, or other contributions to the partnership, but the business goal should be to achieve a return on the dollars invested. Some investors may require a shorter time line for receiving a return on their investments. The business entity should be capable of allowing these individuals to have their dollars invested in tax lien certificates with shorter redemption periods. Other investors may be willing to wait out the longer redemption periods, particularly if there are high rates of return expected on the redemption amounts or the property is a valuable property for which research indicates a high potential to foreclose the right of redemption. The goal of the business should be to provide a return on dollars invested by both types of investors.

Contributions

No matter what form of partnership is chosen, the collaborating partners must be capable of contributing something to the partnership and must be in agreement with the role of the partners, as defined by the terms of the partnership agreement. While it is expected that partners make a financial contribution to the business partnership, not all partners need to contribute financially. Partners may be sought who are capable of bringing physical assets and knowledge to the business. The partner or partners who are most skilled in tax lien certificates would be best suited to present such potential partners with the plan of action for the partnership and the terms for repayment of the funds invested. Expertise in tax lien certificates should be demonstrated with a presentation that focuses on the potential rates of interest and yields involved in tax lien certificate investing. The high rates of return for tax lien certificates, as compared to those achieved in other types of investment opportunities, will lure partners into the partnership.

Finances

Needless to say, it is wise to include partners who are capable of investing liquid capital in an investment partnership. Potential partners with liquid assets to invest may require that the partnership be secured. The language of a promissory agreement should specify that investment properties provide security for the promissory agreement in the same fashion as properties provide security for acquired tax lien certificates. Some potential partners may not have liquid capital to contribute to the partnership, but they may be in a position to provide other types of assistance in the area of finance. Partners may contribute by providing the following assets to the partnership:

- Strong financial statements that may be used to obtain loans for the partnership. Strong financial statements serve as a cosigner in applying for investment loans.

- Assets tied to other long-term investments, such as certificates of deposit. Partners may borrow against existing assets by using them as collateral for the loan. The contributing partners maintain their assets while also generating investment revenue for the partnership.

- Existing and open lines of credit that may be converted to cash for the purchase of tax lien certificates or used in negotiations with delinquent property owners to gain ownership prior to a property tax sale. The purchase of tax lien certificates usually requires payment in cash or certified funds. Investors need to have cash readily available for the purchase of tax lien certificates. Also, when investors attempt to negotiate with property owners who are delinquent in paying property taxes to acquire ownership of the property before the property is auctioned at tax sale, the property owners will require a cash equity offer.

- Credit card accounts where the creditor is willing to extend large lines of credit. These partners must be convinced that the rate of return offered by tax lien certificates will exceed the rate of interest charged by the credit card company. Since the purchase of tax lien certificates usually requires cash or some form of certified funds, the line of credit offered by credit card companies must be converted to cash. Most credit card companies charge relatively low interest rates on purchases to credit card holders in good standing. However, the interest rate for cash advances may be a considerably higher rate. Rates may be as high as 24 percent. Other credit card companies allow cash advances to be made at the same interest rate as purchases.

Other Contributions

Partners may contribute other assets to the partnership outside of cash and financial contributions. A partnership requires office space, office equipment, legal counsel, bookkeeping, and a host of other services and skills. The contract agreement should specify the particular services, skills, or equipment contributed to the partnership by each partner. The contract should also specify how the proceeds from profits will be distributed among the partners who are responsible for providing physical assets, skills, and services as opposed to finances. The partners must be capable of determining the worth of partners that provide these types of assets. Having these assets provided by partners has the effect of reducing the operational costs of the partnership, allowing the individual partners to retain more of the profits.

Distribution of Profits

The contract agreement should clearly specify how profits are to be distributed to each of the partners. It should also specify a time frame for the distribution of such proceeds. In contrast to distributing profits, the contract agreement should spell out the procedure to use in the case of losses. The financial contributors are not necessarily the partners who should absorb the financial loss. The partners who are paid for in-house skills and services, for example, may be required to accept a reduced fee for such services.

Account Access

The contract agreement must stipulate when and how withdrawals are to be made from accounts of the partnership. The expense account, for example, should have specific and documented instructions with respect to who has access to the account, the types of activity to be funded by the account, when withdrawals are to be made, and the party responsible for tracking and managing the account. The terms of access and parties responsible for all other accounts of the partnership must also be specified. The contract agreement should stipulate that withdrawals from partnership accounts be capped at the amount of the individual partner's initial contribution to the partnership before any profits are disbursed to partners from the account. As another example, in-house services could be stipulated with a time frame for completion. The language of the contract agreement could then be structured such that withdrawals from the partnership account are disbursed to the servicing partner only upon the completion of such services. All funds brought into the partnership must be recorded and tracked. Likewise, all funds expended by the partnership must be recorded and tracked. Even when expenses are paid to partners for their in-house services, the payments must be recorded and tracked just as other expenses paid to outside parties are accounted for. Income and expenses should be documented in the partnership's balance sheet. It is recommended that a software program designed to record assets, liabilities, income, capital, and expenses (ALICE) be used to balance the books and perform all other bookkeeping functions of the partnership.

General Management

The duties and responsibilities of each partner should be clearly defined. The successful operation of the partnership is dependent upon an organized collaboration of thoughts, ideas, and procedures. The contract agreement should specify the parties responsible for each specific business function, the hierarchy of the partners, and the circumstances for which a vote or decision by all partners is necessitated.

Dispute Resolution

Every partnership agreement should include language that defines the process for the resolution of disputes. It is recommended that the partners engage in methods of arbitration or binding arbitration as an alternative to judicial methods. Arbitration is a more cost-effective method of resolving disputes, and it prevents disputes from being made public. When disputes are argued and settled through judicial hearings, the process leaves the partnership as well as its partners vulnerable to public scrutiny.

Sale and Assignment

The partnership agreement must include language that specifies the terms for selling or assigning a partner's interest in the partnership. Sometimes partnerships just don't work out, and one or more of the partners may want to separate from the partnership. The partnership agreement should indicate a mutually agreed-upon dollar value for each of its partners. It is recommended that existing partners be given first right of refusal in buying the interest of a departing partner.

Expulsion

It may become necessary to expel a partner, against his or her will, when he or she does not or cannot live up to the terms of the partnership. An expulsion is one the most unfavorable actions that must be executed in the best interests of a business entity. In addition, an expulsion can be costly, nasty, and difficult to carry out even when the procedures to implement such an action are defined in the language of the partnership agreement. To avoid the hassle and loss of productivity that expulsion may create for a partnership, it may be in the best interests of both the partners and the business unit to provide the unwanted partner with a financial incentive to leave the partnership. Though the partnership agreement should clearly define the terms of expulsion and the amount of money to be provided to the departing partner, the partners may decide to provide the departing partner with an amount in excess of that specified in the terms of the partnership agreement. The extra incentive is designed to reduce or avoid any disruptions to the operations and functions of the business entity.

Loss of a Partner

The partnership agreement should specify the procedures to be used in the case that a partner becomes severely ill, dies, or willfully withdraws from the partnership. The partnership agreement should indicate a mutually agreed-upon dollar value to be paid to each of the partners under such conditions. The business is still expected to function under such adverse conditions. The partnership agreement should address the common occurrence of life issues and define the partnership's position in such circumstances. For example, a partnership interest may be willed to heirs in the case of a death of one of the partners, or a partner may file bankruptcy and have his or her assets frozen. A partner may also endure a long-term illness or just decide to abandon all interest in the partnership. The partnership agreement should address these types of situations.

Additional Partners

Should it become necessary or desirable to include additional partners in an existing partnership, the existing partnership agreement should indicate the terms and procedures necessary to accommodate the additional partners. A new or modified partnership agreement may need to be established, clearly defining the role of the new partner and the modification of roles of the existing partners as a result of the addition.

Dissolution

At some time, the partnership will come to an end. It is recommended that the partnership agreement specify and designate a time frame for starting and ending the partnership.

Even when a successful partnership has acquired all of its initial goals and continues to thrive, the partnership should be ended. If agreeable, the partners can always establish a new partnership.

chapter eight

Return on Investment Dollars

Usually, if an investor invests in tax lien certificates, he or she seeks one of three outcomes:

1. To profit from the return mandated for redemption amounts.

2. To assign the certificate to another party for a fee.

3. To take ownership of the property securing the certificate.

The first outcome requires that the investor seek liens against properties that are likely to be redeemed. The second requires that he or she seek liens that present a favorable opportunity for other investors. The latter requires the investor to seek properties that are the least likely to be redeemed. While the first and second outcomes may produce a relatively lucrative return on investment dollars, the second presents a more favorable opportunity for some investors: property ownership at a fraction of its value.

Investors may also contact property owners who are delinquent in paying their property taxes before the property incurs a tax lien that is offered for sale at the annual tax sale. In this scenario, the investor attempts to engage the property owner in an equity-buying or equity-sharing agreement that would extinguish existing debts against the property in exchange for a quitclaim deed to the property or a share of the equity in the property. Furthermore, the investor, upon engaging in such a contract with the property owner, may assign or flip the contractual agreement to another investor for a profit. Though the investor seeks to engage in this type of activity before a tax lien certificate is sold for the securing property, he or she may also engage property owners in agreements to buy and share equity during the tax lien certificate redemption period, particularly when the property owner indicates an inability to pay the debts of the property. This type of contractual agreement offers the benefit of eliminating the time and expense required for obtaining the deed and foreclosing on the property. A foreclosure through the normal tax sale process may not be executed until the redemption period has expired, but this type of contractual agreement provides the investor with the opportunity to acquire ownership earlier and, thus, the opportunity to rent and produce income or sell the property for profit much earlier.

Interest Rates

There are two types of return that are measured by the investor seeking to profit from the return on redemption amounts: interest rate and rate of yield. State statutes require property owners to pay penalties, interest, or both in order to redeem a tax lien certificate. The interest rate on redemption amounts is usually assessed as a fixed rate. The dollar amount to be returned to the investor is dependent upon the accumulated interest that is applicable at the time the tax lien certificate is redeemed. The penalty amount, however, is usually applied at the same rate, regardless of when the redemption takes place and is usually a one-time payment to be applied at redemption. Some states allow the penalty to be staggered during the redemption period, such that the penalty rate is increased for additional years of delinquency. The penalty amount is established according to the statute devised for a particular state or municipality.

Indiana, for example, is a tax lien state that engages in premium bidding. The premium amount is the amount paid by a bidder that is in excess of the opening bid amount. Both the opening bid amount and the premium amount are subject to interest upon redemption. The interest assessed upon redemption is dependent upon how long after the tax sale the redemption takes place as well as the premium amount necessary to win the bid. Indiana also imposes a penalty of 5 percent on the opening bid amount. If the redemption takes place soon after the tax sale, the interest amount may not offer much of a return, particularly for small tax liens. However, the 5 percent penalty assessed on the opening bid amount is guaranteed upon redemption, no matter when the redemption takes place.

As another example, New Jersey engages in competitive bidding down of tax lien certificates. Bidding is started at 18 percent interest on the tax lien certificate amount and bid down to the lowest percentage that a bidder is willing to accept. In addition, a penalty is imposed based on the cost of the certificate. Certificates that are sold for less than $5,000 incur a 2 percent penalty; those that cost from $5,000 to $9,999 incur a 4 percent penalty, while those in excess of $10,000 incur a 6 percent penalty. As such, a tax lien certificate purchased for $1,000 and bid down to 10 percent interest upon redemption would be redeemed for a maximum of 12 percent (10 percent + 2 percent) interest if the redemption occurs within the first year of the redemption period.

When working with interest rates, investors apply the Rule of 72 to determine how long funds need to be invested at a particular interest rate in order to double the amount invested. The time frame to double an investment under the Rule of 72 is calculated as follows:

$$72 \div Interest\ Rate = Time$$

An interest rate of 12 percent per annum doubles the amount invested in $72 \div 12\% = 6$ years. The rule may also be used to do reverse calculations to determine what interest rate is needed to double an investment amount within a given time frame, as follows:

$$72 \div Time = Interest\ Rate$$

The interest rate necessary to double an investment amount in 5 years is $72 \div 5 = 14.4\%$.

Percentage Yield

In addition to interest rates, investors are concerned with maximizing the rate of return, also known as yield. As a rate of return, yield measures how quickly an investor receives a return on the investment amount. The more quickly he or she is capable of receiving a return on an investment, the more quickly the acquired dollars may be used for more investment purposes. Investors use yield to determine the suitability of investment opportunities. When yield is positive, it represents the percentage of profitability of the investment. When yield is negative, it represents the percent of loss in the investment. Unlike interest rates, which are fixed, applied annually, or prorated for the portion of the year or month in which redemption takes place, yield is a calculated measure that takes into consideration the timeliness of the return from redemption.

In states where redemption requires that interest be applied to the redemption return on a tax lien certificate and the redemption amount is paid before the first year of redemption period expires, the value of yield is computed as an annual return. The percent of yield is always equal to the annual interest at the end of a one-year period. The percentage of yield is always greater than the interest rate when the redemption takes place before the end of one year. The increase in yield depends upon how soon the property owner redeems the tax lien certificate after an investor acquires the certificate. The yield for a $1,000 tax lien certificate that earns 12 percent interest upon redemption and is redeemed in one month is calculated as follows:

Cost of Tax Lien Certificate:	*$1,000*	
Annualized Redemption Interest:	*12%*	*= 1% per month*
Tax Lien Redeemed After Tax Sale:	*1 month*	
Actual Interest Paid After 1 Month:	*$10*	*= $1,000 x .01*
Percentage Return:	*1%*	*= $10 ÷ $1,000*
Percentage Yield:	*12%*	*= 1% x 12 months*

States that also apply penalties to the redemption of tax lien certificates provide a method of increasing the yield on investments, which, in turn, provides investors with an incentive to purchase certificates. Using New Jersey as an example, the interest to be applied to redemption is 18 percent per annum. The established bidding down process reduces the interest rate on redemption to 1 percent for the winning bidder. No matter what interest rate is bid by the winning bidder, the property owner is still required to pay a statutory 4 percent penalty. For a tax lien certificate purchased at $10,000 and bid down to 1 percent interest upon redemption, the investor would receive a maximum of 5 percent interest on the investment if the tax certificate is redeemed in the first year. The penalty amount is the fixed amount that assures the investor of receiving a fair return on the purchase of the certificate. The more analytic value—yield—varies depending upon when the certificate is redeemed. If the certificate is redeemed within one month of the tax sale, the yield would be 60 percent, calculated as follows:

Cost of Tax Lien Certificate:	*$10,000*	
Annualized Redemption Interest:	*1%*	*= .083% per month*
Penalty on Lien Certificate:	*4%*	
Tax Lien Redeemed After Tax Sale:	*1 month*	
Actual Interest Paid After 1 Month:	*$83*	*= $10,000 x .0083*
Penalty Paid After 1 Month:	*$400*	*= $10,000 x .04*
Percentage Return:	*5%*	*= $483 ÷ $10,000*
Percentage Yield:	*60%*	*= 4.8% x 12 months*

Though the interest is fixed at 1 percent throughout the redemption period, the amount of interest to be paid by the property owner after one month is $83, and the amount increases by 1 percent (or $83) per month over the redemption period. The yield, however, is highest during the first month of redemption and is calculated as 60 percent at one month and continues to decrease throughout the redemption period.

As another example, statutes of Wyoming provide for interest and penalties to be applied to the redemption amount. State laws provide for the property owner to pay the following upon redemption:

- The amount paid for the tax lien at the annual tax sale.

- 3 percent penalty on the amount paid at the tax sale.

- 15 percent annual simple interest on the amount paid and calculated from the date of the sale.

The property owner is given four years to redeem a tax lien certificate, and the annual interest is calculated and assessed from the date of the tax sale to the date of redemption. Table 5 below shows the yield that is returned to the investor for each month of the four-year redemption period.

Table 5

WYOMING PERCENTAGE YIELDS FOR REDEEMED TAX LIENS							
Months Held	Percent-age Yield	Months Held Past 1 Year	Percent-age Yield	Months Held Past 2 Years	Percent-age Yield	Months Held Past 3 Years	Percent-age Yield
1	51.0	1	17.8	1	16.4	1	16.00
2	33.0	2	17.6	2	16.4	2	15.90
3	27.0	3	17.4	3	16.3	3	15.90
4	24.0	4	17.3	4	16.3	4	15.90
5	22.2	5	17.1	5	16.2	5	15.90
6	21.0	6	17.0	6	16.2	6	15.90
7	20.1	7	16.9	7	16.2	7	15.80
8	19.5	8	16.8	8	16.1	8	15.80
9	19.0	9	16.7	9	16.1	9	15.80

WYOMING PERCENTAGE YIELDS FOR REDEEMED TAX LIENS							
Months Held	Percent- age Yield	Months Held Past 1 Year	Percent- age Yield	Months Held Past 2 Years	Percent- age Yield	Months Held Past 3 Years	Percent- age Yield
10	18.6	10	16.6	10	16.1	10	15.80
11	18.3	11	16.6	11	16.0	11	15.80
12	18.0	12	16.5	12	16.0	12	15.75

Note that the interest rate remains fixed at 15 percent throughout the redemption period. The yield, however, is calculated at 51 percent at the end of one month and decreases to equal the interest rate plus the penalty amount of 18 percent after one year. The yield continues to decrease for the remainder of the redemption period. If a tax lien certificate is for $10,000, the corresponding yields for one-month, one-year, and three-year redemption periods would be calculated as follows:

ONE-MONTH REDEMPTION

Cost of Tax Lien Certificate:	$10,000	
Annualized Redemption Interest:	15%	= 1.25% per month
Penalty on Lien Certificate:	3%	
Tax Lien Redeemed After Tax Sale:	1 month	
Actual Interest Paid After 1 Month:	$125	= $10,000 x .0125
Penalty Paid After 1 Month:	$300	= $10,000 x .03
Percentage Return:	4.25%	= $425 ÷ $10,000
Percentage Yield:	51%	= 4.25% x 12 months

ONE-YEAR REDEMPTION

Cost of Tax Lien Certificate:	$10,000	
Annualized Redemption Interest:	15%	= 1.25% per month
Penalty on Lien Certificate:	3%	
Tax Lien Redeemed After Tax Sale:	1 year	

Actual Interest Paid After 1 Year: $1,500   = $10,000 x .15
Penalty Paid After 1 Year: $300   = $10,000 x .03
Percentage Return: 18%   = $1,800 ÷ $10,000
Return per Month: 1.5%   = $1,800 ÷ 12
Percentage Yield: **18%**   = 1.5% x 12 months
The percentage return and percentage yield are equal.

THREE-YEAR REDEMPTION

Cost of Tax Lien Certificate: $10,000
Annualized Redemption Interest: 15%   = 1.25% per month
Penalty on Lien Certificate: 3%
Tax Lien Redeemed After Tax Sale: **3 years**
Actual Interest Paid After 3 Years: $4,500   = $10,000 x .15
Penalty Paid After 3 Years: $300   = $10,000 x .03
Percentage Return: 48%   = $4,800 ÷ $10,000
Return per Month: 1.3%   = $4,800 ÷ 36
Percentage Yield: **15.75%**   = 1.3% x 12 months
The percentage return exceeds the percentage yield.

Note that the percentage yield exceeds 51 percent of the cost of the tax lien certificate if the certificate is redeemed at any time prior to the end of one month. Also, the percentage yield is an analytical value that does not represent a dollar amount. For an investor to receive the dollar equivalent of the yield percentage, he or she would have to reinvest the redemption amount immediately at the same rate of interest, with the same redemption period. This idealistic situation is not necessarily realistic. The percentage yield, therefore, represents the percentage of return that the investor would gain if he or she were realistically able to do so.

States that impose high interest rates as well as penalties, fees, assessments, and other costs on the redemption amount are in a position to provide the higher rates of yield. States that are positioned to provide rates of yield in excess of 10 percent include the following: (Ref. 4)

	STATE	YIELD POTENTIAL
1	Alabama	12
2	Arizona	16
3	Connecticut	18
4	Delaware[1]	20
5	District of Columbia	18
6	Florida	18
7	Georgia	20
8	Territory of Guam	12
9	Hawaii	12
10	Indiana	15
11	Iowa	24
12	Kentucky	12
13	Louisiana	17
14	Maryland[2]	10-24
15	Massachusetts	16
16	Mississippi	17
17	Missouri	10
18	Montana	12
19	Nebraska	14
20	New Hampshire	18
21	New Jersey	18
22	Ohio	18
23	Commonwealth of Puerto Rico	20
24	Rhode Island	16
25	South Carolina	8-12
26	South Dakota	12
27	Tennessee	10

	STATE	YIELD POTENTIAL
28	Vermont	12
29	Virgin Islands	12
30	West Virginia	12
31	Wyoming	18

[1]Includes the counties of Kent and Sussex.

[2]Includes Baltimore City and the counties of Frederick, Worcester, Baltimore, Cecil, Charles, Harford, Queen Anne's, Somerset, Carroll, Allegany, Anne Arundel, Howard, Kent, Montgomery, and Prince George's.

The yield potential shown represents the yield that would be achieved if a property owner redeemed a tax lien certificate at the end of one year. If the redemption occurs sooner, the yield increases exponentially. If the redemption occurs later, the yield decreases.

Flipping

Flipping is a transfer of ownership that may be applied to tax lien certificates and equity purchasing contracts. Investors who contract with property owners prior to the property tax sale to purchase their equity in a property in exchange for paying the delinquent property taxes may flip the contract to another party for a profit. Using the example from Chapter 6, a property owner has an outstanding mortgage of $80,000 and is delinquent in paying $4,200 worth of property taxes on a property valued at $200,000. The owner's equity is $115,800 (that is, $200,000 – $80,000 – $4,200). An investor offers to buy the owner's equity in the property for $50,000. In exchange for paying the outstanding mortgage loan, the delinquent property taxes, and $50,000 in cash, the property owner provides the investor with a quitclaim deed to the property. The property owner is thus relieved of the obligation to pay the outstanding mortgage, avoids having a tax lien placed against the property for the delinquent property tax, and receives $50,000 in cash. The investor purchases the property for an amount equal to the following:

Equity Offer:	*$50,000*
Loan Balance:	*80,000*
Delinquent Property Tax:	*4,200*
TOTAL PURCHASE PRICE	**$134,200**

Rather than following through on the contractual agreement with the property owner, the investor may flip the agreement to purchase the property to another investor. By flipping the property before the tax sale occurs, the initial investor is relieved of paying the delinquent property tax. The new investor would take on the tax debt. Continuing with the example above, the initial investor decides to flip the $200,000 property to another investor for $150,000. Since the initial investor is relieved of paying the delinquent property tax, the original purchase price is reduced by $4,200 to $130,000. The initial investor's return on investment dollars would be calculated as follows.

Flipped Price	*$150,000*
Purchase Price	*$130,000*
RETURN	**$20,000**

Assignment

If, instead of flipping the contract, the initial investor assigns the contract made with the property owner to another investor, the initial investor profits from the sale of the assignment without having to incur any of the expenses required by the

contract. As the assignee of the contract, the new investor is
held responsible for fulfilling the contractual obligation and
paying the outstanding mortgage, delinquent property tax, and
equity payment. Continuing with the example above, the initial
investor decides to assign the equity contract that was made
with the property owners to a new investor for a fee of $5,000.
The new investor purchases the property owner's $115,800
equity in the $200,000 property and receives a quitclaim deed to
the property just as the original investor would have. The new
investor's cost of ownership is as follows:

Assignment Fee:	*$5,000*
Equity Offer:	*50,000*
Loan Balance:	*80,000*
Delinquent Property Tax:	*4,200*
TOTAL PURCHASE PRICE	**$139,200**

The original investor's return is $5,000 on an investment for
which he or she contributed nothing except the time and
expense of engaging the property owners to enter into the
equity contract.

chapter nine

Steps Toward Purchasing Tax Lien Certificates

Investors can approach the purchase of tax lien certificates as a series of steps. Though it is more difficult for investors to purchase tax lien certificates at delinquent property tax sales than to purchase them over-the-counter, these steps allow investors to achieve success with either method of acquiring tax lien certificates.

- Step 1: Understand state laws and procedures governing the taxing municipality.

- Step 2: If a chosen state engages in over-the-counter offers of tax lien certificates, eliminate those states that are not likely to have certificates available for offer after the annual delinquent property tax sale has ended.

- Step 3: Seek over-the-counter tax lien certificates in order of the oldest to newest.

- Step 4: Determine the bidding system used by each state and within the various municipalities of the state.

- Step 5: Bid for tax lien certificates in states where the bidding process does not significantly affect the price that would have to be paid should the property owner fail to redeem the tax certificate.

- Step 6: Acquire the listing of delinquent properties that will secure tax lien certificates offered for sale.

- Step 7: Determine those tax lien certificates that are less likely to be redeemed during the redemption period.

Step 1: Understand State Laws and Procedures Governing the Taxing Municipality

Each state has laws and statutes governing property tax delinquencies. Many states engage in an annual delinquent property tax sale where tax lien certificates, secured by the property, are offered for sale. Other states engage in the sale of tax deeds, which transfers ownership of the property from the delinquent property owner to the tax deed purchaser. Researching the laws and procedures governing the various states indicates those states that engage in the sale of tax lien certificates. When tax lien certificates are offered for sale, the sale is usually held annually. In many instances, states hold tax sales for the sale of tax lien certificates on the same day of the year for all municipalities of the state. This system makes it virtually impossible for an investor to participate in more than one tax sale. Research also indicates that in most tax lien states, tax certificates are sold or assigned to the state or participating municipality when they are not sold at the annual tax sale. They are then offered for sale to the public over-the-counter. An investor must be capable of identifying states that offer tax lien certificates for sale over-the-counter when the certificates are not sold at the tax sale. Those states that offer tax lien certificates for sale over-the-counter include the following: (Ref. 1)

Table 6

STATES THAT OFFER UNSOLD TAX LIEN CERTIFICATES FOR SALE OVER-THE-COUNTER	
Alabama	
Holder of unsold tax lien certificates:	Alabama.
Status of unsold tax lien certificates:	Judge of probate purchases tax liens for no less than the opening bid amount, on behalf of the state.
The jurisdiction's comptroller examines each tax lien certificate for the sufficiency of the sale. If the sale is found to be in error, the comptroller declares the tax lien certificate void and charges the officer who made the error an amount equal to the delinquent tax, interest, and costs involved in the sale. The county tax assessor is directed to assess the property as an escape for the years it was wrongfully assessed as delinquent. If the sale is rightfully engaged, the property may not be assessed until the tax lien is redeemed or sold.	
State-held lien certificates are assignable in writing or by endorsement from the land commissioner upon payment of the bid amount; interest of 12 percent, calculated from the date of sale to the date of assignment; plus any taxes that have incurred since the tax sale; and 12 percent interest on the newly assessed taxes. The assignee is entitled to all rights and title that were held by the state. Certificates may also be offered over-the-counter to investors. The taxing authority is mandated to make notice of over-the-counter sales.	
Arizona	
Holder of unsold tax lien certificates:	Arizona.
Status of unsold tax lien certificates:	Assigned to the state by the county treasurer for no less than the opening bid amount.
Annual tax sales commence on a specified and advertised date in the month of February. Tax lien certificates are bid and re-bid for a number of days, until all tax liens are sold or until the county treasurer is satisfied that no more sales can be made. The treasurer assigns unsold tax lien certificates to Arizona for the amount of the tax, interest, and costs of the sale. The county treasurer is mandated to sell or assign state-held certificates to any purchaser who pays the amount of the certificate, subsequent taxes, and an assignment fee of one dollar. State liens have priority over tax liens.	

STATES THAT OFFER UNSOLD TAX LIEN CERTIFICATES FOR SALE OVER-THE-COUNTER

Colorado

Holder of unsold tax lien certificates:	Colorado municipality governing the tax sale.
Status of unsold tax lien certificates:	Assigned, sold, or transferred at the discretion of county commissioners.

Tax lien certificates may be assigned, sold, or transferred, as determined by resolution of the particular county commissioners, for rights, title, and interest to the property held as security against the lien certificate. State laws do not mandate the sale of unsold tax lien certificates. The tax sale administrator must specifically approve certificates sold for property with delinquent taxes in excess of $10,000.

Florida

Holder of unsold tax lien certificates:	Florida.
Status of unsold tax lien certificates:	Assigned to the state by the county treasurer.

Unsold tax lien certificates are offered over-the-counter; however, state laws do not provide for the property to be held as security against the lien certificate. If the property owner does not redeem the property, the tax lien certificate holder has no vested interest in the property. The property is auctioned to the highest bidder in a subsequent "deed with right of redemption" auction. The investor must engage in legal actions to recover the cost of the lien or to foreclose the property. If the property is not sold at the "deed with right of redemption" auction, the state commissioner may make deed to the tax lien certificate holder.

Kentucky

Holder of unsold tax lien certificates:	Kentucky.
Status of unsold tax lien certificates:	Assigned to the state by the county treasurer.

Unsold tax lien certificates are offered over-the-counter; however, state laws do not provide for the property to be held as security against the lien certificate. If the property owner does not redeem the property, the tax lien certificate holder has no vested interest in the property. The property is auctioned to the highest bidder in a subsequent "deed with right of redemption" auction. The investor must engage in legal actions to recover the cost of the lien or to foreclose the property. If the property is not sold at the "deed with right of redemption" auction, the state commissioner may make deed to the tax lien certificate holder.

Maryland

Holder of unsold tax lien certificates:	Maryland municipality governing the state.

STATES THAT OFFER UNSOLD TAX LIEN CERTIFICATES FOR SALE OVER-THE-COUNTER

Status of unsold tax lien certificates:	Issued by the tax collector to the mayor and city council of Baltimore City or the governing body of a particular county.

Unsold lien certificates may be sold or assigned, but there is no mandate governing the sale of such certificates. The investor or governing body is given the right to foreclose the right of redemption.

Montana

Holder of unsold tax lien certificates:	Montana municipality governing the state.
Status of unsold tax lien certificates:	Assigned to the county by the county treasurer for no less than the opening bid amount.

Unsold tax lien certificates are assigned to the county. Certificates must be sold to any purchaser upon payment of all delinquent taxes, interest, and other costs.

Nebraska

Holder of unsold tax lien certificates:	Nebraska municipality governing the tax sale.
Status of unsold tax lien certificates:	Assigned to the county by the county treasurer.

Unsold tax lien certificates are assigned to the county. Certificates may be sold to any purchaser upon payment of all delinquent taxes, interest, and other costs.

North Dakota

Holder of unsold tax lien certificates:	North Dakota municipality governing the tax sale.
Status of unsold tax lien certificates:	Assigned to the county by the county treasurer.

The county treasurer, on behalf of the county, bids unsold tax lien certificates. The county acquires all legal and equitable rights to the property that secures the lien. Certificates may be sold to any purchaser upon payment of all delinquent taxes, interest, and other costs.

Oklahoma

Holder of unsold tax lien certificates:	Oklahoma.
Status of unsold tax lien certificates:	Assigned to the state by the county treasurer.

Unsold tax liens are mandated to be offered for sale to the first purchaser willing to pay the taxes, interest, costs of the sale, and transfer as calculated up to the day of sale.

STATES THAT OFFER UNSOLD TAX LIEN CERTIFICATES FOR SALE OVER-THE-COUNTER

Oklahoma

Holder of unsold tax lien certificates:	Oklahoma.
Status of unsold tax lien certificates:	Assigned to the state by the county treasurer.

Unsold tax liens are mandated to be offered for sale to the first purchaser willing to pay the taxes, interest, costs of the sale, and transfer as calculated up to the day of sale.

South Carolina

Holder of unsold tax lien certificates:	South Carolina municipality governing the tax sale.
Status of unsold tax lien certificates:	Assigned to the forfeited land commission.

The county treasurer is mandated to sell unsold tax lien certificates at a private sale to any person willing to pay the taxes, interest, and costs of the sale. The treasurer may make bid, in the name of the county, for the sale of properties, which secure unsold lien certificates. The treasurer is mandated to sell properties for which delinquent taxes have not been paid in the preceding one or more years. In short, the county treasurer may make bid to purchase the property at minimal cost or to sell the property if the county holds it for more than one year.

South Dakota

Holder of unsold tax lien certificates:	South Dakota county treasurer.
Status of unsold tax lien certificates:	Held for sale by the county treasurer.

The county treasurer is mandated to sell unsold tax lien certificates at a private sale to any person willing to pay the taxes, interest, and costs of the sale. The treasurer may make bid, in the name of the county, for the sale of properties, which secure unsold lien certificates. The treasurer is mandated to sell properties for which delinquent taxes have not been paid in the preceding one or more years. In short, the county treasurer may make bid to purchase the property at minimal cost or to sell the property if the county holds it for more than one year.

Wyoming

Holder of unsold tax lien certificates:	Wyoming municipality governing the tax sale.
Status of unsold tax lien certificates:	Purchased in the name of the county by the county treasurer.

The county may sell or assign unsold tax lien certificates at either a public or private sale to any person willing to pay the taxes, interest, and costs of the sale.

Step 2: Eliminate States That Are Not Likely to Have Certificates Available for Offer

Having identified those states that offer tax lien certificates for sale when they are not sold at the annual delinquent property tax sale, the investor must be capable of identifying those states that are most likely to have a significant number of tax lien certificates to offer over-the-counter. As with all investment opportunities, adequate research is necessary for good investing. Understanding state laws and procedures governing a taxing municipality should be part of the initial step in the tax lien certificate investment process. Understanding such laws and procedures also allows the investor to identify and eliminate those states that are not likely to have certificates available to offer over-the-counter. States that are not likely to have certificates available for sale after the tax sale include the following:

- **States that allow for attractive rates of return for redemption.** Tax liens sold by states that allow investors to collect the most attractive rates of return on redemption amounts have high turnover rates at their municipal tax sales. Investors usually purchase most or all available tax lien certificates at the annual tax sale in an effort to profit from the high rates of return.

- **States that have laws that prevent the sale of over-the-counter certificates following the tax sale.** Laws that permit the purchase of tax liens over-the-counter do not govern all states. There are seven states with laws and statutes that are not designed to provide an opportunity for the purchase of tax lien certificates over-the-counter. Currently, Illinois, Indiana, Iowa,* Mississippi, Missouri, New Jersey, and Vermont do not offer over-the-counter sales of tax lien certificates. The investor should be sure to check into the laws applicable to a particular state, since such laws are subject to change or modification from year to year. The seven tax lien states that do not offer over-the-counter sales of tax lien certificates are listed below: (Ref. 8)

Table 7

STATES THAT PROHIBIT OVER-THE-COUNTER OPPORTUNITIES
Illinois
Illinois holds an annual tax sale for the sale of tax lien certificates. Tax lien certificates that are not sold at the annual tax sale are forfeited to Illinois and offered for public sale again at an Illinois collector's scavenger sale. The collector's scavenger sale is mandatory for counties with more than three million residents and must be ordered by resolution in the remaining counties. The collector's scavenger sale is held for properties with two or more years of tax delinquency, including the tax year in which the collector's scavenger sale is advertised and held. If a property tax lien certificate is not sold at the collector's scavenger sale or confirmed by a court, the lien certificate is offered annually at the collector's scavenger tax sale until sold. An exception to Illinois state laws applies to mineral rights. If the lien certificate to mineral rights is not confirmed by a court or sold at the collector's scavenger tax sale for 10 consecutive years, it is no longer offered for sale.
Indiana
Indiana does not engage in over-the-counter sales of tax lien certificates. Tax lien certificates that are unsold at the annual tax sale or bid for an amount that is less than the opening bid amount are either offered for sale at the next annual tax sale or offered for sale at a special sale. A special sale is held between January 1 and March 31 of the year following the annual tax sale. The annual tax sale is usually held during the month of August or September. The particular county treasurer and county auditor must agree to hold the special tax sale, and this sale must be held, at a minimum, 90 days after the initial tax sale. If a tax lien certificate is not sold at the special tax sale or the offered price is not sufficient to cover the minimum amount established as the opening bid amount, the tax lien certificate is bought and held by the county for the opening bid amount. The county may hold unsold tax lien certificates for acquisition by a metropolitan development commission in a consolidated city or for use by a nonprofit corporation.

STATES THAT PROHIBIT OVER-THE-COUNTER OPPORTUNITIES

Iowa

If tax sale certificates are not sold in Iowa during the annual tax sale, the certificates are offered for sale at subsequent adjournments of the tax sale. The first adjourned sale is held within two months of the tax sale. Subsequent adjournments are held, at a maximum, within two months of previous adjourned sales. These adjourned sales are continued until all properties have been sold or until the next annual tax sale is held. State laws dictate that notice of adjourned sales be posted in the county treasurer's office. Iowa state laws do not dictate a need for any other type of public notice. As such, investors must contact the particular treasurer's office of interest to obtain information about adjourned sales. Iowa has 99 such county treasurers. State laws provide for the various counties to engage in three basic systems of adjourned sales, including:

1. Daily adjourned sales.
2. Monthly adjourned sales.
3. Bimonthly adjourned sales.

* When a municipality engages in the daily sales method, it has the same effect as allowing investors to buy tax lien certificates (over-the-counter).

Tax lien certificates that are not sold at adjourned sales prior to the next annual tax sale are offered for sale at a public bidders sale. The public bidders sale is advertised and conducted in the same manner and on the same date as the annual tax sale. If a tax lien certificate is not sold at the public bidders sale or the bid amount is not sufficient to cover the amount due as predetermined by the treasurer, the board of supervisors of the particular municipality decides the disposition of the tax lien certificate. The board may either allow the particular county to bid the property for the opening bid amount, or the board may make a written compromise and assignment of the certificate to the county. In most instances, tax certificates that are unsold and bid or assigned to the county are secured by properties that are the least attractive of the county's base of real properties.

Mississippi

In Mississippi, tax liens that are not sold at the annual delinquent property tax sale are struck off to Mississippi. The tax collector is responsible for striking off tax liens to the county, which provides the county with title to the property without right of possession. Property owners are entitled to redeem tax lien certificates. The tax collector may also assign a certificate to any assignee as named and specified by written approval of the property owner. Upon payment of the tax lien certificate and all associated costs, the assignee is given first lien against the property. The assignee may sell the property to satisfy the lien. If the property is neither redeemed nor assigned within a specified period of time, the state land commissioner may sell the property itself, not the tax lien certificate. The

STATES THAT PROHIBIT OVER-THE-COUNTER OPPORTUNITIES

property must be sold for a minimum of $2 per acre, unless otherwise specified and approved by the land commissioner and the state governor.

Missouri

Missouri records properties that are held as security for tax lien certificates in the state's back-tax book when tax lien certificates are not sold at the annual delinquent property tax sale. If the delinquent property taxes are not paid or any subsequent taxes become delinquent by the next annual tax sale, tax lien certificates for the securing properties are offered for sale again at the next annual delinquent property tax sale.

New Jersey

New Jersey provides for tax lien certificates that are not sold at annual delinquent property tax sales to be struck off and sold to the particular municipality offering tax lien certificates for sale. State laws provide for the striking off of properties only in the case that the particular municipality has not received 15 percent of the total revenue that should be realized by the municipality through tax sales. Tax lien certificates may be purchased by bid that is sufficient to cover the cost of the tax lien, or they may be purchased at 18 percent of the property's value. The tax lien certificate is then subject to redemption. If the property owner fails to redeem the tax lien certificate, the lien-holding city or county may exercise the right to make deed to the property and foreclose the property. New Jersey state law prohibits tax liens held by municipalities from being assigned or sold over-the-counter. Government-held tax lien certificates are offered at subsequent tax sales, as directed by a resolution of the municipality's governing body. Existing and newly assessed taxes, interest, and other costs are added as additional lien amounts before the tax lien certificate is offered at the subsequent tax sale. The property owner must pay existent and newly assessed amounts before the tax lien certificate can be redeemed. Interest is calculated on the newly assessed amounts from the date of the new tax sale. Amounts are recalculated and assessed in the name of the property owner as if the original delinquent property tax sale had never taken place.

Vermont

The state laws of Vermont permit the tax collector to collect on delinquent taxes by seizing and selling the property. The property owner, mortgage holder, or assignee is given a one-year period of right of redemption. If the property is not redeemed within the one year allowed, the tax collector may make title to the property. Vermont laws do not make mention of or provide for the assignment of tax lien certificates.

Counties in Wyoming are examples of municipalities that offer very few, if any, over-the-counter sales of tax lien certificates, because the rate of return is so attractive to investors that they buy all or most tax lien certificates that are offered at the annual delinquent property tax sale.

In contrast to Wyoming, Oklahoma offers a low rate of return on redemption amounts to be paid by property owners. Counties in Oklahoma offer all or most of their lien certificates for sale over-the-counter because the rate of return on redemption is not attractive enough for investors to bid on tax liens at the annual tax sale. The redemption amount to be paid by the property owner includes the following:

- The amount paid for the tax lien at the annual tax sale or the amount paid for the over-the-counter tax liens.

- All subsequent taxes assessed.

- Annual simple interest of 8 percent calculated from the date of the tax sale or purchase of the over-the-counter certificate.

- Costs of the sale and transfer.

Oklahoma state laws do not permit competitive bidding, which means the cost of a tax lien certificate is simply the delinquent tax amount, interest, and any associated costs. There are no additional penalties assessed, and the cost cannot be bid up. The property owner is given two years to redeem the tax lien certificate, and the annual interest is calculated and assessed from the date of the tax sale to the date of redemption.

State statutes dictate the rate of return to be assessed by states that offer over-the-counter certificates. Those rates are summarized in Table 8. States are listed in order of lowest annualized interest rate to the highest.

Table 8

	ANNUALIZED REDEMPTION RATES FOR OVER-THE-COUNTER TAX LIEN CERTIFICATES DICTATED BY STATE STATUTE	
	State	**Interest Rate on Redemption**
1	Maryland	6% per annum, except as "fixed" by the municipality's governing body.
2	Oklahoma	8% per annum.
3	South Carolina	8% to 12% per annum dependent upon when the property is redeemed and whether the property is the legal residence of the property owner. The redemption period is one year, and the annual interest is computed at 8% within the first six months and 12% in the last six months. The state also classifies real property. Redemption statutes apply to property that is less than five acres and occupied by owners or family members of the owners. Owners may hold title to the property in whole or in part.
4	North Dakota	9% per annum.
5	Montana	10% per annum.
6	Alabama	12% per annum.
7	South Dakota	12% per annum.
8	Colorado	9% above the discount rate, as established on September 1 of the year in which the tax sale is held. The discount rate is defined as the rate of interest that commercial banks pay to the Federal Reserve Bank of Kansas City using government bonds or other securities. The amount is rounded to the nearest percent.
9	Nebraska	14% per annum.
10	Michigan	15% to 50% per annum depending upon the date of redemption. If redemption occurs within one year of the tax sale, the redemption rate is 15%. After one year, an additional 50% penalty is assessed.
11	Arizona	16% per annum.

ANNUALIZED REDEMPTION RATES FOR OVER-THE-COUNTER TAX LIEN CERTIFICATES DICTATED BY STATE STATUTE		
12	Wyoming	18% to 51% per annum depending upon the date of redemption. If the redemption occurs within one year of the tax sale, the annualized rate ranges from 18% to 51%. The minimum annualized rate is computed as 15% per annum interest plus 3% penalty. If redemption occurs after the first year, but before the fourth year, the rate may range from 15.75% to 17.8% per year.
13	Iowa	24% per annum.

Municipalities in Maryland offer some of the lowest annual interest rates on redemption. However, the rates vary depending upon the taxing municipality. As Table 9 below shows, most municipalities have statutes that dictate a 6 percent rate; a few have statutory 10 percent rates, while only one has a 14 percent statutory rate. However, with the exception of St. Mary's county, that rate may be "fixed" by the governing body or ordinances enacted by the governing body. As such, the fixed per annum interest rates for Maryland may range from 6 percent to 24 percent, making Maryland a state that offers some of the lowest as well as some of the highest interest rates on redemption. Interest rates established by statute and those fixed by governing authorities for each of Maryland's taxing municipalities are shown in Table 9 listed by fixed interest rates.

Table 9

PER ANNUM INTEREST RATES FOR MUNICIPALITIES IN MARYLAND		
Municipality	**Per Annum Interest Established by Statute**	**"Fixed" Interest Rate**
Baltimore City	6% a year or as fixed by a law of the city council.	24% per annum computed from the date of the sale.

PER ANNUM INTEREST RATES FOR MUNICIPALITIES IN MARYLAND		
Montgomery County	6% a year or as fixed by a law of the county council.	24% per annum computed from the date of the sale.
Prince George's County	6% a year or as fixed by a law of the county council.	20% per annum computed from the date of the sale.
Allegheny County	6% a year or as fixed by the county commissioners.	18% per annum computed from the date of the sale.
Anne Arundel County	6% a year or as fixed by a law of the county council.	18% per annum computed from the date of the sale.
Howard County	6% a year or as fixed by a law of the county council.	18% per annum computed from the date of the sale.
Kent County	6% a year or as fixed by the county commissioners.	18% per annum or 1.5% per month or fraction thereof, calculated from the date of sale.
Cecil County	6% a year or as fixed by a law of the county council.	12% per annum or 1% per month or fraction thereof.
Baltimore County	6% a year or as fixed by a law of the county council.	12% per annum or 1% per month or fraction thereof.
Queen Anne's County	6% a year or as fixed by a law of the county council.	12% per annum or 1% per month or fraction thereof.
Somerset County	6% a year or as fixed by the county commissioners or by a law of the county council.	12% per annum.
Charles County	6% a year or as fixed by the county commissioners or by a law of the county council. 6% a year or as fixed by a law of the county council.	12% per annum.
Harford County	6% a year or as fixed by a law of the county council.	12% per annum.
Worcester County	6% a year or as fixed by the county commissioners or by a law of the county council.	10% per month or fraction thereof.

PER ANNUM INTEREST RATES FOR MUNICIPALITIES IN MARYLAND		
Frederick County	6% a year or as fixed by the county commissioners.	10% computed daily.
Wicomico County	6% a year or as fixed by the county commissioners or by a law of the county council.	8% per annum.
Washington County	6% a year or as fixed by the county commissioners.	8% per annum.
Talbot County	6% a year or as fixed by a law of the county council.	8% per annum.
Calvert County	10% a year or as fixed by the county commissioners	8% per annum.
Caroline County	10% a year or as fixed by the county commissioners.	8% per annum.
Dorchester County	10% a year or as fixed by the county commissioners.	8% per annum.
Garrett County	10% a year or as fixed by the county commissioners.	8% per annum.
Carroll County	14% a year or as fixed by the county commissioners.	8% per annum.
St. Mary's County	6% a year.	8% per annum.

Step 3: Seek Over-the-Counter Lien Certificates in Order of the Oldest to Newest

One of the objectives of investors in purchasing over-the-counter tax lien certificates is to reduce the amount of time that investment dollars are vested in tax lien certificates. States provide property owners with an opportunity to redeem tax lien certificates, and the redemption period may range from months to years. If an investor purchases tax lien certificates at annual state tax sales, the investor may be required to wait anywhere from 6 to 60 months before receiving a return from the redemption of the tax lien certificate. The investor who seeks older lien certificates, which have been held by the state for the longest period of time, benefits from a more immediate return on investment dollars.

Statutory redemption periods for over-the-counter tax lien certificates are listed in Table 10, in order of shortest to longest possible redemption period.

Table 10

REDEMPTION PERIODS ESTABLISHED BY STATE STATUTES FOR OVER-THE-COUNTER TAX LIEN CERTIFICATES	
Redemption Period	Position After Redemption Period
Maryland	
6 months. Exception: The property is certified as needing substantial repairs to comply with building codes. The investor may file a complaint to foreclose the right of redemption within 60 days of the sale of the tax lien certificate.	File complaint to foreclose the right of redemption.
Michigan	
1 year	Initiate processes to obtain a tax deed.
Iowa	
1 year. Following annual tax sale. 9 months. Following public bidders sale.	Held by the county for offer at the next year's public bidders sale.

REDEMPTION PERIODS ESTABLISHED BY STATE STATUTES FOR OVER-THE-COUNTER TAX LIEN CERTIFICATES

Redemption Period	Position After Redemption Period
Mississippi	
2 years. Exception: The property owner is an infant who inherited the property or an individual of unsound mind. The property may be redeemed within 2 years of attaining legal age or being restored to sanity. The redemption amount includes the cost of any permanent improvements made in the 2 years following the tax sale.	
New Jersey	
6 months. If the municipality makes purchase at the annual tax sale.	
Oklahoma	
2 years.	County treasurer issues a deed for unredeemed land upon the property owner's failure to respond to a lien holder's final notice requesting redemption within 60 days.
Alabama	
3 years.	
Colorado	
3 years.	
Montana	
3 years.	Lien holder is issued a deed upon the property owner's not responding to the lien holder's final notice to the property owner requesting redemption within 60 days of the final notice.
Nebraska	
3 years.	The lien holder has 6 months to initiate the process of obtaining a deed.

REDEMPTION PERIODS ESTABLISHED BY STATE STATUTES FOR OVER-THE-COUNTER TAX LIEN CERTIFICATES	
Redemption Period	**Position After Redemption Period**
North Dakota	
3 years. If the property is located within the limits of any municipality.	Initiate the process of obtaining a deed.
South Dakota	
3 years. If the property is located within the limits of any municipality.	Initiate the process of obtaining a deed.
4 years. If the property is located outside the limits of any municipality.	Initiate the process of obtaining deed
Wyoming	
4 years.	Foreclose the right to redemption.
Arizona	
3 years. Judicial foreclosure.	File legal action to foreclose.
5 years. Nonjudicial foreclosure.	Apply with the county treasurer to receive a deed if the tax lien certificate was purchased prior to January 1, 1999.

When redemption periods have expired, the investor is required, in most states, to follow some prescribed procedure for foreclosing the property owner's right to redemption and making deed to the securing property. Some states, however, offer more immediate methods of getting title to a property that secures a tax lien certificate.

Arizona allows unsold tax lien certificates to be sold or assigned to the state, rather than the particular municipality (see Table 7 on pages 134–136). Investors are provided two opportunities to foreclose tax lien certificates. Following a three-year redemption period, an investor may judicially foreclose the right to redemption and obtain a deed to the property. Following a five-year redemption period, an investor may administratively foreclose the right to redemption and receive a deed to the property; however, this statute is being phased out and only applies to property tax liens acquired before 1999. An investor who purchases an over-the-counter tax lien certificate, which has been held by the state for more than three years, may immediately put processes in place to gain a deed to the property. While these certificates offer an investor the opportunity to realize a fast return on investment dollars, other state laws reduce the likelihood that the state will have any unsold tax lien certificates available to offer for sale. Arizona offers an attractive 16 percent interest on redemption amounts. The high redemption rate ensures that interested investors will make bids at the annual tax sale, particularly for improved properties. When tax lien certificates are available for over-the-counter sales, the offer of sale is not always immediate, depending on the workload of the particular county treasurer's office. Interested investors must contact the treasurer of individual municipalities to find out when, if any, sales of state-held over-the-counter tax lien certificates are being made.

Step 4: Determine the Bidding Systems Used

An investor needs to determine the bidding system used by the state or a municipality before bidding on tax lien certificates. The investor wishing to gain ownership should buy tax lien certificates in those states that engage in noncompetitive bidding, which does not adversely affect the price that must be paid for the property if the property owner fails to redeem the tax lien certificate. States that engage in the competitive premium bidding of tax lien certificates are not likely to provide an opportunity for an investor to purchase liens for the minimum of tax, interest, and cost of the sale. States that engage in this type of competitive premium bidding include Alabama, Maryland, Missouri, South Carolina, and Vermont.

Since an investor or investment group is not likely to be able to attend all annual delinquent property tax sales to bid on available tax lien certificates, the investor or investment group is left to engage in the purchase of leftover certificates that are offered over-the-counter by the taxing authority. Properties purchased over-the-counter offer the benefit of being acquired at minimum cost, particularly in states that engage in the competitive bidding down of ownership in the securing property. In these states, no competitive bidding is used when tax lien certificates are offered over-the-counter and the investor bids for 100 percent ownership of the property. An investor may purchase tax lien certificates for an amount equal to the delinquent tax amount, interest, penalty, and any associated fees and costs. Over-the-counter sales offer the investor the benefit of receiving tax lien certificates secured by 100 percent of the property for the minimum cost.

Maryland allows competitive bidding and offers its tax lien certificates to the highest bidder. The system ensures that no investor may acquire a lien certificate unless no one else is willing to bid a higher price. The state, however, does not require that the full amount of the bid be paid initially. Only the opening bid amount is paid to the tax collector, and the balance of the bid amount (the premium amount) is considered a credit. If the property owner fails to redeem the tax lien certificate, the premium amount and all newly assessed taxes, interest, penalties, and costs must be paid before the lien holder may obtain a deed. Maryland statutes provide for a redemption interest of 6 percent, but also provide for the governing body of a jurisdiction to increase the amount at will. Most jurisdictions, particularly Baltimore City, have opted to impose substantially higher rates, attracting investors who wish to profit from the high rate of return. The Maryland system offers investors the benefit of having a vested interest in a tax lien certificate without ever having to invest more than the minimum opening bid amount if the tax lien certificate is redeemed. The ability of the governing body to override the interest rate established by state statute also provides the benefit of a lucrative rate on return for redeemed tax lien certificates. Maryland municipalities with the highest interest rates on redemption include the following, listed in order of highest to lowest rates:

Table 11

MARYLAND'S HIGHEST REDEMPTION RATES	
Municipality	Per Annum Simple Interest *Computed from the Date of Sale*
Baltimore City	24%
Montgomery County	20%
Prince George's County	20%
Allegany County	18%
Anne Arundel County	18%
Howard County	18%
Kent County	18%

While these municipalities present opportunities for the investor interested in profiting from the high yield required for redemption, these municipalities are not cost effective for investors seeking to gain property ownership. The high yield expected from redemption is converted to high costs for the investor who wishes to foreclose the property owner's right of redemption. In order to begin the process of obtaining a deed and foreclosure, the investor is required to pay the premium amount bid to acquire the tax lien certificate as well as any newly incurred taxes, penalties, and interest. The interest is paid at the "fixed" interest rate established by the taxing municipality.

Statutes established for the state put Maryland in the unique position of offering some of the highest and lowest interest rates for redemption. Investors interested in gaining homeownership should concentrate on the Maryland municipalities that offer low redemption interest rates. Municipalities with the lowest interest rates include those shown in Table 12 below.

Table 12

MARYLAND'S LOWEST REDEMPTION RATES	
Municipality	Per Annum Simple Interest *Computed From the Date of Sale*
St. Mary's County	6%
Talbot County	6%
Washington County	6%
Wicomico County	8%

Step 5: Bid Where the Bidding Process Does Not Significantly Affect Price

Some states are governed by statutes that provide for the bidding up of premiums on tax lien certificates if more than one individual is interested in purchasing the certificate. However, the implementation of such statutes does not necessarily mean that the price paid by investors to foreclose the right of redemption and acquire ownership of the property is significantly increased. States where this bidding process does not significantly drive up the cost of obtaining title and possession of foreclosed properties include Colorado,

Mississippi, and Indiana. These states engage in desirable methods of bidding when ownership of a property is the objective.

Desirable Competitive Premium Bidding

Colorado engages in the competitive bidding up of premiums. The winner is the bidder willing to pay the largest premium amount in cash above the opening bid. Upon redemption, the property owner is required to pay the opening bid amount plus interest from the date of sale. The redemption interest rate is set at 9 percent plus the federal discount rate that is established for a particular year. The tax lien certificate holder is not reimbursed for the premium amount used to win the bid; nor does the certificate holder receive interest on the premium amount invested. If a property owner is quick to redeem a tax lien certificate after the tax sale, it is likely that the investor may suffer a loss from the investment. If the premium amount bid and paid by the investor is significantly more than the amount received from interest on the redemption amount, the investor takes a loss. As an example, an investor bids $1,200 for a tax lien certificate. The opening bid amount is $1,000, but the investor bids up the premium to $200.

Opening Bid:	*$1,000*
Premium Bid:	*200*
Total Cost of Tax Lien Certificate	***$1,200***

The property owner redeems the tax lien certificate with a 12 percent interest rate one month after the tax sale. Upon redemption, the investor receives the following:

Tax Lien Cost:	$1,000	Opening bid does not include the premium amount
Interest on Opening Bid:	10	12% per annum (1% per month)
Total Returned:	$1,010	
TOTAL LOSS	**−$190**	$1,010 − $1,200

Because the premium amount and interest on the premium amount are excluded from the redemption amount, and the premium ($200) does not exceed the amount paid in interest ($10), the investor takes a loss. If, on the other hand, the property owner fails to redeem the tax lien certificate, the investor would obtain the deed to the property for the opening bid amount plus the premium amount and any newly accrued taxes, which is substantially cheaper than purchasing the property in the real estate market.

Mississippi also engages in the competitive bidding up of premiums. The winning bidder is the one willing to pay the largest premium amount in cash above the opening bid amount. Upon redemption, the premium amount is refunded to the tax lien certificate holder, but no interest is paid on the premium amount. The property owner is required to pay the following:

- The opening bid amount.

- Interest at 18 percent of the opening bid amount computed at 1.5 percent per month or any fractional part thereof, calculated from the date of the tax sale.

- Any taxes that have accrued since the date of the sale.

- Interest on the newly accrued taxes computed at 1 percent per month or any fractional part thereof calculated from the date of the tax sale.

If a $1,000 tax lien certificate were bid up in premium to $1,200, the investor would receive the following from redemption 1 month after the tax sale:

Tax Lien Cost:	*$1,000*	*Opening bid*
Refund of Premium:	*200*	
Interest on Opening Bid:	*15*	*18% per annum (1.5% per month)*
Total Returned:	*$1,215*	
TOTAL GAIN	**$15**	*$1,215 – $1,200*

If the property is redeemed quickly, no new taxes are likely to accrue, as in the example above. However, if the redemption occurs after subsequent taxes are assessed, the investor may not receive much return on the investment or may even take a loss. If, on the other hand, the property owner fails to redeem the tax lien certificate, the investor may obtain deed to property for the minimum of the opening bid amount, the premium amount, and any newly accrued taxes — still significantly cheaper than purchasing property through normal real estate channels.

Bidders in Colorado and Mississippi realize that early redemptions may create low gains or losses, so they make an effort to keep premiums low. Not only does this type of premium bidding have the potential to create a loss when tax lien certificates are redeemed early, control of the premium bid amount may offer a benefit should the property owner fail to redeem the tax lien certificate. Should the tax lien certificate investment lead to property ownership, ownership would be acquired at substantially lower costs than would be required to purchase property through normal real estate channels.

Indiana engages in the competitive bidding up of premiums much like that of Mississippi, except that the tax lien investor must file a verified claim with the county auditor to recover the premium amount from the county's tax sale surplus fund. Also, Indiana does not require property owners to pay any interest on redemption amounts but requires that they pay a penalty on both the opening bid and premium. Upon redemption, the property owner is required to pay the following:

- The opening bid amount.

- A 10 percent penalty on the opening bid amount if the redemption occurs in the first six months.

- A 10 percent penalty on the opening bid amount if the redemption occurs after six months.

- A 10 percent penalty on the premium amount.

- Any taxes that have accrued since the date of the sale.

If a $1,000 tax lien certificate is bid up in premium to $1,200, the investor would receive the following from redemption one month after the tax sale:

Tax Lien Cost:	$1,000	*Opening bid*
Refund of Premium:	200	
Penalty on Opening Bid:	100	*10%*
Penalty on Premium:	2	*10% per annum (0.83% per month)*
Total Returned:	$1,302	
TOTAL GAIN	**$1,102**	*$1,302 – $1,200*

Not only does the tax sale process provide for the investor to profit from the redemption amount paid, it also provides for the investor to acquire property without substantially increasing the cost of ownership. If the tax lien certificate is not redeemed, the investor may obtain a deed to property for the minimum tax, interest, penalty, sale costs, and any newly accrued taxes, which is substantially cheaper than if he or she bought the property in the real estate market.

Desirable Bidding Down of Interest Rates

Some states assign tax lien certificates to the bidder who purchases the certificate at the opening bid and also bids down the lowest percentage of interest to be paid upon redemption. Arizona, Illinois, and New Jersey engage in this type of bidding process. Arizona and Illinois sell tax lien certificates at the exact amount of the opening bid. When there is more than one bidder for a particular property, the successful bidder is the one who bids down the lowest redemption interest to be paid, if and when the tax lien certificate is redeemed. In New Jersey, a successful bidder of the competitive bidding down process is decided by bidding down the redemption interest and then engaging in a competitive bidding up of premium amounts.

Both Arizona and Illinois have been identified as states that are not likely to have tax lien certificates available to offer over-the-counter. Investors wishing to profit from the high-yielding redemption rates of 16 percent and 18 percent, respectively, usually attend the tax sales held in these states. Bidders in these states are not likely to bid down too far because it would defeat the purpose of receiving the high rates of interest. Statutes governing Arizona provide for a 16 percent per annum redemption interest. A bidder may bid down to accept an interest rate that is less than the statutory 16 percent but not too much more. If, however, the property owner fails to redeem the tax lien certificate, the investor's cost to obtain deed to the property is, at a minimum, an amount equal to the opening bid and any newly accrued taxes. The same holds true for Illinois, except that the interest rate is 18 percent.

New Jersey uses a similar process, except that limits are established for redemption rates. State statutes dictate that redemption rates may not exceed 18 percent. Also, should more than one bidder offer to purchase a tax lien certificate and the bid down process results in a redemption rate that is less than 1 percent, the successful bidder is the one who pays the highest premium over the opening bid. If, however, the property owner fails to redeem the tax lien certificate, the investor's cost to obtain a deed to the property is, at a minimum, an amount equal to the opening bid, the premium bid, and any newly accrued taxes.

Desirable First-Come, First-Served Bidding

Kentucky, Montana, and Oklahoma engage in first-come, first-served methods of offering tax lien certificates for sale. There are no premium amounts to be paid, and the opening bids may not be bid up or bid down. The opening bid is the final bid.

In Kentucky, tax lien certificates are not secured by real property. If a tax lien certificate is not redeemed within the redemption period, the tax lien certificate is offered for sale again at a subsequent auction. The successful bidder at the subsequent tax sale is the bidder who, based upon the judgment of the sheriff, makes the first offer to pay cash for the lien certificate. However, the initial lien holder is given preference in the subsequent tax sales.

Montana laws dictate that tax lien certificates be sold to any purchaser willing to pay the opening bid amount. Most municipalities engage in a first-come, first-served method of offering tax lien certificates for sale.

In Oklahoma, the successful bidder is the bidder who, based

upon the decision of the county treasurer, makes the first offer to purchase a tax lien certificate. The county treasurer, using his or her own discretion, is required to implement fair and impartial methods of determining the successful bidder when multiple bidders wish to purchase the same tax lien certificate.

Undesirable Bidding Down of Ownership

Some states engage in competitive bidding that results in investors' having to bid down the percentage of ownership in property used as security for tax lien certificates. The investor does not obtain 100 percent ownership in the property should the property owner fail to redeem the tax lien certificate. Iowa, Michigan, Louisiana, Massachusetts, New Hampshire, and Rhode Island engage in this type of competitive bidding.

In Iowa, the tax lien certificate purchaser is the bidder who offers to pay the lien for the smallest portion of ownership in the property used to secure the tax lien certificate. This portion of ownership is designated an undivided portion. The remaining portion of ownership in the property belongs to the property owner. When two or more investors wish to bid on the same tax lien certificate, the percentage of ownership in the securing property is bid down until no other bidder wishes to bid. Iowa state statutes provide for a 24 percent per annum redemption rate. If a tax lien certificate is not redeemed within the one-year, nine-month redemption period, the investor may foreclose the owner's right to redemption. The lien holder is granted a treasurer's deed for the percentage of interest that was bid to obtain the tax lien certificate. Because a treasurer's deed entitles both the investor and the property owner to a percentage of tenancy-in-common, an investor is not likely to obtain full ownership. Very specific and time-consuming processes must be followed to sell the property and receive a return on the investment.

Undesirable Random Selection Bidding

Some states implement a system of randomly selecting bidders to purchase tax lien certificates. Wyoming and certain municipalities of Colorado and Iowa engage in a random selection process. First-come, first-served methods that allow each purchaser to bid on all available tax lien certificates that have not been purchased are more desirable than selection processes in which bidders are randomly chosen to purchase a particular tax lien certificate. Random selection bidding offers investors very low or no odds of being able to invest in specific or valuable properties. The random selection process reduces the odds of being able to bid on a particular property to one out of the number of total bidders participating in the tax sale. An investor has virtually no chance of being able to bid on a property of choice.

Though Iowa is not governed by statutes that allow for random selection, some municipal treasurers are favorable to such a process rather than engaging in the mandatory system of bidding down ownership established by the state. Likewise, the statutes established for Wyoming provide for the bidding down of the percentage of interest in tax lien certificates. However, all 15 municipalities of Wyoming choose to engage in a random selection process. Wyoming also provides bidders with an opportunity to purchase tax lien certificates over-the-counter. When tax lien certificates are available for over-the-counter sales, the bid-down process and the random selection process are eliminated.

Step 6: Acquire the Listing of Delinquent Properties

Most delinquent property tax sales are mandated to be held on a particular date or within a particular time frame. Other states allow tax sale dates to be determined by the governing body responsible for the sale. Statutory dates that are established by states are as shown in Table 13 below. Investors must contact those states and municipalities that do not have laws or statutes governing delinquent property tax sales to determine when the particular taxing municipality holds its annual tax sale.

All tax lien certificates offered for sale in a given municipality must be published in a local newspaper of general circulation in the particular municipality where the tax sale is held. The treasurer's office of each municipality decides which newspaper to use for the publication of tax lien certificates. An investor may request that the treasurer indicate which newspaper it intends to use by addressing a simple letter to the treasurer's office. A prepaid and self-addressed envelope should be included with the letter to cover the expense of mailing a response. Once the newspaper and date of publication have been determined, the investor may order the particular issue of the newspaper directly from the publisher to begin research.

Table 13

	STATUTORY TAX SALE DATES	
	State	**Statutory Date of Sale**
1	Arizona	Month of February. Each municipality establishes its own day in the month of February. Most municipalities choose dates near the end of the month.
2	Colorado	Before the second Monday in December. Sales are typically held during the month of November.
3	Illinois	No date is specified in the statutes; sales are typically held during the month of November.
4	Indiana	Between August 1 and October 31, but must not extend beyond October 31.
5	Iowa	Third Monday in June.
6	Maryland	As specified by the particular municipality.
	Baltimore County	Within four months of the first Monday in February.
	Cecil County	First Monday in June.
	Hartford County	Third Monday in June, after 10 a.m.
	Montgomery County	Second Monday in June.
	Prince George's County	Second Monday in May, after 10 a.m.
	Queen Anne's County	Third Tuesday in May.
7	Michigan	Third Tuesday in May.
8	Missouri	Fourth Monday in August.
9	Mississippi	Last Monday in August or, at the discretion of the tax collector, the first Monday in April.
10	Montana	No date is specified in the statutes; sales are typically held during the month of July. Notice of a pending sale must be published once a week, beginning before the last Tuesday in June and continue, once a week, for three consecutive weeks. The tax sale must occur within 21 to 28 days of publication.

STATUTORY TAX SALE DATES	
State	Statutory Date of Sale
11	North Dakota	Second Tuesday in December, after 10 a.m.
12	Oklahoma	First Monday in October, 9 a.m. to 4 p.m.
13	South Dakota	Third Monday in December, 9 a.m. to 4 p.m.

January 00, 2006

Treasurer's Office
123 Street Address
Anytown, USA 00000

Dear Treasurer,

I am requesting information regarding the upcoming 2006 annual property tax sale. Would you please provide the name, address, and phone number of the newspaper that will be used by your office to publish the listing of certificates for offer? In addition, would you please provide the dates for which your office plans to list certificates in the publication? I have enclosed a self-addressed, stamped envelope for your response.

Thank you for your assistance.

Sincerely,
Your Name

Step 7: Determine Properties Less Likely to Be Redeemed

Though redemption offers the investor the benefit of profiting from the redemption interest and penalties applied to tax lien certificates, the ultimate goal of some investors is acquire ownership of a property that secures a tax lien certificate. Having acquired a listing of all tax lien certificates for offer at the delinquent property tax sale, the investor must identify those tax lien certificates that he or she would like to pursue in an attempt to gain ownership. In order to gain ownership, an investor needs to identify those properties that are less likely to be redeemed by the property owner, and the investor should attempt to buy tax lien certificates from those municipalities that engage in desirable bidding processes. Tax lien certificates document a priority lien, which means they are given priority over all other liens except liens held by the state in which the property is located and certain liens held by the federal government. When tax lien certificates are not redeemed, the investor must obtain a tax deed to the securing property and foreclose to gain ownership. Since most states provide for two- to three-year redemption periods, property ownership may be acquired for an amount equal to the real property taxes and costs assessed during the redemption period (typically, three years), the expenses of applying for a deed, and the expenses required for foreclosure. Typical real property taxes are assessed in the range of 1 percent to 4 percent of the real property's market value. Accumulated interest, penalties, costs, and fees over a three-year redemption lien could increase the cost of ownership from as little as 4 percent to as much as 15 percent of the market value of a property.

When a tax lien is sold for delinquent taxes, the property may be redeemed by anyone having any type of secured interest in the property. This is inclusive of anyone having ownership interest or security interest in the property. Ownership interest is the interest of any party named on the deed to the property. Security interest is the interest of any party having a lien against the property, such as a mortgage company.

States such as Oklahoma require that the tax lien holder make notice of the intent to foreclose not only to property owners but also to any lenders with outstanding loans against the property before making application for a deed to the property. Thus the investor seeking to gain property ownership is reliant upon both the owner and lender to fail to respond to the notice and abandon responsibility for the property. The investor must be skillful in identifying those tax lien certificates that are not likely to be redeemed. Few property owners will allow their valuable properties to be foreclosed because of delinquent taxes, and lenders are not likely to forfeit security on their loans for the relatively small cost of redeeming a tax lien certificate. Usually when a seemingly valuable property is not redeemed, the owner or lender with security interest in the property has intentionally or unintentionally abandoned the property. If the property is intentionally abandoned, it is likely to have some peculiarities that are not cost effective or time effective to deal with. A property may be assessed with the same value as other similar properties in an area, but research indicates that the property contains some environmental hazard or the property may have been severely damaged by fire and the property owner had no insurance to cover the loss. Valuable properties are rarely abandoned intentionally. Unintentional abandonment, on the other hand, may be caused by a number of factors. The property owner could have passed away and left no will that would indicate the disposition of the property. The party responsible to pay property taxes could have moved and not provided the tax collector with a forwarding address. The property owner could be facing a long-term illness, and relatives are irresponsible in paying bills on his or her behalf. Any number of reasons could cause unintentional abandonment.

In general, the investor attempting to gain ownership should seek properties that are:

- High in market value.

- Free of any lender liens.

- Abandoned by the owner.

Whether tax lien certificates are purchased at annual tax sales or purchased over-the-counter, the investor is required to engage in research to determine whether properties are likely to be redeemed. That research should indicate the following:

1. **If the tax lien certificate is secured by a valuable parcel of real estate.** The amount of taxes due and delinquent, as published in the tax sale listing, may provide some indication of the market value of a property. Evidence from an inspection, as outlined in Step 11 on page 173, will also help in determining market value. In general, taxes are higher on more valuable real property. The published annual tax sale listing indicates an amount of delinquent taxes, but that amount may also include the associated penalties, interest, and other costs that are due. Listings may also include a single amount with no indication as to the number of years of delinquency. An investor must be sure to interpret the listed values according to the tax sale laws and procedures of the given municipality. To be more precise in determining market value, the investor may examine the tax assessor's records, which indicate a property's appraised market value. In addition, records held by the municipality's tax assessor indicate the owner's name and legal description or account number, which can be queried against the owner and legal description identified in the tax sale listing. A computer-generated output of the assessor's information pertaining to a tax lien certificate may contain information similar to the following:

Market/Use		
Assessed Land --------	[9,234]	[876]
Improvements ---------	[38,831]	[5,042]
Mobile home ----------	[]	[]
Total ------------------>	48,065	5,918

The output indicates a valuation of fair market value equal to $48,065, land valued at $9,234, improvements valued at $38,831, and the property does not include a mobile home. An improvement can be a house or other structure. As a rule of thumb, if the assessed value of the land is more than 40 percent of the total assessed value, the property may offer no value. The output shows that the assessed value of the land, relative to the total property value is 19 percent ($9,234 ÷ $48,065). The output, therefore, represents a property where most of the worth is in the structure. This type of property is likely to be of value to an investor. If the output is reversed and the structure is assessed at 19 percent of the total property's worth, the land would hold the greater percentage of worth. The property is likely to be a parcel of land with a small structure, such as a shed or a larger structure that is below par. Only a visual inspection of the property will determine the suitability of such a property for investment purposes. Other records available from the assessor's office may be used to determine the use of a property as well as other specific characteristics of the property. The file of the property file may indicate all or some subset of the following:

- Use of the property; for example, single-family home.

- Lot size.

- Size of additions to the land.

- Composition of the exterior, foundation, roof, fireplace, and utilities.

- Composition of the foundation.

- Photographs of the property.

Clearly, if records indicate that a property represents a single-family home, but the property assessment assigns 80 percent of the worth to the land, there are likely to be problems with the structure identified as a single-family home, or there was some error in the recording of the assessment values. Investors must remember that assessors are not immune from making mistakes in their assessments or in recording assessment data.

2. **If the real property is owned free of any lender liens.** The investor must be capable of researching the title to the property as held by the registrar of deeds, recorder's office, or county clerk of the municipality. Properties that are used as security against lender loans are most likely to be redeemed since a tax lien has priority over a lender's loan. In order for a lender to move its loan into highest priority and prevent it from being discarded, the lender must extinguish any outstanding tax lien certificates by redeeming them. In order to research the outstanding debt held against a parcel of property, the investor must be capable of using the property description and other information provided in the tax sale listing to locate information contained and

recorded in public records. The investor must be capable of researching properties using the particular state's method of indexing properties. States index properties using either a tract indexing system or a grantor-grantee indexing system.

Tract Indexing

In states like Oklahoma, a tract indexing method is used to index mortgages by the legal property description of the property for which they are held. Tax sale listings may provide a legal description of a property in one of two different formats. Either the state subdivision name is listed along with the block and lot number, or a government survey description is provided. The county clerk of each municipality maintains a book or database of all mortgages held against each parcel of real property in the particular municipality. Mortgages are indexed by the property's legal description. The legal description provided in a tax sale listing may be used to query against the legal descriptions used to index mortgaged properties. If the property specified in the tax sale listing has an existing mortgage, it will be documented in the records held by the county clerk. An example of a government survey legal description for a parcel of real property, as published in a tax sale listing, is as follows:

SMITH, JOHN Q. ET UX. 10 21N 03E, E2 NW4 LESS N 466 FT of E 466 FT

The actual legal description is the series of numbers and characters, "10 21N 03E, E2 NW4 LESS N 466 FT of E 466 FT," that follows the named party to the mortgage note. The legal description signifies the location of the property as Section 10, Township 21 North and Range 3 East. The party to the mortgage (grantee) is named as John Q. Smith and his wife (ET UX).

Other information that may be contained in the file or record for a particular property includes the following:

- The named lender or grantor.

- The type of instrument recorded; that is, mortgage. The entry "Mtg" indicate if a mortgage was ever held against the property. The entries "Mtg Rel" or "Rel Mtg" are used to signify that the mortgage was paid off or released.

- The location of the copy of the mortgage note; that is, book and page number.

For a computerized system, the location may be a link to a stored file position in a database.

The following states make use of a tract indexing system:

- Nebraska

- North Dakota

- Oklahoma

- South Dakota

- Wyoming

Grantor-Grantee Indexing

With the exception of Ohio, states that use grantor-grantee indexing are able to identify properties by the names of the grantor (borrower), grantee (lender), or their equivalents. A legal description of the property is not used as the index. Instruments documented and recorded under this system are indexed under the names of individuals associated with the document.

Arizona, for example, maintains an indexed record of instruments for each property in each of its municipalities. The record contains, as a minimum, the following indices for each instrument recorded:

- Date of recording

- Page number

- Grantor (borrower)

- Grantee (lender)

Records may be indexed by either single or multiple indices. The identifying names used to index official records are stored and arranged in alphabetical order using some form of storage and retrieval system. Indices must be accessible to the public yet protected from compromise when electronic storage and retrieval systems are used. Both the grantor and grantee or their equivalents must have indexed instruments for each of the following categories:

- Transference of real property

- Mortgage

- Mortgage release

- Miscellaneous

- Lease

- Secured transactions

- Assignments of mortgages

- Leases

- Governmental liens

- Nongovernmental liens

- Attachments

- Judgments

- Agreements

Instruments may also be categorized according to the following optional categories:

- Powers of attorney

- Official bonds

- Executions

- Lis pendens

- Mine location notices

- Partnerships

- A description or code indicating the type of instrument recorded

Arizona uses two types of grantor/grantee indexes, as follows:

- A combined general grantor/grantee index in which all documents of a specific type are indexed under the grantor and grantee in one separate volume.

- Separate indexes for each type of recorded document. All documents of a specific type that pertain to a particular grantor are indexed in one volume, while documents of a specific type that pertain to a particular grantee are indexed in another volume.

Instruments are categorized according to the type of instrument. Documents indexed as miscellaneous do not fall into the established types of instruments. In Arizona, lenders are likely to hold deeds of trust as well as mortgages as security interest in a property. The investor seeking to invest in tax lien certificates in Arizona must be sure to research both types of documents. As an example, if an investor wants to determine whether a deed of trust or mortgage is being held as a lien against a property, the investor would need to research the grantor-grantee indexing system using the name of the property owner, as published in the tax sale listing. If an entry is found for the grantor, grantee, or both, the investor may use the indicated document number or book and page number to locate the specified document. The document indicates a legal description for the property that should be identical to the legal description of the property published in the tax sale listing. If the legal descriptions match, an outstanding lien is being held against the property.

3. **If outstanding liens against the property are discharged by tax sale process.** In general, a real property tax lien is the first lien against a property, with the exception of states that allow liens assessed by the state to be given higher priority and certain liens held by the federal government. Before an investor purchases a tax lien certificate, he or she must research the title to the property to determine if any other liens are senior to the tax lien.

In Oklahoma and Arizona, for example, state-held liens are senior to tax liens. State-held liens include liens assessed by commissions, boards, and officers with the power to make loan of public funds or any funds held as security for real estate and under the control of the state. Should an investor obtain ownership of real estate through the tax sale process, he or she would also assume any outstanding liens held by the state. The property would not be acquired free and clear. This is in contrast to a lien held by a private institution, such as a mortgage lender. Tax lien certificates are senior to lender liens, and in all likelihood, the lender would redeem the property before the investor exercised his or her right to foreclose the right of redemption. In the case that the lender, for whatever reason, fails to redeem the tax lien certificate, the investor obtains ownership, free and clear of the lender's lien against the property.

4. **Liens that indicate abandonment, such as violations of building codes or liens for services performed.** Some municipalities are governed by statutes that allow them to abate properties that are not maintained, such as vacant lots, vacant houses, and transient housing. In general, the process of abatement involves notifying the property owner to correct the situation and assessing liens against the property for the cost of correcting the situation when the property owner fails to comply. This type of lien instrument is generally indexed, classified, and recorded as a "notice of lien" in the municipality's public records. Any such recorded entries are potential indicators of an abandoned property. In other states, the abatement is not recorded, but the amount is added to the real property tax bill as part of the delinquent tax amount.

5. **If the property was inherited or given as a gift.**
Oftentimes, properties are inherited or given away to individuals, free and clear, but the individuals do not pay the property tax or other costs that may be assessed by the municipality against the property. An investor may research the method in which title was acquired. If a property is given by a gift of deed or inherited, a decree of distribution is recorded with the taxing municipality.

6. **If tax bills and notices have been returned undeliverable.**
When tax bills are returned to the treasurer's office by the postal system as undeliverable, the property may have been abandoned. Returned postage usually includes some type of endorsement, such as moved, left no address, vacant, or deceased. These endorsements will help in the research to identify abandoned properties. If certified mailings, with return receipts, are not deliverable, the party serving the notice may be required to publish his or her notice, depending upon the type of correspondence that is being delivered. If a public notice is required to advertise the correspondence, it is likely that property ownership will be obtainable. Most notices that must be published by statute are generally not published with widespread circulation to the general public, which means that the property owner is not likely to see the notice or respond to it.

7. **If the property owners have out-of-state or out-of-country mailing addresses.** If mail is delivered out-of-state or out-of-country to the property owner and the mail is returned undeliverable, the likelihood of ownership increases, particularly when a tax lien certificate is purchased near the end of the redemption period.

8. **If mailings to the property address are forwarded to another.** If mail is addressed in care of another, it is likely that the intended party may not get the mail or the mail will be returned undelivered.

9. **If the property owners are a named defunct corporation, LLC, limited partnership, or entity of trust.** Property held under the name of a corporation, LLC, limited partnership, or investment trust is usually required to register with some agency of the state. When the particular entity fails to register, it may be an indication that the entity is defunct, which means it is no longer a legal entity. In this situation, the property or properties held by the entity may be abandoned.

10. **Information provided about the owners from the treasurer's or collector's office.** In less populated municipalities, it may be advantageous to speak with personnel at the treasurer's office to try to gain information about specific properties. In more populated municipalities, especially large cities, the effort may be wasted.

11. **Evidence obtained from inspecting the property for market value.** The investor must be responsible for inspecting a chosen property before attempting to purchase a tax lien certificate that is secured by it. Sometimes, records are incorrect or out-of-date. An assessed value may be the result of an old assessment that was completed before the roof of the property was blown away and the garage caught fire. If possible, an investor should attempt to gain entry to the property or talk to the occupants of the property. If access to the occupants is not possible, the investor may try to talk to

others who have examined the inside of the property, such as neighbors or persons who have made repairs. The investor should be sure to examine the front, sides, and rear of the property. Many times, curb appeal can be deceiving. While examining a property in an unfamiliar neighborhood, the investor should note advertised real estate postings and make contact with such realtors to gain a better understanding of the market potential of the area.

12. **Evidence obtained from inspecting the property for abandonment, usually a report of curb appeal.** It is not unusual for a property to be listed as an improved property, but a visual inspection proves the property to be just a vacant lot. Some properties, particularly raw land, have no street address, are landlocked, and are difficult, if not impossible, to locate. The investor should acquire a parcel map from the assessor's office to assist in locating properties.

13. **The availability of tax lien certificates for other neighboring and vacant or improved properties.** While inspecting a chosen property location, the investor should take note of any neighboring vacant, valuable, and improved properties and then determine the availability of a tax lien certificate for purchase.

14. **Whether an estate has been opened when the owner is deceased.** Probate records should indicate whether an estate has been established for a vacant property. If an estate has been established, the owner is deceased and the heirs of the owner are likely to redeem the tax lien certificate.

15. **Whether the listed owner has any other abandoned properties.** If research indicates that an owner has, in fact, vacated a property, the investor should check with the assessor to determine if the owner has abandoned any other properties for which tax lien certificates are available.

chapter ten

Making Use of Tax Lien Certificates

Purchasing tax sale certificates at annual tax sales, purchasing tax lien certificates over-the-counter at some time after the annual tax sale, or making assignment of tax lien certificates are just parts of the process necessary to make money from tax lien certificates. To profit from the purchase of tax lien certificates, the investor must be capable of understanding and following procedures established by the municipalities of each state. The investor must understand how to assign, redeem, and foreclose tax lien certificates such that the return on investment is maximized.

Tax Lien Certificate Assignments

Tax lien certificates are a form of real estate contract, and like all real estate contracts, they may be assigned to another party for a fee. An assignment transfers all rights to purchase real estate under a real estate contract from the assignor to the assignee. Assignments represent an easy and quick method of flipping a parcel of real estate. A tax lien certificate holder may assign his or her rights, responsibilities, and interest in a tax lien certificate to another investor. The tax lien certificate holder assigns the certificate by making a contractual agreement with another party to receive the assigned lien certificate. The other party, the assignee, contractually obligates him or herself to pay the cost of the lien certificate plus a fee for the tax lien certificate assignment. Like tax lien certificates, tax lien certificate assignments are also a form of real estate contract. As such, they may also be assigned to another party. The assignment and reassignment of tax lien certificates must be recorded by the taxing municipality to become valid. The taxing authority in the property that secures the tax lien certificate will usually record an assignment for a nominal fee of a couple of dollars. Tax lien certificates offered for sale by a taxing authority at an annual tax sale and certificates that are offered for sale over-the-counter after the tax sale represent real estate contracts. When the taxing authority sells a tax lien certificate, it actually assigns the tax lien certificate to the purchaser for a fee. In most instances, the fee includes the delinquent tax amount, penalty, interest, and costs. That assignment can then be reassigned to another party for a fee. In situations where an investor engages in a contract with a property owner to buy equity, share equity, or lease the property prior to the tax sale, the established contract represents a real estate contract. The contract may be assigned to another party for a fee.

Tax lien certificates may be assigned to assignees during the redemption period, and the assignment entitles the assignee to all rights and responsibilities with regard to redemptions, initiating processes to obtain a deed, and foreclosing the property held as security for the tax lien certificate. Upon redemption, the assignee receives the penalty, interest, and other costs that accrue during the redemption period. If the property owner fails to redeem the lien certificate, the assignee is entitled to foreclose the right of redemption just as the original lien holder would have. The newly established property owner may make use of the property to provide living space, rental income, appreciation, or for whatever purpose he or she deems appropriate.

If the assignment is made after issuance of a tax deed, the tax deed holder may assign the property at foreclosure. The assignee is issued an assignment deed (or quitclaim deed) for a fee.

Collecting Redemption Amounts

When tax lien certificates are acquired for delinquent property taxes, the investor is assigned a lien certificate, which indicates that the named lien holder holds indebtedness against the property that secures the tax lien certificate. Depending upon the tax sale system used in a particular municipality, the investor has to allow time for the delinquent property owner to redeem the tax lien certificate. The redemption period may range from 60 days to 4 years. Some municipalities provide investors with a physical tax lien certificate to be held as evidence of the purchase and assignment of the certificate. Other states record the paid assignment but do not provide the actual certificate. This works in the best interests of the investor in the event that a property owner decides to redeem the tax lien certificate.

When tax lien certificates are redeemed, the tax collector is responsible for collecting the payment from the property owner and recording the assignment in his or her records. In most states, the tax collector notifies the tax lien certificate holder of the redemption and requests that the certificate is returned to the collector. Following receipt of the tax lien certificate, the tax collector issues the tax lien certificate holder a check for the amount of proceeds received for redemption. The period of time from which the property owner redeems the tax lien certificate and the time in which the tax collector issues a check to the investor may be a matter of days or weeks, depending upon the workload of the tax collector's office. During this period, no interest is earned. In states where the tax lien is recorded, but the actual certificate is held by the tax collector, the time frame from redemption to reimbursement may be severely shortened. This shortened time frame provides investors with a faster turnover rate, which increases the rate of return for the investment and allows the investor to reinvest redeemed dollars more quickly. Investors are cautioned to notify tax collectors of any address change. Some states have a time limit in which a tax lien certificate holder may respond to the request to return a tax lien certificate in return for the redemption amount. If the notice is delivered to the wrong address or returned undeliverable, the investor risks exceeding the time limitation imposed and may suffer a loss of the redemption amount.

When the redemption period associated with a lien certificate extends beyond one year and the property owner fails to redeem the property within the first year, new real estate taxes are assessed against the property in subsequent years.

Some municipalities require the tax lien certificate holder to pay subsequent taxes that accrue over the redemption period, if the property owner fails to do so. In other states, it is optional for the tax lien certificate holder to pay subsequent taxes. If the newly assessed property taxes are not paid, the property may go to tax sale again. In this situation, a second investor may acquire the tax lien certificate that is offered for sale for newly assessed and delinquent tax amounts. As such, the delinquent property becomes security for two distinct and separate tax liens. In order to maintain ownership of the property, the property owner would have to satisfy the redemption amounts associated with both tax liens. This process will continue to manifest itself until the redemption period has expired. The redemption period for the first tax lien certificate will expire before any subsequent tax lien certificates. The owner of the first tax lien certificate will have the first opportunity to foreclose the property owner's right of redemption in accordance with the laws of the particular municipality. In order to foreclose, however, the first tax lien certificate holder must redeem the second tax lien certificate as well as any subsequent tax lien certificates. This process ensures that dollars invested in any tax lien certificates are always protected. Second and subsequent tax lien certificate holders may never get an opportunity to gain ownership of the securing property unless the previously held tax lien certificate fails to engage in a foreclosure. Investors who engage in the purchase of tax lien certificates that are subsequent to previously held tax lien certificates are guaranteed of having the redemption amount satisfied by the previous tax lien certificate holder, or they will be given the opportunity to foreclose.

Lien Priorities

Tax lien certificates are but one type of indebtedness for which a property may be held as security. Liens against the real estate title may be held by federal, state, or local government entities. Liens may also be placed against the title to a property if the property owner is the losing party in a civil lawsuit. Real estate cannot be sold free and clear until all liens against the property are satisfied. The IRS may place tax liens against real estate owned by individuals who fail to pay required federal income taxes. State tax liens may be placed by state taxing authorities for unpaid state income taxes. Local taxing authorities may place liens against real estate for unpaid property taxes or the nonpayment of services performed by the local government. Liens against a parcel of property are set in priority, and tax liens are generally in first position against a property. This is because real property taxes are used to pay for local services. Tax rates are set and assessed against real property to fund budgets that pay the expenses of the local municipality. Without such funds, the municipality would not be capable of funding its share of police protection, emergency services, public schools, public libraries, court systems, local roadways, or salaries for the jurisdiction's local employees. When a property owner loses a civil lawsuit to another party, the other party may file a lien against the property owner's property and everything else that he or she owns. If the property owner fails to redeem a tax lien certificate secured by the property, this type of lien, which is junior to a tax lien, is wiped out by the foreclosure of a tax lien certificate.

In the states of New Mexico and Arizona, state-held liens against a property are given priority over tax liens. One of several reasons for engaging in the research of properties before acquiring tax lien certificates is to discover if any outstanding debts are in place against a chosen parcel of property. When a lien exists and is in excess of the market value of a property, the property is considered to be over-encumbered. If a property is over-encumbered by a state-held lien and the state's lien is given priority over tax liens, then the security of the tax lien certificate is nonexistent. As an example, an investor, without researching a particular property, purchases a $3,000 tax lien secured by a property valued at $46,000 in Arizona. At foreclosure, the investor learns that Arizona also has a lien against the property for $45,000. If the investor pays the state lien, he or she would have $1,000 worth of security in a property for which was purchased for $3,000. The property is over-encumbered by $2,000. Rather than acquiring free and clear title to the property, the investor would be required to pay for the property at $2,000 above its fair market value to gain title to it. This scenario is a far cry from obtaining ownership for pennies on the dollar.

Fair Market Value:	*$46,000*	
State Lien:	*$45,000*	
Tax Lien:	*$3,000*	
Total Required for Foreclosure:	*$48,000*	*= $45,000 + $3,000*
Over-encumbered:	*$2,000*	*= $48,000 - $46,000*

State Lien Priority

With the exception of certain government liens, tax liens have first priority over other liens, such as those assessed for the nonpayment of mortgage or other instruments where the property is held as security for the instrument. Other liens are prioritized according to their recording dates. As an example, a property in Arizona is valued at $100,000, with property taxes equal to $1,600. The property has several other liens against it: a first mortgage with a balance of $50,000, a second mortgage with a balance of $20,000, and a $300 lien assessed by the state for the nonpayment of state income taxes. Arizona offers a three-year redemption period when neither the first tax lien certificate holder nor the property owner pays the property taxes for subsequent tax years. As such, two other certificates are sold to recoup the loss to the municipality for the delinquent property taxes in subsequent years. In Arizona, state-held liens are given priority over tax liens. Following the expiration of the three-year redemption period for the first tax lien certificate, the order of precedence for liens against the property is as follows:

1. *State Lien:*   *$300 plus interest*
2. *First Tax Lien:*   *$1,600 plus interest and costs*
3. *Second Tax Lien:*   *$1,600 plus interest and costs*
4. *Third Tax Lien:*   *$1,600 plus interest and costs*
5. *First Mortgage:*   *$50,000*
6. *Second Mortgage:*   *$20,000*

- If the second mortgage company forecloses the property for nonpayment of the mortgage note, all other liens must be paid before the foreclosure can be completed.

- If the first mortgage company forecloses, the state lien and the three tax liens must be paid before the mortgage company can complete its foreclosure. The second mortgage is wiped out and not paid.

- If the first tax lien holder forecloses, the second tax lien, third tax lien, and the state lien must be paid. Both mortgages are wiped out and neither is paid.

The second and third tax lien holders are not in a position to foreclose, because the period of redemption has not expired for their lien certificates. If the state forecloses, no other liens will be paid; however, it is not likely that the state will foreclose, because Arizona mandates that individual county treasurers sell tax lien certificates. The attractive 16 percent interest rate that is applied to redemption amounts ensures that the certificates will be sold.

If, by rare circumstance, neither of the mortgage companies forecloses and the first tax lien certificate holder also fails to foreclose within one year of the expiration of the redemption period, the second tax lien holder is put in a position of being able to foreclose. When the redemption period of the second tax lien certificate has expired, the second certificate holder is put a position of being able to foreclose by paying the first tax lien, third tax lien, and the state lien. Neither mortgage lien would have to be paid. The second lien holder would then acquire ownership of the property, free and clear.

Given that tax liens are given first priority over mortgage liens, a foreclosure by a tax lien certificate holder wipes out any mortgage liens. Mortgage companies will redeem tax liens should the delinquency of the property owner lead to such a circumstance. Because the amount necessary to redeem a tax sale certificate is relatively small compared to the loss of the mortgage amount. In this example, the first mortgage company would have paid the required redemption amount rather than have the mortgage wiped out. In fact, unless some bizarre occurrence prevents the mortgage company from becoming aware of the delinquent tax amount, the situation in this example would never really happen.

Federal Lien Priority

The federal government may also assess liens against real property for the nonpayment of a government debt by the property owner. An IRS lien has priority immediately following the expiration of the first redemption period. Once the redemption period has expired and a deed sale has been completed, the IRS is given 120 days from the date of the deed sale to redeem all lien certificates. If the IRS redeems a property, it must pay all tax lien amounts. However, the IRS is only required to pay interest on the redemption amount at 6 percent per annum, from the date of the tax sale. The IRS is also required to pay expenses of the tax sale and any expenses to maintain or provide protection for the property if those expenses exceed any income that may be generated by the property. If the IRS does not redeem during this 120-day time frame, its lien is extinguished. An IRS lien has no ability to wipe out tax liens.

Bankruptcy and Lien Priorities

Bankruptcies affect the process of redeeming and foreclosing tax lien certificates by increasing the time line to receive a return on the investment. Federal bankruptcy laws allow judges to order a stay of claims against the individual who has filed for bankruptcy as well as a stay of claims against property that is owned by such individuals. A stay order halts all claims by creditors, including tax lien certificate holders. For the purposes of bankruptcy, tax lien certificate holders are considered secured creditors. As such, any processes that are initiated as a result of the sale, purchase, or assignment of tax lien certificates are stayed. Even during bankruptcy, property tax liens have the highest priority of liens against real property of bankrupt property owners. The tax lien will remain in first position throughout the bankruptcy proceedings unless a bankruptcy judge orders that all property of the bankrupt individual be sold. In this situation, all secured creditors will receive a prorated amount of their claims, based upon the proceeds from the sale of the property. The judge may also require creditors to file an "answer" in response to requests for information about their claims. The answer requires lien holders to acquire legal services and present their positions during bankruptcy court proceedings. When the certificate is secured by the property of a bankrupt party, the tax lien certificate holder must consider whether a prorated redemption amount plus the cost of engaging necessary legal services is cost effective in pursuing the return offered by a particular tax lien certificate.

chapter eleven

Foreclosing Unredeemed Properties

T ax lien states extend property owners an opportunity to redeem tax lien certificates. Some deed states also offer property owners an opportunity to redeem properties that are sold at tax deed sales. When the property owner or other vested party fails to redeem a tax lien certificate, the investor may foreclose the right to redemption of the certificate and obtain title to the property. Before an investor is able to foreclose the right of redemption, the foreclosing investor must pay all delinquent taxes, penalties, interest, and costs. The longer the redemption period on a tax lien certificate, the greater the amount that must be paid. Arizona offers the longest redemption period of four to five years. The accumulated taxes, interest, and other costs will far exceed those required for a foreclosure in some municipalities of Maryland. Certain Maryland municipalities offer the shortest redemption period of just six months. The right to foreclose a property owner's right of redemption does not guarantee that the investor will gain title to the property. Some states may limit the investor's return by ensuring that the cost of the tax lien certificate and any interest, penalties, costs, and fees are reimbursed to the tax lien certificate holder as a result of a foreclosure sale, but allow any remaining equity in the property to be returned to the property owner.

In general, there are two types of foreclosures. The first type provides for the investor to obtain title to the property free and clear; that is, without payment of any additional liens or consequences. This type of foreclosure is considered to be an administrative filing of foreclosure. The second type of foreclosure requires the tax lien certificate holder to force a sale of the property at a tax deed sale. This type of foreclosure is known as a force of sale foreclosure. The fees associated with both types of foreclosures may include the following:

- Attorney's fees when court proceedings are necessary

- Filling fees

- Court costs

- Fees required of the taxing authority

- Title expenses

Administrative Filing of Foreclosure

An administrative filing of foreclosure is the process used by most tax lien states to foreclose the right of redemption of a tax lien certificate. This type of foreclosure is also considered a nonjudicial foreclosure, since no court proceedings are required to foreclose. The investor must be diligent in following the processes defined by public notices and other state requirements established for foreclosure or risk forfeiting rights to the property. The process usually involves the following steps, once the redemption period of a tax lien certificate has expired:

- **Notify the municipality of the desire to foreclose.** In some states, an investor need only apply to the taxing authority for a tax deed once the redemption period has expired. Upon receiving and verifying the application, the tax collector will issue a tax deed in the name of the party on record as holder of the tax lien certificate.

- **Pay any administrative fees required to file for foreclosure.** Foreclosure is not immediate or without costs. Most states that provide investors with the capability to foreclose the right of redemption also charge a fee to administer the tax deed.

- **Complete necessary paperwork required by the municipality.** The investor is usually required to complete certain paperwork before the issuance of a tax deed.

- **Send a notice of intent to the property owner or publish legal notice in a local paper.** Various states have differing requirements for making notice of a foreclosure. The investor may be required to provide the taxing authority or court with specific details as to the information included in the notice; who was notified by the notice and how those parties were notified. Some states require that only the persons named on the property record as property owners be notified. Other states insist that the documented owners be notified as well as occupants of the property and mortgage holders. In addition, heirs of the property owner and other lien certificate holders may need to be notified. Some states require that notice be posted on the particular property or posted at a public location or both. In most states, if the property owner can be located, the state may require that the he or she be notified by "personal service." The investor is expected to bear the expense of hiring a process server to make delivery of the notice. The particular state statute indicates whether personal service, certified mail, or registered mail is an acceptable form of delivering notice. All states accept service by publication when the property owner cannot be located. Some states may require both personal service and service by publication to make the notice available to any other person who may have an interest in the property. The courts do not look favorably on investors who resort to trickery in making notice of a foreclosure. Tactics such as placing notice in a foreign paper will cause the notice to be thrown out of court. The requirements for foreclosure can be very restrictive, requiring, for example, that the full name, as specified on the property deed, be used and not an individual's initials. At a minimum, the notice of foreclosure must detail the following:

- An adequate description of the property to be foreclosed.

- When the foreclosure proceedings are to be held.

- Where the foreclosure proceedings are to be held.

- Name of the property owner.

- The types of taxes that are due.

When the notice is determined to be inadequate, the courts lack jurisdiction, which allows the property owner or mortgage holder to contest the deed, even if they are not present at the court proceedings. If, on the other hand, a party to the foreclosure is not properly notified yet appears in court for the proceedings, that party is considered to be properly notified.

- **Pay all other tax liens and government liens, if required.**
  In order for a tax lien certificate holder to foreclose the right of redemption, the investor must pay all other tax liens held against the property. In addition, if any liens are superior to the investor's tax lien, the investor must satisfy those liens as well. Such liens may include state-held liens and federal liens held against the property.

Even when states allow an investor to engage in an administrative foreclosure process, he or she may still have to engage the services of an attorney. Title companies are not always willing to insure a property title acquired through a judicial foreclosure process. Some title companies wait one year after foreclosure to see if any claims are filed against the property before issuing a title policy. Most investors are not willing to wait for the extended time period. In such instances, the investor may have to engage the services of an attorney to bring the matter before a judge and obtain a court order of foreclosure through a quiet title action. When a court order is necessary to foreclose a tax lien certificate, the foreclosure is considered to be a judicial foreclosure.

Force of Sale Foreclosure

A foreclosure that requires a tax lien certificate holder to force a sale of the securing property is used in most tax deed states. The lien holder must follow the same process as outlined above for an administrative filing of foreclosure. However, the participating municipality, not the lien holder, is responsible for handling the issuance of all notices. The municipality also establishes and sets the date for the sale. The property owner is given additional time, up to the date of the deed sale, to redeem the property. If the property owner fails to redeem, the property is auctioned on the specified and published date. The party named on the tax deed receives preference at the sale and is given a credit for holding the first position lien. The credit is an amount equal to the following:

- First position lien, plus interest

- Costs to buy out subsequent liens, plus interest

- Filing fees

- Other administrative costs

A winning bid at the tax sale auction is the bid that exceeds the credit amount established for the party named on the tax deed. If no one bids above the lien credit amount, the named party to the tax deed acquires the property free and clear. If a bidder bids in excess of the lien credit amount, the named party to the tax deed may compete in bidding up the cost of the property. The winning bidder acquires the property, free and clear. If the winning bidder is someone other than the named party to the tax deed, the named party to the tax deed is paid the credit amount, and the winning bidder acquires ownership of the property, free and clear. It is for this reason that many investors choose to engage primarily in the sale of tax deeds. The investor does not have to vest dollars in the investment throughout a redemption period, and any money invested at the deed sale receives either an immediate return of the money invested or property ownership.

Quiet Title

A force of sale foreclosure, like an administrative foreclosure, may be nonjudicially processed in some states and judicially processed in others. It is recommended that investors bear the expense of hiring legal representation to ensure that the very specific procedures required for a foreclosure are followed and complied with, even when states do not require it. Investors are encouraged to file a legal claim against any potential claimants of the foreclosed property. By doing so, the investor engages in what is known as a quiet title action. Such an action, when successfully pursued, provides the investor with a court declaration that the title to the property is good. The courts will determine whether documents are properly completed, whether they include all required information, and whether the proper notices of foreclosure were put into place. Given that all procedures are followed and all paperwork is complete, claimants, including the former property owner, can do very little to disrupt the foreclosure. Should the investor choose to sell the foreclosed property, the court declaration protects the investor against any challenges to the foreclosure process and assures any potential buyer that the title was properly and legally acquired. Some title companies require such a declaration from the courts before they will insure the title to a foreclosed property.

Hindrance to Foreclosure

While a successful foreclosure to gain ownership of valuable property is a goal of investors, there are situations that may arise that and delay efforts to foreclose on valuable properties. In most instances, judicial foreclosures are default proceedings, which means that the foreclosure proceeds with no one opposing the foreclosure action. The governing tax authority issues a deed in the name of the investor only after the court is satisfied that all procedures have been followed and that the foreclosure should have taken place. Occasionally, a property owner may successfully halt a foreclosure action when it is determined that he or she paid the required property tax or properly redeemed the tax lien certificate but was not given credit for such actions. Attempts to challenge the tax assessment, property tax amount, or foreclosure procedures are usually dismissed by the courts during this phase of the tax sale process. However, when property owners are able to provide proof that some form of fraud made cause for a foreclosure, they may be successful in stopping foreclosure actions.

Bankruptcies, destruction, and environmental issues may adversely affect the property used to secure a tax lien certificate. Bankruptcy may have the effect of delaying the foreclosure process and significantly reducing the yield on a tax lien certificate investment. Environmental issues and property destruction may significantly reduce the value of the securing property and, in some cases, render it worthless.

Bankruptcy

When a property owner files a petition for bankruptcy, the bankruptcy may delay or eliminate any effort to foreclose a tax lien certificate. There are two categories of bankruptcy: liquidation under Chapter 7 of the U.S. Bankruptcy Code and reorganization under Chapters 11 and 13 of the U.S. Bankruptcy Code.

Chapter 7 bankruptcies provide for the property owner to turn over all nonexempt assets to a court-appointed trustee of the bankruptcy court. The trustee is required to liquidate all nonexempt assets of the property owner. The bankruptcy court first freezes the nonexempt assets of the property owner and then liquidates them. The proceeds gained from liquidation of the property owner's assets are used to pay creditors. For the purpose of bankruptcy, tax lien certificate holders are considered creditors. As creditors, tax lien certificate holders hold first lien priority and are paid all costs associated with acquiring the tax lien certificate. Liquidation by the bankruptcy court eliminates any opportunity for an investor to foreclose the right to redeem a tax lien certificate and gain ownership of the property.

Chapters 11 and 13 provide for the property owner to reorganize his or her financial obligations by continuing to make payments to creditors. The property owner is also required to make up any back payments with interest through a modified and extended payment schedule. Chapter 13 is intended for individuals, while Chapter 11 is intended for corporations and partnerships. As such, court proceedings under Chapter 11 are the most complex, time consuming, and costly. Unlike bankruptcy under Chapter 7 liquidation, bankruptcies under Chapters 11 and 13 have no time limits for subsequent petitions to be filed. When the property owner files a petition for bankruptcy, the bankruptcy court enacts a legal moratorium called an automatic stay. The stay prevents a tax lien certificate holder and all other creditors from engaging in any legal actions against the property owner to satisfy a debt. The mere act of filing a petition for bankruptcy creates an automatic stay, and many property owners have been known to continuously file such petitions under Chapters 11 or 13 in an effort to delay foreclosure. While this process has proven successful in delaying foreclosures in the past, in recent years, courts have tended to lift recurring stays.

Relief of Stay

If a foreclosure sale occurs after the property owner has filed a bankruptcy petition, the bankruptcy court will order the foreclosure to be null and void. As a creditor, the lien certificate holder may file a petition to seek relief from the automatic stay imposed by the bankruptcy court. The bankruptcy court has a legal obligation to hear the relief case within 30 days; otherwise, the stay is lifted and the tax lien certificate holder is allowed to continue with the foreclosure. This, however, is not likely to happen. In all likelihood, the bankruptcy court will hear all requests for relief from stay. The court usually considers the amount of equity in a property in making a decision as to granting a relief from stay. When the property has significant value and the owners have significant equity in the property, the court is more likely to deny a relief of stay. It is anticipated that all creditors will be better served if the property is sold and the proceeds used to satisfy creditors. If, on the other hand, the property owners have very little equity in the property, the court is more likely to grant a relief from stay to the foreclosing creditor. Because the tax lien certificate holder holds a first priority lien against the property does not necessarily mean the tax lien certificate holder will be the creditor that the bankruptcy court allows to foreclose.

In many instances, there is at least one mortgage lender involved in the bankruptcy proceedings of a property owner. The courts may order that a cram-down or short sale provision be imposed on the mortgage lender to assist the property owner with reorganization under Chapters 11 and 13 of the U.S.

Bankruptcy Code. Under such circumstances, the court orders a modification of terms of the mortgage or trust deed, which may include a modification of the payment schedule or a reduction of the principal amount to be paid to the mortgage lender. The tax lien certificate holder is reimbursed for the costs associated with the tax lien certificate, but any plan to acquire deed to the property and foreclose is voided. If a petition for bankruptcy is filed after a foreclosure sale, the court may order the foreclosure null and void if it is determined that the equity in the property could have been more wisely used to pay the debts of creditors. The petition initiates an automatic stay of any foreclosure proceedings. If the stay is lifted, the foreclosure process continues from the point at which the creditor was frozen by the stay.

In instances where the tax lien certificate holder is seeking a relief of stay and there are no mortgage lenders seeking foreclosure, the court may declare that the relatively small amount invested in a tax lien certificate provides too much equity for the tax lien certificate holder when there other creditors with claims against the property owner. The court may order a bankruptcy liquidation sale of the owner's assets, as specified under Chapter 7 of the U.S. Bankruptcy Code. Assets, including the property that secures a tax lien certificate, are auctioned to the highest bidder. The highest bidder for the property receives title to the property, free and clear. The proceeds from the sale of assets are then used to reimburse the tax lien certificate holder for the cost of the tax lien certificate, interest, penalties, fees, costs, and expenses associated with the tax lien. Because the tax lien certificate holder holds the first priority lien against the property, he or she is reimbursed for his or her investment. The remaining proceeds are prorated and distributed to the other creditors. No foreclosure of the right to redeem a tax lien certificate may take place.

Destruction

After having acquired a tax lien certificate but before redemption takes place, there is a possibility that any structures located on the property may be destroyed by fire, vandalism, or a natural disaster, such as a tornado or hurricane. If the property owner holds casualty insurance on the property, the cost of repairs will be covered by the insurance. If the loss results in a total destruction, the insurance company may pay all outstanding liens against the property on behalf of the property owner. In the absence of casualty insurance, the equity in a tax lien certificate may be reduced accordingly. There are some instances, however, where the tax lien certificate may still be secured. The property tax bill issued to property owners by the tax collector indicates assessment amounts allocated for land and improvements on the property. When the land on an improved property is more valuable than the improvements, the value of the land may be sufficient to provide security for the tax lien certificate even though the structures are damaged or destroyed. In instances where the structure is the most valuable part of the property, destruction in the absence of casualty insurance may render the securing property to be worth less than the tax lien certificate held.

Environmental Issues

One of the issues surrounding the availability of tax lien certificates for commercial and industrial properties is the potential for the existence of environmental issues. The Superfund Act enacted by the U.S. Congress makes all property owners and operators responsible for contamination on their

property whether they caused the contamination. Commercial
and industrial properties are the most likely kinds of properties
to suffer contamination from hazardous chemicals. Properties
such as gas stations, chemical plants, and other businesses that
may be contaminated, used to produce contaminants, or that
make use of contaminants, such as gas, toxic wastes, mold, lead
paint, and radon, are often cited by government entities for
the exposure or release of contaminants. If a property is cited
for environmental problems, the property owner or operator
becomes responsible for any necessary environmental analyses
and cleanup efforts. Property owners are forced to incur
large expenses for the detection, removal, or containment of
contaminants. In some instances, property owners default on
paying the property tax associated with such a property to avoid
the expense of an environmental cleanup. It is their intent to rid
themselves of the property and its associated expenses and allow
the tax lien certificate investor to inherit the problems. A property
listing for a property that presents a potential environmental
issue is shown in Form 5 below.

```
                                                        MB   PG  PCL
     ITEM         LEGAL  LATEST                        LASTEST  PARCEL
     NO   NSB#    DESC  ASSESSEE    LOCATION   MIN BID.  IMPS EARLIEST PARCEL


     3719   176    E J   BALDWIN'S   FIFTH   $87,553       Y     8741 011 002
            SUBDIVISION OF  A   PORTION  OF                   81/8741 011 002
            RANCHO LA PUENTE LOT  COM  AT  S
            TERMINUS OF A COURSE IN  W  LINE
            OF VALINDA AVE  PER  MB533-48-49
            HAVING A BEARING OF S 0¢39'50"  W
            AND A LENGTH OF 473.38 FT  TH   N
            0¢39'50" E TO A PT N 0¢39'50"   E
            150 FT FROM E PROLONGATION OF   N
            LINE OF MAPLEGROVE ST PER CSB119      THIS PROPERTY MAY BE CONTAMINATED
            TH N 86¢02'49" W  150   FT   TH   S   INVESTIGATE BEFORE YOU PURCHASE
            0¢39'50" W TO SD  N  LINE   TH   E
            THEREON TO A PT  S  47¢18'35"   W
            23.44 FT FROM BEG TH N 47¢18'35"
            E TO BEG   PART   OF   LOT   349
            ASSESSED     TO
            LOCATION COUNTY OF LOS ANGELES
```

Form 5: Property That Indicates a Potential Environmental Issue

Investors are encouraged to invest in residential properties to avoid the potential loss and complications that environmental issues may add to commercial and industrial properties. Though residential properties are not exempt from environmental contamination, the likelihood of contamination is far less probable for residential properties than commercial and industrial properties. As stated previously, properties under consideration for tax lien certificate investment should be properly researched and evaluated. Some residential properties, for example, that are located in rural communities or communities that were once considered to be rural may have gasoline tanks or underground heating oil tanks installed on or the near the property. Over time, these storage units may leak contaminants. Also, properties that are developed on farmland may be candidates for contamination, particularly when the land has a history of being treated with pesticides or other chemical contaminants. In most instances, farmland must be graded for development, and the process of grading is usually sufficient to dilute contaminants below detectable levels. Time also contributes to the breakdown of contaminants such as pesticides. Properties that are developed on industrial land present more of a risk of contamination, particularly when the developer has failed to record an environmental report for the property. An environmental report indicates the results of an environmental inspection of the land. Investors are encouraged to check the previous history of properties under consideration to determine whether any such inspection reports exist. In the absence of an inspection report, the investor should check public records to determine the use of the property before making an investment decision. Although commercial properties present a high risk of contamination, they also provide a good investment when they are usable and free of contaminants.

Phase 1 Environmental Evaluations

A Phase I environmental evaluation is designed to confirm
whether hazardous substances ever existed on a property.
The process of the evaluation is such that an environmental
consultant requests that property owners provide information
about the environmental history of the property. The consultant
then engages in a walk-through inspection of the property
to seek any visible indications of contamination. Such visible
indicators include sticky vegetation, soil discoloration, and
vent pipes that may be attached to underground storage units.
A search of government records may also be performed to
determine whether the property is listed in one of its many
lists of contaminated properties or whether a permit has ever
been issued for the installation of underground storage units.
A search of government records may also be performed to
locate any existing aerial photographs that may indicate the
previous uses of the property. As helpful as an environmental
inspection is in confirming the existence of contaminants, it is
not likely that a tax lien certificate holder will be given access
to a property to perform such an inspection. As a tax lien
certificate holder, the investor has no right of possession to the
securing property. Unless the property is open to the public, an
inspection is not feasible. The investor will have to rely on the
historical public records of the property to confirm the existence
of environmental contaminants.

Phase II Environmental Evaluations

A Phase II evaluation involves a more scientific approach to
evaluating the property. Samples are taken from the property
and sent to a laboratory for evaluation. This process is necessary
for high-risk properties that indicate some potential for

contamination. This phase of evaluation is much more expensive, since the consultant must first determine where to sample and then what to sample. As with a Phase I evaluation, access to property to perform such an evaluation is likely to be denied by the owners or operators, and a tax lien certificate holder has no authority to override the property owner's decision.

While the Superfund Act holds property owners and operators responsible for environmental contamination, the U.S. Congress exempts lien holders from such a liability. Specifically, the exemption indicates that a lien holder is not an owner or operator as long as he or she is acting in a capacity to protect a security interest in the property and not participating in the management of the property. A tax lien certificate documents such a lien and, by definition, only serves the purpose of protecting the security interest of a property. The certificate does not give an investor any right to participate in the management of a property. The exemption, however, may not carry forward should the property owner fail to redeem a tax lien certificate and the investor forecloses the right of redemption. The EPA requires foreclosing tax lien certificate holders to auction or sell the property or make a good faith effort to sell the property in order to maintain the exemption. If a lien holder outbids, rejects, or fails to accept a cash offer for the property, the exemption may be lost. Furthermore, if within 90 days of a written, legally binding, and reasonable offer of cash, the investor refuses the offer, he or she loses the exemption and becomes the responsible owner of the property. The property must be offered for sale by either listing it through a broker within one year of foreclosure or listing it monthly in an appropriate publication. If the property has an existing business that the investor continues after foreclosure, he or she may retain the exemption as long as no contamination continues under the new ownership.

Unlawful Detainer

After title to a foreclosed property is acquired, the investor may still have problems gaining possession of the property. When an investor forecloses an occupied property, he or she may find that existing occupants are reluctant to leave the property. Occupants who are not owner-occupants may not be aware that a foreclosure has taken place and a change of ownership has been granted. When occupants refuse to leave a foreclosed property, the investor is put in the same position as a landlord whose tenants refuse to leave. The investor must seek a court order to force an eviction and gain possession of the property. Rather than seeking an eviction, such as that used by landlords, the foreclosing investor must engage an unlawful detainer action. Such an action, when successfully pursued, provides the investor with a court declaration granting him or her possession of the property. The order may then be presented to local law enforcement officials who will assist in removing the occupants and their possessions from the property.

When an investor is given reason to believe that the occupants are posed to challenge the newly established title and ownership of the property (usually owner-occupants), the investor is encouraged to engage in the process of both a quiet title action and an unlawful detainer action. An unlawful detainer judgment can be acquired within weeks. A quiet title action or a combination of both actions takes much longer.

Adverse Possession (Squatter's Rights)

In some states, if an individual or group of individuals makes an otherwise unoccupied property into personal living space, the inhabitants may make claim to the property. States have statutes for what is known as adverse possession or squatter's rights. The investor should seek legal advice as to the application of such laws to a particular parcel of property. He or she is encouraged to act upon the rights granted through the tax sale and tax lien foreclosure processes within the time frame allocated to do so, particularly since most states impose statutes of limitation with regard to foreclosure and possession of a property. State and local governments have supported individuals in their claims for adverse possession when their occupancy has been established for a period of years.

After Foreclosure

Foreclosure gives the investor title to the foreclosed property as well as all of the responsibility of home ownership. Upon foreclosure, the investor should acquire hazard insurance to cover any losses that may occur on the property. As the newly established property owner, the investor needs to protect his or her investment against natural disasters, fire, and other causes of damage. Insurance will also prove useful for foreclosed properties that have existing occupants. Occupants of the property may decide to cause damage and destruction to the property if they are requested or forced to leave.

The investor must consider all costs that may be required before he or she is able to take possession of the property. Those costs may include any or all of the following:

- Other tax liens held against the property

- Federal liens

- State liens

- Municipal liens

- Quiet title fees

- Fees for issuance of a deed

- Attorney's fees for judicial foreclosures

- Environmental inspection

- Environmental cleanup

- Hazard insurance

- Eviction of existing occupants

chapter twelve

State Laws

T he following list details the laws and anomalies that apply to each of the 50 states as well as the District of Columbia, the territory of Guam, and the commonwealth of Puerto Rico.

STATE LAWS		
Alabama		
Type of Sale	Tax lien	Certificate of sale or certificate of purchase
Sale Date	May	Property taxes are due in October and delinquent on January 1. The tax sale listing is published after the month of April.
Bid Method	Premium	The premium amount is paid to the property owner or added to the municipality's general fund. Property owners may request that amounts placed in the general fund be paid to them.
Payment Method	Cash or certified funds	
Interest Rate	12% per annum	
Subsequent Taxes	Optional	The tax lien certificate holder must present the tax lien certificate before paying delinquent taxes for subsequent years. The additional amount earns interest at the same rate as the original lien certificate.

STATE LAWS		
Redemption Period	3 years	If the tax lien certificate is not redeemed, a tax deed is delivered to the lien holder who must, in turn, return the lien certificate to the judge of probate.
Over-the-Counter	Yes	Over-the-counter sales are handled by the state commissioner of revenue.
Municipalities	67	Autauga, Baldwin, Barbour, Bibb, Blount, Bullock, Butler, Calhoun, Chambers, Cherokee, Chilton, Choctaw, Clarke, Clay, Cleburne, Coffee, Colbert, Conecuh, Coosa, Covington, Crenshaw, Cullman, Dale, Dallas, Dekalb, Elmore, Escambia, Etowah, Fayette, Franklin, Geneva, Greene, Hale, Henry, Houston, Jackson, Jefferson, Lamar, Lauderdale, Lawrence, Lee, Limestone, Lowndes, Macon, Madison, Marengo, Marion, Marshall, Mobile, Monroe, Montgomery, Morgan, Perry, Pickens, Pike, Randolph, Russell, Shelby, St. Clair, Sumter, Talladega, Tallapoosa, Tuscaloosa, Walker, Washington, Wilcox, Winston
Statute	Code of Alabama	Sections 40-10-15, 20,120,121,187
Alaska		
Type of Sale	Tax deed	
Sale Date	Various	
Bid Method	Determined by the municipality	Only municipalities are present at the tax sale. Properties are transferred to the municipality. The municipality may sell the property after the expiration of the 1-year redemption period. Properties are usually sold according to local ordinances and are usually sold at fair market value.
Payment Method		
Interest Rate	N/A	
Redemption Period	Up to 1 year	
Over-the-Counter	No	

STATE LAWS		
Municipalities	27 Municipalities are termed boroughs	Aleutian Islands East, Aleutian Islands West, Anchorage, Angoon, Barrow, Bethel, Bristol Bay, Cordova-McCarthy, Fairbanks, Haines, Juneau, Kenai-Cook Inlet, Ketchikan, Kobuk, Kodiak, Matanuska-Susitna, Nome, Outer Ketchikan, Prince of Wales, Seward, Sitka, Skagway-Yakutat, Southeast Fairbanks, Upper Ukon, Valdez-Chitina-Whittier, Wade-Hampton, Wrangell-Petersburg, Yukon-Koyukuk
Statute	Alaska statutes	Chapter 48
Arizona		
Type of Sale	Tax lien	Tax lien or certificate of purchase.
Sale Date	February	The tax sale listing must be compiled by December 31 and published at least two weeks prior to the tax sale. The listing of delinquent properties must be published in an officially designated county newspaper. Additional notices are to be posted near the door to the county treasurer's office.
Bid Method	Bid down interest	
Payment Method	Cash	Payment is due on the date of the tax sale.
Interest Rate	16% per annum	Any fraction of the month is counted as a whole month.
Redemption Period	3 years	Property owners may redeem after foreclosure has been initiated and before the foreclosure judgment is made. The redemption amount includes additional costs for "reasonable" attorney's fees.
Over-the-Counter	Yes	Tax lien certificates that are not purchased at the tax sale are offered for sale every day until all tax liens are sold or the treasurer is convinced that no more liens can be sold. The remaining tax lien certificates are assigned to the state and reassigned to the buyer willing to pay the delinquent tax, interest, penalties, and charges.

STATE LAWS

Subsequent Taxes	Optimal	The tax lien certificate holder must present the tax lien certificate before paying delinquent taxes for subsequent years. The additional amount earns interest at the same rate as the original lien certificate.
Foreclosure	Within 10 years	A judicial foreclosure must be initiated within 10 years. A nonjudicial foreclosure may be initiated after 5 years.
Municipalities	15	Apache, Cochise, Coconino, Gila, Graham, Greenlee, La Paz, Maricopa, Mohave, Navajo, Pima, Pinal, Santa Cruz, Yavapai, Yuma.
Statute	Arizona revised statutes	Sections 42-312, 390, 393, 410, 451, 462
Arkansas		
Type of Sale	Tax deed	
Sale Date	May 1	The tax sale, called a tax-delinquent sale, is a public oral-bid foreclosure auction of real estate.
Bid Method	Premium bid	The opening bid amount includes the tax lien amount plus the assessed value of the property. The assessed value is calculated as 20 percent of the market value.
Payment Method		
Interest Rate	N/A	
Redemption Period	30 days from date of auction	
Over-the-Counter	No	
Municipalities	75	Arkansas, Ashley, Baxter, Benton, Boone, Bradley, Calhoun, Carroll, Chicot, Clark, Clay, Cleburne, Cleveland, Columbia, Conway, Craighead, Crawford, Crittenden, Cross, Dallas, Desha, Drew, Faulkner, Franklin, Fulton, Garland, Grant, Greene, Hempstead, Hot Spring, Howard, Independence, Izard, Jackson, Jefferson, Johnson, Lafayette, Lawrence, Lee, Lincoln, Little River, Logan, Lonoke, Madison, Marion, Miller, Mississippi, Monroe, Montgomery, Nevada, Newton, Ouachita, Perry, Phillips, Pike, Poinsett, Polk, Pope, Prairie, Pulaski,

STATE LAWS		
		Randolph, Saline, Scott, Searcy, Sebastian, Sevier, Sharp, St. Francis, Stone, Union, Van Buren, Washington, White, Woodruff, Yell
Statute	Arkansas code	Chapter 38
California		
Type of Sale	Tax deed	Tax certificate.
Sale Date	Varies by municipality	The tax sale, called a tax-defaulted land sale, is a public oral-bid foreclosure of real estate. Though state statutes provide for the sale of tax lien certificates, local municipalities have never made use of the statutes. Property owners are allowed to incur 5 years of delinquent property taxes before the local government intervenes and offers the property at a foreclosure sale.
Bid Method	Premium bid	
Payment Method		The tax sale is free of all liens and encumbrances except that special assessments, easements, and IRS liens must be paid.
Interest Rate	N/A	Tax deed
	18%	When tax lien certificates are offered for sale.
Redemption Period	N/A	
	2 years	When tax lien certificates are offered for sale.
Over-the-Counter	No	
Municipalities	58	Alameda, Alpine, Amador, Butte, Calaveras, Colusa, Contra Costa, Del Norte, El Dorado, Fresno, Glenn, Humboldt, Imperial, Inyo, Kern, Kings, Lake, Lassen, Los Angeles, Madera, Marin, Mariposa, Mendocino, Merced, Modoc, Mono, Monterey, Napa, Nevada, Orange, Placer, Plumas, Riverside, Sacramento, San Benito, San Bernardino, San Diego, San Francisco, San Joaquin, San Luis Obispo, San Mateo, Santa Barbara, Santa Clara, Santa Cruz, Shasta, Sierra, Siskiyou, Solano, Sonoma, Stanislaus, Sutler, Tehama, Trinity, Tulare, Tuolumne, Ventura, Yolo, Yuba

STATE LAWS		
Statute	California Revenue and Taxation Code	Chapter 7, Sections: 3691, 3698, 3712
Colorado		
Type of Sale	Tax lien	Tax lien, tax certificate, tax sale certificate, or certificate of purchase.
Sale Date	November, first Thursday	The tax sale must be held on or before the second Monday in December. Notice of the sale must be published beginning four weeks prior to the sale. The tax sale must be published in a local newspaper or, in the absence of a local newspaper, at the treasurer's office.
Bid Method	Premium bid	The premium amount is not returned, and no interest is applied to the premium amount upon redemption.
Payment Method	Cash	The purchaser receives a certificate of purchase that indicates the interest rate.
Interest Rate	9% plus FDR	FDR is the federal discount rate, which is set in September and rounded to the nearest full percent.
Redemption Period	3 years	A fee charged by the taxing authority must be paid before a tax deed is requested. Any outstanding property taxes must be paid by the tax lien certificate holder before a tax deed is acquired.
Over-the-Counter	Yes, with exceptions	Over-the-counter sales are optional, and the jurisdiction of Denver does not offer liens over-the-counter.
Subsequent Taxes	Optional	The tax lien certificate holder must present the tax lien certificate before paying delinquent taxes for subsequent years. The additional amount earns interest at the same rate as the original tax lien certificate.
Foreclosure	Within 5 years	Property owners may dispute the foreclosure up to 5 years after its issuance. Under certain circumstances the period can be extended to 9 years if a quiet title judgment has not been made.
Municipalities	63	Adams, Alamosa, Arapahoe, Archuleta, Baca, Bent, Boulder, Chaffee, Cheyenne, Clear Creek, Conejos, Costilla, Crowley, Custer, Delta, Denver,

	STATE LAWS	
		Dolores, Douglas, Eagle, El Paso, Elbert, Fremont, Garfield, Gilpin, Grand, Gunnison, Hinsdale, Huerfano, Jackson, Jefferson, Kiowa, Kit Carson, La Plata, Lake, Larimer, Las Animas, Lincoln, Logan, Mesa, Mineral, Moffat, Montezuma, Montrose, Morgan, Otero, Ouray, Park, Phillips, Pitkin, Prowers, Pueblo, Rio Blanco, Rio Grande, Routt, Saguache, San Juan, San Miguel, Sedgwick, Summit, Teller, Washington, Weld, Yuma
Statute	Colorado revised statutes	Sections 39-123-103, 39-11-120,122
Connecticut		
Type of Sale	Hybrid tax deed	Collector's deed.
Sale Date	June	Real property is sold at public auction to the highest bidder. A tax deed is executed and delivered to the purchaser within 2 weeks of the tax sale. The deed is not recorded until a 1-year redemption period has expired. The town of New Haven only sells deeds in bulk to qualified buyers.
Bid Method	Premium bid	The premium amount receives 18% interest upon redemption.
Payment Method		
Interest Rate	18% annually	
Redemption Period	1 year	
Over-the-Counter	No	
Municipalities	8	Fairfield, Hartford, Litchfield, Middlesex, New Haven, New London, Tolland, Windham
Statute	General statutes of Connecticut	Section 12-157
Delaware		
Type of Sale	Hybrid tax deed	Deed.
Sale Date	Varies by municipality	The tax sale is a public oral-bid foreclosure sale of real estate.

STATE LAWS		
Bid Method	Premium bid	
Payment Method		
Interest Rate	15% penalty	
Redemption Period	60 days	
Over-the-Counter	No	
Municipalities	3	Kent, New Castle, Sussex
Statutes	9 Del. code	Sections 8721, 8728, 8749, 87650, 8758
Florida		
Type of Sale	Tax lien	The sale of tax lien certificates is an offer to invest. If a tax lien certificate is not redeemed during the redemption period, no foreclosure will take place. A tax deed for the associated property is offered for sale at another auction.
	Tax deed	The tax deed sale is a public oral-bid foreclosure of real estate.
Sale Date	Tax lien: on or before June 1	The tax lien certificate sale must be published in a local newspaper beginning 3 weeks prior to the sale.
	Tax deed	The tax deed sale must be held at least 30 days following the first publication of the sale. Publication is required for 4 consecutive weeks.
Bid Method	Bid down interest	Bids must be placed in increments of 1/4 of 1%.
Payment Method	Cash, certified check, bank draft, money order	A deposit of at least 10% is required prior to bidding, and the balance of all purchases must be received within 48 hours of the sale or within 48 hours of notification from the tax collector that the tax lien has been prepared. Failure to pay within 48 hours results in a forfeiture of the deposit.

STATE LAWS		
Interest Rate	Tax lien: 18% per annum with a 5% minimum	If the sale of a tax lien certificate is voided due to error, the cost of the tax lien certificate is refunded to the purchaser by the municipality with 8% interest.
	Tax deed: 18% per annum	If the tax certificate holder does not win the subsequent tax deed bid, he or she is, instead, refunded the value of the tax lien certificate, application fees, and interest at 18% per annum from the date of the application for a tax deed. The interest rate is fixed during this period, irrespective of the bid down interest rate. If the sale of a tax deed is found to be invalid, the investor is refunded the cost of the deed, legal expenses, fair value of any improvements made to the property, and interest at 12% from the date of issuance of the deed.
Redemption Period	2 years	Tax lien redemption periods are calculated from April 1 of the year in which the lien certificate was purchased. The cost of the tax lien certificate and a minimum 5% penalty are paid upon redemption.
Over-the-Counter	Yes, for liens	Tax lien certificates are offered for sale with an 18% redemption rate; the interest rate is not bid down.
	No, for deeds	
Subsequent Taxes	Optional	
Foreclosure	Within 7 years	Tax lien certificates expire after 7 years. Application for a tax deed must occur within the 7-year expiration period. Making application for a tax deed causes the particular municipality to initiate a sale of the tax deed. The winning bidder must offer a bid in excess of the amount that the tax lien certificate holder invested in the property. If the property is a homestead property, the cost of the tax deed will include 1/2 of the appraised value of the property. A 4-year statute of limitations exists for anyone challenging the tax deed after foreclosure and also for the investor to engage an adverse possession action.

STATE LAWS

Municipalities	67	Alachua, Baker, Bay, Bradford, Brevard, Broward, Calhoun, Charlotte, Citrus, Clay, Collier, Columbia, Dade, Desoto, Dixie, Duval, Escambia, Flagler, Franklin, Gadsden, Gilchrist, Glades, Gulf, Hamilton, Hardee, Hendry, Hernando, Highlands, Hillsborough, Holmes, Indian River, Jackson, Jefferson, Lafayette, Lake, Lee, Leon, Levy, Liberty, Madison, Manatee, Marion, Martin, Monroe, Nassau, Okaloosa, Okeechobee, Orange, Osceola, Palm Beach, Pasco, Pinellas, Polk, Putnam, Santa Rosa, Sarasota, Seminole, St. Johns, St. Lucie, Sumter, Suwannee, Taylor, Union, Volusia, Wakulla, Walton, Washington
Statute	Florida statutes annotated	Section 197

Georgia

Type of Sale	Hybrid tax deed	Sheriff's deed or deed.
Sale Date	First Tuesday of selected month	The tax sale is a public oral-bid foreclosure sale of real estate. Tax sales are advertised for 4 consecutive weeks prior to the tax sale.
Bid Method	Premium bid	
Payment Method	Cash, certified check, cashier's check, money order	Payment is required by the end of the tax sale day.
Interest Rate	10%–20% penalty	The redemption amount is equal to the amount that was paid by the high bidder plus a penalty of 10% per annum of the bid amount. An investor is required to serve notice of the intent to foreclose the right of redemption within the 6 months prior to the end of the redemption period. Notice is issued to the property owner and other parties with interest in the property, as shown in public records. If the redemption takes place after the notice to foreclose has been issued, an additional 10% penalty is added to the redemption amount.

STATE LAWS		
Redemption Period	1 year	If a tax lien certificate is redeemed, the investor must issue the property owner a quitclaim deed to the property. If a creditor or other person with interest in the property redeems the property, that party is given first lien to the property for the redemption amount expended.
Subsequent Taxes	Optional	Subsequent tax bills are sent to the property owner of record as well as the tax deed purchaser. The first tax deed purchaser is the superior lien holder. Subsequent tax deed purchasers become lien holders and are listed as owners along with the prior tax deed holders.
Foreclosure	Within 7 years	Tax deeds purchased before July 1, 1989, ripen to a fee simple title in 7 years. No notice of intent to foreclose the right of redemption needs to be sent to the property owner or persons with interest in the property, as found in public records.
	Within 4 years	Tax deeds purchased after July 1, 1989, ripen to a fee simple title in 4 years. No notice of intent to foreclose the right of redemption needs to be sent to the property owner or persons with interest in the property, as found in public records. An administrative and nonjudicial process is followed to foreclose the right to redemption. The tax deed is recorded upon following the established process; however, the deed cannot be executed for 4 years from the date of recording.
Over-the-Counter	No	
Municipalities	159	Appling, Atkinson, Bacon, Baker, Baldwin, Banks, Barrow, Bartow, Ben Hill, Berrien, Bibb, Bleckley, Brantley, Brooks, Bryan, Bulloch, Burke, Butts, Calhoun, Camden, Candler, Carroll, Catoosa, Charlton, Chatham, Chattahoochee, Chattooga, Cherokee, Clarke, Clay, Clayton, Clinch, Cobb, Coffee, Colquitt, Columbia, Cook, Coweta, Crawford, Crisp, Dade, Dawson, DeKalb, Decatur, Dodge, Dooly, Dougherty, Douglas, Early, Echols, Effingham, Elbert, Emanuel, Evans, Fannin, Fayette, Floyd, Forsyth, Franklin, Fulton, Gilmer, Glascock,

STATE LAWS

		Glynn, Gordon, Grady, Greene, Gwinnett, Habersham, Hall, Hancock, Haralson, Harris, Hart, Heard, Henry, Houston, Irwin, Jackson, Jasper, Jeff Davis, Jefferson, Jenkins, Johnson, Jones, Lamar, Lanier, Laurens, Lee, Liberty, Lincoln, Long, Lowndes, Lumpkin, Macon, Madison, Marion, McDuffie, McIntosh, Meriwether, Miller, Mitchell, Monroe, Montgomery, Morgan, Murray, Muscogee, Newton, Oconee, Oglethorpe, Paulding, Peach, Pickens, Pierce, Pike, Polk, Pulaski, Putnam, Quitman, Rabun, Randolph, Richmond, Rockdale, Schley, Screven, Seminole, Spalding, Stephens, Stewart, Sumter, Talbot, Taliaferro, Tattnall, Taylor, Telfair, Terrell, Thomas, Tift, Toombs, Towns, Treutlen, Troup, Turner, Twiggs, Union, Upson, Walker, Walton, Ware, Warren, Washington, Wayne, Webster, Wheeler, White, Whitfield, Wilcox, Wilkes, Wilkinson, Worth
Statute	Official code of Georgia annotated	Annotated Sections 48-240; 48-319, 20; 48-4-42, 45
Hawaii		
Type of Sale	Hybrid tax deed	Conveyance deed or tax deed.
Sale Date	June and November or December	The tax sale is a public oral-bid foreclosure sale of real estate. Tax sales are held twice a year. The county of Hawaii has both an east and west office. The east office is responsible for handling the more remote locations of the island. The west office handles the more populated areas.
Bid Method	Premium bid	
Payment Method		
Interest Rate	12% per annum	
Redemption Period	1 year	The redemption period is within 1 year of recording of the tax deed. The tax deed may be recorded within 60 days of the tax sale. The redemption amount includes all costs incurred by the deed purchaser to acquire the deed. If the deed is not recoded within the 60-day time frame, the redemption period may be extended to 1 year

STATE LAWS

		beyond the date on which the tax deed is recorded. Interest is not applied to the redemption amount during the period of time that the redemption is extended.
Over-the-Counter	No	
Municipalities	5	Hawaii, Honolulu, Kalawao, Kauai, Maui
Statute	Hawaii revised statutes	Section 246-60

Idaho

Type of Sale	Pure tax deed	Real property with delinquent taxes is foreclosed and acquired by the municipality in which the property is located. The municipality is then authorized to offer for sale any property that is not necessary for use by the municipality.
Sale Date	May	
Bid Method	Premium bid	The particular municipality determines opening bid amounts. Some municipalities include the lien amount plus any pending issue fees, certifications, special assessments, recording fees, and cost of publication of the sale notice. Other municipalities may also include the current market value, as determined by the tax assessor.
Payment Method		
Interest Rate	N/A	
Redemption Period	N/A	
Over-the-Counter	No	
Municipalities	44	Ada, Adams, Bannock, Bear Lake, Benewah, Bingham, Blaine, Boise, Bonner, Bonneville, Boundary, Butte, Camas, Canyon, Caribou, Cassia, Clark, Clearwater, Custer, Elmore, Franklin, Fremont, Gem, Gooding, Idaho, Jefferson, Jerome, Kootenai, Latah, Lemhi, Lewis, Lincoln, Madison, Minidoka, Nez Perce, Oneida, Owyhee, Payette, Power, Shoshone, Teton, Twin Falls, Valley, Washington
Statutes	Idaho statute	Sections 31-808; 63-1003-1011

STATE LAWS

Illinois

Type of Sale	Tax lien	Certificate of purchase or tax sale certificate
Sale Date	Varies by municipality	Tax liens that are not sold at the annual tax sale are offered for sale at what is termed a scavenger sale. Scavenger sales are held in odd years for properties with 2 years of delinquent taxes.
Bid Method	Annual tax sale: bid down interest with penalties	Penalties are assessed as a percentage of the bid amount and are staggered across the redemption period.
	Scavenger sale: premium bid	Interest upon redemption is only applied to the opening bid amount. Redemption does not allow for a refund of the premium amount or that interest be applied to the premium amount.
Payment Method	Annual tax sale	Pre-registration procedures require that a deposit be made 10 days prior to the tax sale in order to participate in the bidding. The balance of all purchases is due immediately upon winning a bid. Larger municipalities may require a letter of credit or bond for 1.5 times the amount of taxes and penalties for bids.
	Scavenger sale	Pre-registration requires a $50 to $100 registration fee, paid 5 business days in advance of the sale. The minimum bid is $250, one-half of the tax amount or $500, and is due on the date of sale. If the bid is above the minimum, the balance of the bid is due the next day. Failure to pay the bid amount results in a forfeiture of the minimum bid amount and a possible lawsuit.

STATE LAWS		
Interest Rate	Annual tax sale: 18% penalty per 6 months	The penalty amount increases by the same amount that was bid, every 6 months.
	Scavenger sale: 24% per annum	Staggered penalty rates allow for differing payments, depending upon the date of redemption. The penalty to be applied to the redemption amount is calculated as a percentage of the certificate amount. If the interest upon redemption is bid down to 12%, the penalty is applied as follows: Within 2 months: 3% of the purchase amount per month. After 2 months, on or before 6 months: 12% of the purchase amount; 12% is the bid interest. After 6 months, on or before 1 year: 24% of the purchase amount; 24% is equivalent to 2 times the bid interest. After 1 year, on or before 18 months: 36% of the purchase amount, 36% is equivalent to 3 times the bid interest. After 18 months, on or before 2 years: 48% of the purchase amount; 48% is equivalent to 4 times the bid interest. After 2 years: 48% plus 6% per year thereafter.
Redemption Period	2–3 years	The typical redemption period is 2 years. However, the tax lien certificate holder may extend the redemption period to 3 years beyond the annual tax sale by filing notice with the particular municipality. Improved residential properties with between one and six residential units have a redemption period of 2 years and 6 months. Improved residential properties with more than six residential units have a redemption period of 6 months, if the taxes are delinquent for more than 2 years. Vacant properties may be void of a redemption period and foreclosed by a petition filed with the courts.
Subsequent Taxes	Optional	If a tax lien certificate holder fails to pay back taxes, the property may be auctioned at a scavenger sale. Subsequent taxes are included in the calculation of the minimum bid for the scavenger sale.

STATE LAWS		
Foreclosure		A tax lien certificate becomes void if a petition for deed and record of the deed is not filed within 5 months of the end of the redemption period. Property owners may dispute a foreclosure up to 5 years after its issuance. Under certain circumstances and in the absence of a quiet title judgment, the period may be extended to 9 years. Foreclosed properties are free of liens and encumbrances, but not easements, such as those assessed by utility companies.
Over-the-Counter	No	
Municipalities	102	Adams, Alexander, Bond, Boone, Brown, Bureau, Calhoun, Carroll, Champaign, Christian, Clark, Clay, Clinton, Coles, Cook, Crawford, Cumberland, DeKalb, DeWitt, Douglas, Dupage, Edgar, Edwards, Effingham, Fayette, Ford, Franklin, Fulton, Gallatin, Greene, Grundy, Hamilton, Hancock, Hardin, Henderson, Henry, Iroquois, Jackson, Jasper, Jefferson, Jersey, Jo Daviess, Johnson, Kane, Kankakee, Kendall, Knox, La Salle, Lake, Lawrence, Lee, Livingston, Logan, Macon, Macoupin, Madison, Marion, Marshall, Mason, Massac, McDonough, McHenry, McLean, Menard, Mercer, Monroe, Montgomery, Morgan, Moultrie, Ogle, Peoria, Perry, Piatt, Pike, Pope, Pulaski, Putnam, Randolph, Richland, Rock Island, Saline, Sangamon, Schuyler, Scott, Shelby, St. Clair, Stark, Stephenson, Tazewell, Union, Vermilion, Wabash, Warren, Washington, Wayne, White, Whiteside, Will, Williamson, Winnebago, Woodford
Statute	33 Illinois compiled statutes	205/238, 200/21-350, 355, 385
Indiana		
Type of Sale	Tax lien	Certificate of sale or tax sale certificate.
Sale Date	On or after 1 August, but before 1 November	Notice of the tax sale is displayed in a public location for 21 days and published once a week for 3 weeks.

STATE LAWS		
Bid Method	Premium bid	The premium bid amount is referred to as a tax sale overbid. The premium amount is held in the municipality's tax sale surplus fund.
Payment Method		Payment is required immediately upon winning the bid. Failure to pay results in a 25% penalty on the bid amount and also a lawsuit.
Interest Rate	10%–15% penalty; no interest	Staggered interest rates allow for differing payments, dependent upon the date of redemption. The penalty to be applied to the redemption amount is calculated as follows: Within 6 months: 10% of the opening bid amount. After 6 months, on or before 1 year: 15% of the opening bid amount. After 1 year: 25% of the opening bid amount. The premium amount incurs no interest. Subsequent taxes and assessments incur interest at 12% per annum.
Redemption Period	1 year	The premium amount is refunded to the investor upon redemption. Between 3 to 5 months before the end of the redemption period, the investor must give notice of the tax sale, the redemption period, the redemption amount, and the intent to petition for a deed. Notice must be delivered by certified mail to all individuals with interest in the property, as specified in public records. If an address is unknown, notice must be published for 3 consecutive weeks. If notice with specified details is not provided, the tax lien certificate expires 30 days after the end of the redemption period. A tax deed must be acquired within 4 years of filing a petition for it; otherwise, the tax lien certificate terminates.
Subsequent Taxes	Optional	Subsequent taxes earn interest at 12%.
Foreclosure		Upon foreclosure, the property owner may file a claim to obtain the premium bid amount that was placed in the tax sale surplus fund. If the amount is not claimed within 5 years, the amount is forfeited and transferred from the municipality's surplus fund to its general fund.
Over-the-Counter	No	

STATE LAWS		
Municipalities	92	Adams, Allen, Bartholomew, Benton, Blackford, Boone, Brown, Carroll, Cass, Clark, Clay, Clinton, Crawford, Daviess, DeKalb, Dearborn, Decatur, Delaware, Dubois, Elkhart, Fayette, Floyd, Fountain, Franklin, Fulton, Gibson, Grant, Greene, Hamilton, Hancock, Harrison, Hendricks, Henry, Howard, Huntington, Jackson, Jasper, Jay, Jefferson, Jennings, Johnson, Knox, Kosciusko, Lagrange, Lake, La Porte, Lawrence, Madison, Marion, Marshall, Martin, Miami, Monroe, Montgomery, Morgan, Newton, Noble, Ohio, Orange, Owen, Parke, Perry, Pike, Porter, Posey, Pulaski, Putnam, Randolph, Ripley, Rush, Scott, Shelby, Spencer, St. Joseph, Starke, Steuben, Sullivan, Switzerland, Tippecanoe, Tipton, Union, Vanderburgh, Vermillion, Vigo, Wabash, Warren, Warrick, Washington, Wayne, Wells, White, Whitley
Statute	Indiana code	Sections 6-1, 1-24 and 6-1.1-25
Iowa		
Type of Sale	Tax lien	Certificate of purchase or tax sale certificate.
Sale Date	June, third Monday	The tax sale listing is published 1 to 3 weeks prior to the sale.
Bid Method	Random or rotational	Random or rotational bidding is used in lieu of bidding down ownership.
Payment Method		A nonrefundable fee may be required to register for the sale. Payment is required immediately upon winning the bid. If payment is not made, the tax lien certificate is offered for sale again.
Interest Rate	24% per annum	
Redemption Period	1 year and 9 months	If the tax lien on a property is more than 1 year old when it is acquired, the redemption period is 9 months. Only the property owner or other individuals with recorded interest in a property may redeem a tax lien certificate.
Subsequent Taxes		

STATE LAWS		
Foreclosure	3 years	Ninety days prior to the expiration of the redemption period, the lien certificate holder must inform the property owner that the right of redemption is to expire in 90 days. The tax deed must be acquired within 3 years of the tax sale date. If the tax lien certificate holder does not notify the property owner within 1 year and 9 months or obtain a tax deed within the specified 3-year time frame, the tax lien certificate expires, and any amounts used to acquire the lien certificate are forfeited to the municipality.
Over-the-Counter	No	Unsold tax lien certificates are adjourned and repeatedly offered for sale at 2-month intervals until the next annual tax sale, when the process of repeatedly offering certificates for sale begins again.
Municipalities	99	Adair, Adams, Allamakee, Appanoose, Audubon, Benton, Black Hawk, Boone, Bremer, Buchanan, Buena Vista, Butler, Calhoun, Carroll, Cass, Cedar, Cerro Gordo, Cherokee, Chickasaw, Clarke, Clay, Clayton, Clinton, Crawford, Dallas, Davis, Decatur, Delaware, Des Moines, Dickinson, Dubuque, Emmet, Fayette, Floyd, Franklin, Fremont, Greene, Grundy, Guthrie, Hamilton, Hancock, Hardin, Harrison, Henry, Howard, Humboldt, Ida, Iowa, Jackson, Jasper, Jefferson, Johnson, Jones, Keokuk, Kossuth, Lee, Linn, Louisa, Lucas, Lyon, Madison, Mahaska, Marion, Marshall, Mills, Mitchell, Monona, Monroe, Montgomery, Muscatine, O'brien, Osceola, Page, Palo Alto, Plymouth, Pocahontas, Polk, Pottawattamie, Poweshiek, Ringgold, Sac, Scott, Shelby, Sioux, Story, Tama, Taylor, Union, Van Buren, Wapello, Warren, Washington, Wayne, Webster, Winnebago, Winneshiek, Woodbury, Worth, Wright
Statute	Code of Iowa	Chapters 446, 447.13
Kansas		
Type of Sale	Tax deed	
Sale Date	Varies by municipality	The tax sale is a public oral-bid foreclosure sale of real estate.

STATE LAWS		
Bid Method	Premium bid	Some municipalities have no established minimum for bids. Bidding may start as low as $50, and properties may be purchased for less than the tax lien amount, that is, the delinquent tax, penalties, and costs.
Payment Method		
Interest Rate	N/A	
Redemption Period	N/A	
Over-the-Counter	No	
Municipalities	105	Alien, Anderson, Atchison, Barber, Barton, Bourbon, Brown, Butler, Chase, Chautauqua, Cherokee, Cheyenne, Clark, Clay, Cloud, Coffey, Comanche, Cowley, Crawford, Decatur, Dickinson, Doniphan, Douglas, Edwards, Elk, Ellis, Ellsworth, Finney, Ford, Franklin, Geary, Gove, Graham, Grant, Gray, Greeley, Greenwood, Hamilton, Harper, Harvey, Haskell, Hodgeman, Jackson, Jefferson, Jewell, Johnson, Kearny, Kingman, Kiowa, Labette, Lane, Leavenworth, Lincoln, Linn, Logan, Lyon, Marion, Marshall, McPherson, Meade, Miami, Mitchell, Montgomery, Morris, Morton, Nemaha, Neosho, Ness, Norton, Osage, Osborne, Ottawa, Pawnee, Phillips, Pottawatomie, Pratt, Rawlins, Reno, Republic, Rice, Riley, Rooks, Rush, Russell, Saline, Scott, Sedgwick, Seward, Shawnee, Sheridan, Sherman, Smith, Stafford, Stanton, Stevens, Sumner, Thomas, Trego, Wabaunsee, Wallace, Washington, Wichita, Wilson, Woodson, Wyandotte
Statute	K.S.A.	Section 79-2801
Kentucky		
Type of Sale	Tax lien	Certificate of delinquency or tax claims.
Sale Date	April to May	The tax sale must be published 15 days prior to the tax sale date.
Bid Method	Premium bid	Bidding is not established by state statute.
Payment Method		Payment is due immediately upon winning a bid.

STATE LAWS		
Interest Rate	12% per annum	Interest is calculated monthly with no consideration for portions of a month. The interest computed for the first day of the month is the same as that computed for any other day of the month.
Redemption Period	1 year	After one year, the tax lien certificate holder may pursue formal collection from the property owner for amounts necessary to acquire the lien certificate or engage in enforcing the right to foreclose any right of redemption of the tax lien certificate. Tax deeds are obtained through a judicial foreclosure. The property owner must be notified of the intent to foreclose and the required redemption amount that will accrue 50 days prior to the date of the foreclosure.
Over-the-Counter	No	
Municipalities	120	Adair, Alien, Anderson, Ballard, Barren, Bath, Bell, Boone, Bourbon, Boyd, Boyle, Bracken, Breathitt, Breckinridge, Bullitt, Butler, Caldwell, Calloway, Campbell, Carlisle, Carroll, Carter, Casey, Christian, Clark, Clay, Clinton, Crittenden, Cumberland, Daviess, Edmonson, Elliott, Estill, Fayette, Fleming, Floyd, Franklin, Fulton, Gallatin, Garrard, Grant, Graves, Grayson, Green, Greenup, Hancock, Hardin, Harlan, Harrison, Hart, Henderson, Henry, Hickman, Hopkins, Jackson, Jefferson, Jessamine, Johnson, Kenton, Knott, Knox, Larue, Laurel, Lawrence, Lee, Leslie, Letcher, Lewis, Lincoln, Livingston, Logan, Lyon, Madison, Magoffin, Marion, Marshall, Martin, Mason, McCracken, McCreary, McLean, Meade, Menifee, Mercer, Metcalfe, Monroe, Montgomery, Morgan, Muhlenberg, Nelson, Nicholas, Ohio, Oldham, Owen, Owsley, Pendleton, Perry, Pike, Powell, Pulaski, Robertson, Rockcastle, Rowan, Russell, Scott, Shelby, Simpson, Spencer, Taylor, Todd, Trigg, Trimble, Union, Warren, Washington, Wayne, Webster, Whitley, Wolfe, Woodford
Statute	K.R.S.	Section 134.460

STATE LAWS		
Louisiana		
Type of Sale	Hybrid tax deed	Tax deed or deed of sale
Sale Date	January to April	The tax sale date is not established by state statute.
Bid Method	Bid down interest	
Payment Method	Cash	Payment is required immediately upon winning the bid.
Interest Rate	12% per annum and 5% penalty	
Redemption Period	3 years	The redemption period may be overridden, because Louisiana allows tax deed purchasers to petition the court for immediate possession of a property. Abandoned or blighted properties have the redemption period reduced to 18 months.
Subsequent Taxes		
Foreclosure		Statute does not dictate when a tax deed must be recorded, but a tax deed must be recorded after the sale, and the property owner is given 3 years from the date of the tax deed recording to redeem the property.
Over-the-Counter	No	
Municipalities	64 Municipalities are called parishes	Acadia, Alien, Ascension, Assumption, Avoyelles, Beauregard, Bienville, Bossier, Caddo, Calcasieu, Caldwell, Cameron, Catahoula, Claiborne, Concordia, De Soto, East Baton Rouge, East Carroll, East Feliciana, Evangeline, Franklin, Grant, Iberia, Iberville, Jackson, Jefferson, Jefferson Davis, La Salle, Lafayette, Lafourche, Lincoln, Livingston, Madison, Morehouse, Natchitoches, Orleans, Ouachita, Plaquemines, Pointe Coupee, Rapides, Red River, Richland, Sabine, St. Bernard, St. Charles, St. Helena, St. James, St. John the Baptist, St. Landry, St. Martin, St. Mary, St. Tammany, Tangipahoa, Tensas, Terrebonne, Union, Vermilion, Vernon, Washington, Webster, West Baton Rouge, West Carroll, West Feliciana, Winn
Statute	L.R.S	Section 47:2181, 2183

STATE LAWS

Maine

Type of Sale	Tax deed	Municipalities place liens against real property for delinquent property taxes. If the property owner does not redeem the property, the municipality may retain ownership of the property or sell the property. When the municipality decides to sell property, title to the property is offered for sale through a tax lien foreclosure or sewer lien foreclosure.
Sale Date	Varies by municipality	
Bid Method	Sealed	The municipality offers property for sale that it has taken ownership of, because the property owner failed to redeem the delinquent taxes assessed against him or her. The municipality uses its own discretion in accepting sealed bid offers or rejecting sealed bid offers as inadequate.
Payment Method		
Interest Rate	N/A	
Redemption Period	N/A	
Over-the-Counter	No	
Municipalities	16	Androscoggin, Aroostook, Cumberland, Franklin, Hancock, Kennebec, Knox, Lincoln, Oxford, Penobscot, Piscataquis, Sagadahoc, Somerset, Waldo, Washington, York
Statute	Maine revised statutes	Title 36

Maryland

Type of Sale	Tax lien	Tax sale certificate or certificate of sale.
Sale Date	Varies by municipality	The particular municipality establishes the tax sale date and the listing is published 30 to 60 days prior to the tax sale.
Bid Method	Premium bid	

STATE LAWS		
Payment Method		Only the opening bid amount is required on the day of the tax sale. The tax lien certificate purchaser never pays the premium amount if the lien certificate is redeemed. If the lien certificate is redeemed, the premium amount must be paid in order to foreclose the right of redemption.
Interest Rate	6% to 24%	
Redemption Period	6 months	A redemption period is not established by statute. However, the lien certificate holder may judicially foreclose and end the redemption period 6 months after the tax sale, but before 2 years have expired. If the complaint is not filed within 2 years of the tax sale date, the tax lien certificate expires, and the purchaser forfeits all money used to acquire the certificate.
Subsequent Taxes		
Foreclosure	Within 2 years	Foreclosure must be accomplished within 2 years, except in Baltimore City. Vacant or abandoned buildings or buildings in violation of building codes must be foreclosed within 1 year.
Over-the-Counter	Yes	
Municipalities	23	Allegany, Anne Arundel, Baltimore, Calvert, Caroline, Carroll, Cecil, Charles, Dorchester, Frederick, Garrett, Harford, Howard, Kent, Montgomery, Prince George's, Queen Anne's, Somerset, St. Mary's, Talbot, Washington, Wicomico, Worchester and Baltimore City
Statute	Annotated code of the public laws of Maryland	Section 14-817, 818, 820, 831, 833, 844
Massachusetts		
Type of Sale	Hybrid tax deed	Collector's deed, deed, or deed of the land.
Sale Date	Varies by municipality	Notice of the tax sale must be published at least 14 days prior to the sale in a local newspaper and in two or more publicly accessible places.

STATE LAWS		
Bid Method	Bid down ownership	
Payment Method		A good-faith deposit is required immediately upon winning the bid, or else the sale is void. Full payment is required within 20 days of the sale, or the sale is void and the deposit is forfeited.
Interest Rate	16% per annum	
Redemption Period	6 months	A redemption period is not established by statute. The redemption amount may be paid to either the treasurer, the tax deed purchaser, a representative designated by the tax deed purchaser, or an assignee of the tax deed purchaser. If a redemption payment is made to the treasurer for less than the full amount, the purchaser may sue for the balance within 3 months. Property owners are allowed to make payment in installments. Each installment must be at least 25% of the total redemption amount with the exception of the last installment payment, which should cover the balance of the amount due. When installment payments are made, the redemption period increases by 1 year. The tax deed holder must initiate a judicial foreclosure to end the redemption period. The tax deed holder may initiate the foreclosure 6 months after the tax sale date.
Subsequent Taxes		
Foreclosure		The tax deed must be recorded within 60 days of the sale. The property owner is given 6 months to redeem the property, or the tax deed purchaser may foreclose on the property. Because of backlogs and the number of property owners requesting an extension of the redemption period, the actual foreclosure may be delayed up to 3 years. If a foreclosure is found to be invalid, the investor is refunded the amount of the purchase plus 6% interest for up to 2 years.
Over-the-Counter	No	Unsold tax deeds are sold at another auction.

STATE LAWS		
Municipalities	14	Barnstable, Berkshire, Bristol, Dukes, Essex, Franklin, Hampden, Hampshire, Middlesex, Nantucket, Norfolk, Plymouth, Suffolk, Worcester
Statute	Annotated law of Massachusetts	Sections 45, 62

Michigan

Type of Sale	Tax deed	
Sale Date	May, first Tuesday	Tax lien certificates are offered for sale for properties in the third year of delinquency.
Bid Method	Bid down ownership	
Payment Method	Cash, certified check, or money order	Payment is required at the end of the tax sale day.
Interest Rate	First year, 15% Second year, 50% penalty	The interest rate of 15% applies to redemption in the first year after the tax sale. Redemption at any point in the second year, but before the 6-month redemption period that is initiated by the issuance of a tax deed, incurs a 50% penalty. The purchaser must provide the property owner with a quitclaim deed upon redemption.
Redemption Period	1 year	The property owner may redeem the tax lien certificate up until the time that a tax deed is obtained. The issuance of a tax deed initiates a new 6-month redemption period.
Subsequent Taxes	Required	The time frame for converting a tax lien certificate into a tax deed is 6 months after the end of the redemption period. During this time frame, the purchaser is required to pay all subsequent taxes.
Foreclosure		The tax deed expires in 5 years if a tax deed is not acquired and proper procedures are not followed to obtain title to the property.
Over-the-Counter	Yes	Unsold tax lien certificates are bought and offered for sale by the state. Tax lien certificates are offered for sale up to April 19 of the following year. The price includes interest at a rate of 15% per annum or 1.25% per month.

STATE LAWS		
Municipalities	83	Alcona, Alger, Allegan, Alpena, Antrim, Arenac, Baraga, Barry, Bay, Benzie, Berrien, Branch, Calhoun, Cass, Charlevoix, Cheboygan, Chippewa, Clare, Clinton, Crawford, Delta, Dickinson, Eaton, Emmet, Genesee, Gladwin, Gogebic, Grand Traverse, Gratiot, Hillsdale, Houghton, Huron, Ingham, Ionia, Iosco, Iron, Isabella, Jackson, Kalamazoo, Kalkaska, Kent, Keweenaw, Lake, Lapeer, Leelanau, Lenawee, Livingston, Luce, Mackinac, Macomb, Manistee, Marquette, Mason, Mecosta, Menominee, Midland, Missaukee, Monroe, Montcalm, Montmorency, Muskegon, Newaygo, Oakland, Oceana, Ogemaw, Ontonagon, Osceola, Oscoda, Otsego, Ottawa, Presque Isle, Roscommon, Saginaw, Sanilac, Schoolcraft, Shiawassee, St. Clair, St. Joseph, Tuscola, Van Buren, Washtenaw, Wayne, Wexford
Statute	Public Acts	Act 123 of 1999; Act 206 of Public Acts 1893 Sections 140-143
Minnesota		
Type of Sale	Tax deed	Municipalities place liens against real property for delinquent property taxes. If the property owner does not redeem the property, the municipality may retain ownership of the property or sell the property. The municipality may: - Offer the property for sale at public auction. - Offer the property for sale to an adjacent property owner if the parcel of land is too small to build on. - Transfer ownership to the city for authorized public use. - Place the property on hold for an environmental review.
Sale Date	Varies by municipality	
Bid Method	Premium bid	Properties offered for sale at the public auction are sold to the highest bidder willing to pay the highest amount above the appraised market value of the property.

STATE LAWS		
Payment Method		Some municipalities may finance the purchase of tax deeds at a rate of 10% per annum for up to 10 years.
Interest Rate	N/A	
Redemption Period	N/A	The property owner loses title to the property as a result of foreclosure; however, the property owner may make application to repurchase the property. The municipality uses its own discretion in determining whether to accept or reject the application.
Over-the-Counter	Yes	
Municipalities	87	Aitkin, Anoka, Decker, Beltrami, Benton, Big Stone, Blue Earth, Brown, Carlton, Carver, Cass, Chippewa, Chisago, Clay, Clearwater, Cook, Cottonwood, Crow Wing, Dakota, Dodge, Douglas, Faribault, Fillmore, Freeborn, Goodhue, Grant, Hennepin, Houston, Hubbard, Isanti, Itasca, Jackson, Kanabec, Kandiyohi, Kittson, Koochiching, Lac Qui Parle, Lake, Lake of the Woods, Le Sueur, Lincoln, Lyon, Mahnomen, Marshall, Martin, McLeod, Meeker, Mille Lacs, Morrison, Mower, Murray, Nicollet, Nobles, Norman, Olmsted, Otter Tail, Pennington, Pine, Pipestone, Polk, Pope, Ramsey, Red Lake, Redwood, Renville, Rice, Rock, Roseau, Scott, Sherburne, Sibley, St. Louis, Stearns, Steele, Stevens, Swift, Todd, Traverse, Wabasha, Wadena, Waseca, Washington, Watonwan, Wilkin, Winona, Wright, Yellow Medicine
Statute	Minnesota statutes	Sections 281, 282
Mississippi		
Type of Sale	Tax lien	Receipt showing the amount paid.
Sale Date	April, first Monday or September, third Monday	The tax sale listing must be published in a local newspaper or posted for two weeks.

STATE LAWS		
Bid Method	Premium bid	Interest upon redemption is only applied to the opening bid amount. Redemption does not allow for a refund of the premium amount or interest on the premium amount.
Payment Method	Cash, certified check, money order or cashier's check	
Interest Rate	12% per annum plus 5% penalty	The 5% penalty is applied only once, in the first year of redemption. If the tax sale is found to have occurred in error, the investor receives a refund of the amount of the purchase with 12% interest and 5% penalty.
Redemption Period	2 years	The premium amount is refunded to the tax lien certificate holder.
Subsequent Taxes		
Foreclosure		Tax deeds must be requested upon expiration of the redemption period. The investor is provided a deed with title and immediate possession of the property.
Over-the-Counter	No	
Municipalities	82	Adams, Alcorn, Amite, Attala, Benton, Bolivar, Calhoun, Carroll, Chickasaw, Choctaw, Claiborne, Clarke, Clay, Coahoma, Copiah, Covington, Desoto, Forrest, Franklin, George, Greene, Grenada, Hancock, Harrison, Hinds, Holmes, Humphreys, Issaquena, Itawamba, Jackson, Jasper, Jefferson, Jefferson Davis, Jones, Kemper, Lafayette, Lamar, Lauderdale, Lawrence, Leake, Lee, Leflore, Lincoln, Lowndes, Madison, Marion, Marshall, Monroe, Montgomery, Neshoba, Newton, Noxubee, Oktibbeha, Panola, Pearl River, Perry, Pike, Pontotoc, Prentiss, Quitman, Rankin, Scott, Sharkey, Simpson, Smith, Stone, Sunflower, Tallahatchie, Tate, Tippah, Tishomingo, Tunica, Union, Walthall, Warren, Washington, Wayne, Webster, Wilkinson, Winston, Yalobusha, Yazoo

STATE LAWS		
Statute	Mississippi code of 1972	Amended Sections 27-41-55, 59 27-45-3
Missouri		
Type of Sale	Tax lien	Certificate of purchase.
Sale Date	August, fourth Monday	The tax sale listing is published 2 to 3 weeks prior to the tax sale.
Bid Method	Bid up ownership	Bidding is limited to residents of the particular municipality only. Nonresidents must designate a resident of the particular municipality to act as a resident agent on their behalf and bid at the tax sale.
Payment Method	Cash, certified check, or cashier's check	Payment is required immediately upon winning the bid, or a penalty may be imposed on the purchaser.
Interest Rate	10% per annum	An 8% interest rate is applied to subsequent taxes paid by the lien certificate holder.
Redemption Period	2 years	The lien certificate holder must apply for a tax deed within 6 months of the expiration of the redemption period.
Over-the-Counter	No	
Municipalities	114	Adair, Andrew, Atchison, Audrain, Barry, Barton, Bates, Benton, Bollinger, Boone, Buchanan, Butler, Caldwell, Callaway, Camden, Cape Girardeau, Carroll, Carter, Cass, Cedar, Charlton, Christian, Clark, Clay, Clinton, Cole, Cooper, Crawford, Dade, Dallas, Daviess, DeKalb, Dent, Douglas, Dunklin, Franklin, Gasconade, Gentry, Greene, Grundy, Harrison, Henry, Hickory, Holt, Howard, Howell, Iron, Jackson, Jasper, Jefferson, Johnson, Knox, Laclede, Lafayette, Lawrence, Lewis, Lincoln, Linn, Livingston, Macon, Madison, Marion, Maries, McDonald, Mercer, Miller, Mississippi, Moniteau, Monroe, Montgomery, Morgan, New Madrid, Newton, Nodaway, Oregon, Osage, Ozark, Pemiscot, Perry, Pettis, Phelps, Pike, Platte, Polk, Pulaski, Putnam, Rails, Randolph, Ray, Reynolds, Ripley, Saline, Schuyler, Scotland, Scott, Shannon,

STATE LAWS

		Shelby, St. Charles, St. Clair, St. Francois, Ste. Genevieve, St. Louis, Stoddard, Stone, Sullivan, Taney, Texas, Vernon, Warren, Washington, Wayne, Webster, Worth, Wright
Statute	Missouri revised statutes	140

Montana

Type of Sale	Tax lien	
Sale Date	July	The tax sale listing must be published in a local newspaper or public place for 3 weeks, beginning no later than the last Monday in June
Bid Method	Random or rotational	
Payment Method	Cash	Payment is required on the day of the sale.
Interest Rate	10% per annum plus 2% penalty	
Redemption Period	3 years	A tax deed is granted to the lien certificate holder upon expiration of the redemption period. The tax deed must then be recorded.
Over-the-Counter	Yes	
Municipalities	57	Beaverhead, Big Horn, Blaine, Broadwater, Carbon, Carter, Cascade, Chouteau, Custer, Daniels, Dawson, Deer Lodge, Fallen, Fergus, Flathead, Gallatin, Garfield, Glacier, Golden Valley, Granite, Hill, Jefferson, Judith Basin, Lake, Lewis and Clark, Liberty, Lincoln, Madison, McCone, Meagher, Mineral, Missoula, Musselshell, Park, Petroleum, Phillips, Pondera, Powder River, Powell, Prairie, Ravalli, Richland, Roosevelt, Rosebud, Sanders, Sheridan, Silver Bow, Stillwater, Sweet Grass, Teton, Toole, Treasure, Valley, Wheatland, Wibaux, Yellowstone, Yellowstone National Park
Statute	Montana code	Annotated Sections 15-16-102; 15-18-211 through 216

STATE LAWS		
Nebraska		
Type of Sale	Tax lien	Certificate of purchase, certificate of sale or tax certificate.
Sale Date	March, first Monday	The tax sale listing must be compiled between 4 and 6 weeks prior to the tax sale date. The listing must be published weekly for 3 consecutive weeks.
Bid Method	Bid down ownership or rotational	The tax lien holder is required to pay subsequent taxes on the securing property. The amounts are added to the tax lien amount.
Payment Method	Payment methods are determined by the particular municipality	Payment is required on the day of the sale.
Interest Rate	14% per annum	
Redemption Period	3 years	A tax lien certificate holder must serve notice to the property owner of the intent to foreclose the right to redemption 3 months prior to making application for a tax deed.
Over-the-Counter	Yes	
Municipalities	93	Adams, Antelope, Arthur, Banner, Blaine, Boone, Box Butte, Boyd, Brown, Buffalo, Burt, Butler, Cass, Cedar, Chase, Cherry, Cheyenne, Clay, Colfax, Cuming, Custer, Dakota, Dawes, Dawson, Deuel, Dixon, Dodge, Douglas, Dundy, Fillmore, Franklin, Frontier, Furnas, Gage, Garden, Garfield, Gosper, Grant, Greeley, Hall, Hamilton, Harlan, Hayes, Hitchcock, Holt, Hooker, Howard, Jefferson, Johnson, Kearney, Keith, Keya Paha, Kimball, Knox, Lancaster, Lincoln, Logan, Loup, Madison, McPherson, Merrick, Morrill, Nance, Nemaha, Nuckolls, Otoe, Pawnee, Perkins, Phelps, Pierce, Platte, Polk, Red Willow, Richardson, Rock, Saline, Sarpy, Saunders, Scotts Bluff, Seward, Sheridan, Sherman, Sioux, Stanton, Thayer, Thomas, Thurston, Valley, Washington, Wayne, Webster, Wheeler, York

STATE LAWS

Statute	Revised statutes of Nebraska	Sections 77-1807, 1824

Nevada

Type of Sale	Tax deed	The tax sale is a public oral-bid foreclosure sale of real estate.
Sale Date	Varies by municipality	
Bid Method	Premium bid	
Payment Method		
Interest Rate	12%	
Redemption Period	120 days 2 years	The redemption period is 120 days for vacant properties and 2 years for developed properties.
Over-the-Counter	No	
Municipalities	17	Carson City, Churchill, Clark, Douglas, Elko, Esmeralda, Eureka, Humboldt, Lander, Lincoln, Lyon, Mineral, Nye, Pershing, Storey, Washoe, White Pine
Statute	Nevada revised statutes	Sections 361.590-595

New Hampshire

Type of Sale	Tax lien	Tax lien.
Sale Date	Varies by municipality	The tax sale listing must be published in at least two places, at least 25 days prior to the tax sale.
Bid Method	Bid down ownership	The tax lien certificate purchaser is required to notify any mortgage holders of record of the purchase of the certificate before the tax sale is considered valid.
Payment Method		Payment is required immediately upon winning the bid.
Interest Rate	18%	
Redemption Period	2 years	Partial payments are allowed for redemption in multiples of $5. Part owners may redeem only their share of the redemption amount.

STATE LAWS

Subsequent Taxes	Optional	The tax lien holder must notify mortgage holders of record of the payment within 30 days of making the payment. Subsequent taxes incur interest at a rate of 18%.
Foreclosure		The lien certificate holder must apply for a tax deed at the expiration of the redemption period. The tax lien holder must serve notice of the lien purchase to the property owner, mortgage company, or other entity with a security interest in the property by certified mail. If the tax lien certificate is still not redeemed within 30 days, a deed is issued to the purchaser. The statute of limitations to contest the tax sale and tax deed is 10 years.
Over-the-Counter	No	
Municipalities	10	Belknap, Carroll, Cheshire, Coos, Grafton, Hillsborough, Merrimack, Rockingham, Strafford, Sullivan
Statute	New Hampshire revised statutes	Annotated Section 80:24
New Jersey		
Type of Sale	Tax lien	Certificate of purchase or certificate of tax sale.
Sale Date	Varies by municipality	The tax sale must be published in a local newspaper for 4 weeks prior to the sale and posted in five of the most public places of the municipality.
Bid Method	Bid down interest or premium bid	If the interest rate is bid down to less than 1%, the bidders may then engage in the bidding up of premiums on the lien amount.
Payment Method		Payment is required immediately upon winning the bid.
Interest Rate	18% per annum plus 2% to 6% penalty	
Redemption Period	2 years	The purchase of a tax lien certificate must be recorded within 3 months of the tax sale in order for the lien certificate to be considered valid. If the tax lien certificate is redeemed, the property

STATE LAWS

		owner is required to pay the following: Within 10 days: cost of lien certificate and 18% interest. After 10 days: cost of lien certificate, 18% interest, and subsequent municipal liens plus penalty on the redemption amount as: 2%, if the redemption amount is in excess of $200; 4%, if the redemption amount is over $5,000; 6%, if the redemption amount is over $10,000. The redemption period is 2 years, provided the property owner is provided written notice of the right to redemption within 18 months of the sale date. If the notice is served after the expiration of 18 months, the redemption period is 6 months from the date of the notice.
Subsequent Taxes	Optional	The lien holder is not required to make subsequent tax payments. Newly assessed and delinquent taxes will cause a new tax lien certificate to be offered for sale.
Foreclosure	Within 20 years	After 20 years, no further action can be taken upon the foreclosure, except when the tax lien certificate holder pays the subsequent taxes. The foreclosure period extends for as long as taxes continue to be paid. Upon expiration of the redemption period, the holder of a valid lien certificate may obtain a deed of conveyance, which indicates that all procedures have been followed with regard to redemption. The investor must issue a 30-day notice of the intent to foreclose. The investor must initiate a judicial foreclosure of the property owner's right of redemption.
Over-the-Counter	Yes	Unsold tax lien certificates are sold at auction at a private sale or public auction for not less than the cost of the lien. If the tax lien is valued at an amount that is more than the assessed value of the property, the tax lien certificate is sold at the assessed value of the property, unless by resolution, the municipality allows the lien certificate to be sold for less than the assessed value.

STATE LAWS		
Municipalities	21	Atlantic, Bergen, Burlington, Camden, Cape May, Cumberland, Essex, Gloucester, Hudson, Hunterdon, Mercer, Middlesex, Monmouth, Morris, Ocean, Passaic, Salem, Somerset, Sussex, Union, Warren
Statute	New Jersey code	Annotated Sections 54:5-32, 54
New Mexico		
Type of Sale	Tax deed	Real property is offered for sale subject to any encumbrances on the property, such as outstanding mortgages.
Sale Date	Varies by municipality	
Bid Method	Premium bid	
Payment Method		
Interest Rate	N/A	
Redemption Period	N/A	The tax lien certificate does not represent a priority lien.
Over-the-Counter	No	
Municipalities	33	Bernalillo, Catron, Chaves, Cibola, Colfax, Curry, De Baca, Dona Ana, Eddy, Grant, Guadalupe, Harding, Hidalgo, Lea, Lincoln, Los Alamos, Luna, McKinley, Mora, Otero, Quay, Rio Arriba, Roosevelt, San Juan, San Miguel, Sandoval, Santa Fe, Sierra, Socorro, Taos, Torrance, Union, Valencia
Statute	New Mexico statutes	Annotated Chapter 7, articles 38-38
New York		
Type of Sale	Deed	Tax lien certificate or tax lien.
Sale Date	Varies by municipality	The city of New York is allowed to offer the sale of tax lien certificates.
Bid Method	Premium bid	
Payment Method		
Interest Rate	14%	

STATE LAWS

Redemption Period	1 year	
Over-the-Counter	No	
Municipalities	62	Albany, Allegany, Bronx, Broome, Cattaraugus, Cayuga, Chautauqua, Chemung, Chenango, Clinton, Columbia, Cortland, Delaware, Dutchess, Erie, Essex, Franklin, Fulton, Genesee, Greene, Hamilton, Herkimer, Jefferson, Kings, Lewis, Livingston, Madison, Monroe, Montgomery, Nassau, New York, Niagara, Oneida, Onondaga, Ontario, Orange, Orleans, Oswego, Otsego, Putnam, Queens, Rensselaer, Richmond, Rockland, Saratoga, Schenectady, Schoharie, Schuyler, Senecca, St. Lawrence, Steuben, Suffolk, Sullivan, Tioga, Tompkins, Ulster, Warren, Washington, Wayne, Westchester, Wyoming, Yates
Statute	Uniform delinquent tax enforcement act	

North Carolina

Type of Sale	Deed	The tax sale is a public oral-bid foreclosure sale of real estate.
Sale Date	Varies by municipality	Any person taking exception or claiming an irregularity of the tax sale may challenge the sale within 10 days of the commissioner reporting foreclosure sales to the court. Also, anyone who wishes to increase the amount that was accepted at bid may file court action to increase the bid. This process is termed an upset bid. The upset bid must increase the bid amount by the maximum of $25 or 10% of the first $1,000 plus 5% of the excess above $1,000. The court will negate the first tax sale purchase and order a "resale" of the property.
Bid Method	Premium bid	
Payment Method		
Interest Rate	N/A	

STATE LAWS		
Redemption Period	N/A	
Over-the-Counter	No	
Municipalities	100	Alamance, Alexander, Alleghany, Anson, Ashe, Avery, Beaufort, Bertie, Bladen, Brunswick, Buncombe, Burke, Cabarrus, Caldwell, Camden, Carteret, Caswell, Catawba, Chatham, Cherokee, Chowan, Clay, Cleveland, Columbus, Craven, Cumberland, Currituck, Dare, Davidson, Davie, Duplin, Durham, Edgecombe, Forsyth, Franklin, Gaston, Gates, Graham, Granville, Greene, Guilford, Halifax, Harnett, Haywood, Henderson, Hertford, Hoke, Hyde, Iredell, Jackson, Johnston, Jones, Lee, Lenoir, Lincoln, Macon, Madison, Martin, McDowell, Mecklenburg, Mitchell, Montgomery, Moore, Nash, New Hanover, Northampton, Onslow, Orange, Pamlico, Pasquotank, Pender, Perquimans, Person, Pitt, Polk, Randolph, Richmond, Robeson, Rockingham, Rowan, Rutherford, Sampson, Scotland, Stanly, Stokes, Surry, Swain, Transylvania, Tyrrell, Union, Vance, Wake, Warren, Washington, Watauga, Wayne, Wilkes, Wilson, Yadkin, Yancey
Statute	North Carolina general statutes	Chapter 44A
North Dakota		
Type of Sale	Tax lien	Tax sale certificate or certificate of sale.
Sale Date	December, second Tuesday	Municipalities place liens against real property for delinquent property taxes. If the property owner does not redeem the property, the municipality may retain ownership of the property or sell the property. Notice of the tax sale must be published in the local newspaper, once each week, for 2 consecutive weeks and posted in at least four public places.

STATE LAWS		
Bid Method	Bid down interest	The board of commissioners of the particular municipality must appraise properties owned and offered for sale prior to the tax sale. If the appraised fair market value is more than the amount due on the property, the opening bid is set to the amount due on the property. If the appraised fair market value is less than the amount due on the property, the opening bid is fixed as determined by the board of commissioners. The property must be sold for at least the opening bid.
Payment Method	Cash	The winning bidder may pay the total bid price or 25% of the bid price with the balance to paid, as set by a contractual agreement, over a period of 10 years.
Interest Rate	9%–12% per annum	The interest rate upon redemption is 12% for the tax lien certificate and 9% for subsequent tax lien certificates purchased.
Redemption Period	3 years	Upon expiration of the redemption period, notice of the redemption is served on the property owner, occupants of the property, mortgage holders, and others with a recorded interest in the property. If any of the parties resides out of state, the notice must be served by registered or certified mail, and it must be published once a week for 3 consecutive weeks in the local newspaper. If no redemption occurs within 90 days of serving notice, a tax deed is issued to the tax lien certificate purchaser. As an exception, individuals with mental challenges, minor children, and prisoners of war are allowed a redemption period that extends 3 years after the end of their disability.
Subsequent Taxes	Optional	Only the purchaser of the original tax lien certificate is entitled to purchase subsequent tax lien certificates.
Foreclosure		Processes to acquire a tax deed and foreclose the right of redemption must be initiated within 10 years of the tax sale.
Over-the-Counter	Yes	Unsold tax lien certificates are offered for sale at 6% per annum interest.

STATE LAWS		
Municipalities	53	Adams, Barnes, Benson, Billings, Bottineau, Bowman, Burke, Burleigh, Cass, Cavalier, Dickey, Divide, Dunn, Eddy, Emmons, Foster, Golden Valley, Grand Forks, Grant, Griggs, Hettinger, Kidder, Lamoure, Logan, McHenry, McIntosh, McKenzie, McLean, Mercer, Morton, Mountrail, Nelson, Oliver, Pembina, Pierce, Ramsey, Ransom, Renville, Richland, Rolette, Sargent, Sheridan, Sioux, Slope, Stark, Steele, Stutsman, Towner, Traill, Walsh, Ward, Wells, Williams
Statute	North Dakota century code	Chapters 57-24, 38
Ohio		
Type of Sale	Tax deed	Tax certificate or certificate.
Sale Date	Varies by municipality	Counties with populations in excess of 200,000 may offer the sale of tax lien certificates. Otherwise, the tax sale is a public oral-bid foreclosure sale of real estate. The courts must confirm all sales.
Bid Method	Premium bid	The opening bid for deed sales is 2/3 of the appraised value of the property.
Payment Method		
Interest Rate	18% per annum (tax liens)	
Redemption Period	1 year 15 days (tax deeds)	Property owners may redeem property up until such time as the sale is confirmed. This usually takes about 15 days.
Over-the-Counter	No	
Municipalities	88	Adams, Alien, Ashland, Ashtabula, Athens, Auglaize, Belmont, Brown, Butler, Carroll, Champaign, Clark, Clermont, Clinton, Columbiana, Coshocton, Crawford, Cuyahoga, Darke, Defiance, Delaware, Erie, Fairfield, Fayette, Franklin, Fulton, Gallia, Geauga, Greene, Guernsey, Hamilton, Hancock, Hardin, Harrison, Henry, Highland, Hocking, Holmes, Huron, Jackson, Jefferson, Knox, Lake, Lawrence, Licking, Logan, Lorain, Lucas, Madison, Mahoning, Marion, Medina, Meigs, Mercer, Miami, Monroe, Montgomery, Morgan,

STATE LAWS

		Morrow, Muskingum, Noble, Ottawa, Paulding, Perry, Pickaway, Pike, Portage, Preble, Putnam, Richland, Ross, Sandusky, Scioto, Seneca, Shelby, Stark, Summit, Trumbull, Tuscarawas, Union, Van Wert, Vinton, Warren, Washington, Wayne, Williams, Wood, Wyandot
Statute	Ohio revised code	Sections 2329.17, 20; 5721.23; 315.251

Oklahoma

Type of Sale	Tax lien	Certificate of purchase or tax sale certificate.
Sale Date	October, first Monday	
Bid Method	Random or rotational	
Payment Method		
Interest Rate	8% per annum	
Redemption Period	2 years	
Over-the-Counter	Yes	
Municipalities	77	Adair, Alfalfa, Atoka, Beaver, Beckham, Blaine, Bryan, Caddo, Canadian, Carter, Cherokee, Choctaw, Cimarron, Cleveland, Coal, Comanche, Cotton, Craig, Creek, Custer, Delaware, Dewey, Ellis, Garfield, Garvin, Grady, Grant, Greer, Harmon, Harper, Haskell, Hughes, Jackson, Jefferson, Johnston, Kay, Kingfisher, Kiowa, Latimer, Le Flore, Lincoln, Logan, Love, Major, Marshall, Mayes, McClain, McCurtain, McIntosh, Murray, Muskogee, Noble, Nowata, Okfuskee, Oklahoma, Okmulgee, Osage, Ottawa, Pawnee, Payne, Pittsburg, Pontotoc, Pottawatomie, Pushmataha, Roger Mills, Rogers, Seminole, Sequoyah, Stephens, Texas, Tillman, Tulsa, Wagoner, Washington, Washita, Woods, Woodward
Statute	68 Oklahoma state statutes	Sections 3107; 3135

STATE LAWS

Oregon

Type of Sale	Tax deed	Municipalities place liens against real property for delinquent property taxes. If the property owner does not redeem the property, the municipality may retain ownership of the property or sell the property.
Sale Date	Varies by municipality	The tax sale is a public oral-bid foreclosure sale of real estate.
Bid Method	Premium bid	Some municipalities may set the opening bid as a percentage of the appraised value of the property.
Payment Method		Some municipalities may finance the purchase of tax deeds.
Interest Rate	N/A	
Redemption Period	N/A	
Over-the-Counter	Yes	Some municipalities offer over-the-counter sales.
Municipalities	36	Baker, Benton, Clackamas, Clatsop, Columbia, Coos, Crook, Curry, Deschutes, Douglas, Gilliam, Grant, Harney, Hood River, Jackson, Jefferson, Josephine, Klamath, Lake, Lane, Lincoln, Linn, Malheur, Marion, Morrow, Multnomah, Polk, Sherman, Tillamook, Umatilla, Union, Wallowa, Wasco, Washington, Wheeler, Yamhill
Statute	Oregon revised statutes	Section 311

Pennsylvania

Type of Sale	Hybrid tax deed	The tax sale is a public oral-bid foreclosure sale of real estate.
Sale Date	Monthly	
Bid Method	Premium bid	Properties are offered for sale at the opening bid amount during an Upset sale. Properties not sold at the Upset sale are offered for sale at a Private sale. If a property is not sold at the Private sale, the property is offered for sale at a Judicial sale, which is governed by court order. If the property is not

STATE LAWS

		sold at the Private sale, the property is offered for sale to county commissioners who bid up the cost of the tax lien at a Repository sale.
Payment Method		
Interest Rate	10% per annum	
Redemption Period	1 year	
Over-the-Counter	Yes	Some municipalities offer over-the-counter sales.
Municipalities	67	Adams, Allegheny, Armstrong, Beaver, Bedford, Berks, Blair, Bradford, Bucks, Butler, Cambria, Cameron, Carbon, Centre, Chester, Clarion, Clearfield, Clinton, Columbia, Crawford, Cumberland, Dauphin, Delaware, Elk, Erie, Fayette, Forest, Franklin, Fulton, Greene, Huntingdon, Indiana, Jefferson, Juniata, Lackawanna, Lancaster, Lawrence, Lebanon, Lehigh, Luzerne, Lycoming, McKean, Mercer, Mifflin, Monroe, Montgomery, Montour, Northampton, Northumberland, Perry, Philadelphia, Pike, Potter, Schuylkill, Snyder, Somerset, Sullivan, Susquehanna, Tioga, Union, Venango, Warren, Washington, Wayne, Westmoreland, Wyoming, York
Statute	Act of assembly	May 16, 1923, P.L. 207; March 15, 1956, No. 388
Rhode Island		
Type of Sale	Hybrid tax deed	Collector's deed or deed.
Sale Date	August	The tax sale must be published in the newspaper and at least two public places for 3 weeks prior to the sale. The purchaser is required to make subsequent tax payments.
Bid Method	Bid down interest or premium bid	
Payment Method		Payment is required immediately upon winning the bid.

STATE LAWS		
Interest Rate	10% penalty	The interest rate upon redemption is 10% of the purchase plus 1% percent month for each month over 6 months.
Redemption Period	1 year	A tax deed is issued immediately and must be recorded within 60 days of the tax sale. The tax deed holder must petition the court to foreclose the owner's right of redemption at the expiration of the redemption period.
Over-the-Counter	No	
Municipalities	5	Bristol, Kent, Newport, Providence, Washington
Statute	Rhode Island general laws	Sections 44-9-12,19,21
South Carolina		
Type of Sale	Tax lien	Receipt for the purchase money or tax sale receipt.
Sale Date	December, third Monday	The tax sale listing must be published within 4 weeks prior to the tax sale.
Bid Method	Premium bid	Payment is required immediately upon winning the bid.
Payment Method		
Interest Rate	8%–12% annum	The interest rate upon redemption is dependent upon when the redemption takes place. - First 3 months: 3% - Months 4 though 6: 6% - Months 7 through 9: 9% - Months 9 through 12: 12%
Redemption Period	1 year and 18 months	If the property owner fails to redeem the tax lien certificate, the lien certificate holder is provided a deed within 30 days of the expiration of the redemption period. Neither the taxing municipality nor the state makes warranty as to the quality of title acquired.
Over-the-Counter	Yes	
Municipalities	46	Abbeville, Aiken, Allendale, Anderson, Bamberg, Barnwell, Beaufort, Berkeley, Calhoun, Charleston, Cherokee, Chester, Chesterfield, Clarendon, Colleton, Darlington, Dillon, Dorchester, Edgefield,

STATE LAWS		
		Fairfield, Florence, Georgetown, Greenville, Greenwood, Hampton, Horry, Jasper, Kershaw, Lancaster, Laurens, Lee, Lexington, Marion, Marlboro, McCormick, Newberry, Oconee, Orangeburg, Pickens, Richland, Saluda, Spartanburg, Sumter, Union, Williamsburg, York
Statute	South Carolina statutes	Section 12-51-90
South Dakota		
Type of Sale	Tax lien	Tax certificate, tax sale certificate, or certificate of sale.
Sale Date	December, third Monday	The tax sale listing must be published in the newspaper and one other public place, once in the week prior to the tax sale.
Bid Method	Premium bid	The tax lien certificate holder has the option of paying subsequent taxes. Subsequent taxes earn 12% interest calculated from the date they would have become delinquent, if not paid.
Payment Method		Payment is required immediately upon winning the bid.
Interest Rate	12% per annum	
Redemption Period	3 or 4 years	The redemption rate is 3% for properties within the limits of the municipality and 4% for properties located outside of the municipality.
Over-the-Counter	Yes	The winning bidder must initiate the process to obtain a tax deed by providing the property owner with a notice of the intent to obtain deed to the property within 60 days and also inform the property owner of the redemption expiration date. The county will issue a tax deed 60 days after making such notice.
Municipalities	66	Aurora, Beadle, Bennett, Bon Homme, Brookings, Brown, Brule, Buffalo, Butte, Campbell, Charles Mix, Clark, Clay, Codington, Corson, Custer, Davison, Day, Deuel, Dewey, Douglas, Edmunds, Fall River, Faulk, Grant, Gregory, Haakon, Hamlin, Hand, Hanson, Harding, Hughes, Hutchinson,

STATE LAWS		
		Hyde, Jackson, Jerauld, Jones, Kingsbury, Lake, Lawrence, Lincoln, Lyman, Marshall, McCook, McPherson, Meade, Mellette, Miner, Minnehaha, Moody, Pennington, Perkins, Potter, Roberts, Sanborn, Shannon, Spink, Stanley, Sully, Todd, Tripp, Turner, Union, Walworth, Yankton, Ziebach
Statute	South Dakota codified laws	Titles 10, 44
Tennessee		
Type of Sale	Hybrid tax deed	Tax deed.
Sale Date	Varies by municipality	
Bid Method	Premium bid	
Payment Method		Payment is required within 24 hours of the tax sale. Failure to pay the bid amount may result in legal action.
Interest Rate	10% per annum	
Redemption Period	1 year	The court must confirm the tax deed sale, and the tax deed may be requested following such confirmation, which usually takes about 30 days.
Over-the-Counter	No	
Municipalities	95	Anderson, Bedford, Benton, Bledsoe, Blount, Bradley, Campbell, Cannon, Carroll, Carter, Cheatham, Chester, Claiborne, Clay, Cocke, Coffee, Crockett, Cumberland, Davidson, Dekalb, Decatur, Dickson, Dyer, Fayette, Fentress, Franklin, Gibson, Giles, Grainger, Greene, Grundy, Hamblen, Hamilton, Hancock, Hardeman, Hardin, Hawkins, Haywood, Henderson, Henry, Hickman, Houston, Humphreys, Jackson, Jefferson, Johnson, Knox, Lake, Lauderdale, Lawrence, Lewis, Lincoln, Loudon, Macon, Madison, Marion, Marshall, Maury, McMinn, McNairy, Meigs, Monroe, Montgomery, Moore, Morgan, Obion, Overton, Perry, Pickett, Polk, Putnam, Rhea, Roane, Robertson, Rutherford, Scott, Sequatchie, Sevier, Shelby, Smith, Stewart, Sullivan, Sumner, Tipton, Trousdale, Unicoi, Union, Van Buren

STATE LAWS		
Statute	Tennessee code	Title 67
Texas		
Type of Sale	Hybrid tax deed	Deed.
Sale Date	Each month, first Tuesday	
Bid Method	Premium bid	
Payment Method		
Interest Rate	25% penalty	The penalty is applied to the lien amount, the premium amount, and any costs associated with the administration of the deed.
Redemption Period	6 months or 2 years	The redemption period is 6 months for nonhomestead and nonagricultural properties and 2 years for homestead and agricultural properties.
Over-the-Counter	Yes	
Municipalities	254	Anderson, Andrews, Angelina, Aransas, Archer, Armstrong, Atascosa, Austin, Bailey, Bandera, Bastrop, Baylor, Bee, Bell, Bexar, Blanco, Borden, Bosque, Bowie, Brazoria, Brazos, Brewster, Briscoe, Brooks, Brown, Burleson, Burnet, Caldwell, Calhoun, Callahan, Cameron, Camp, Carson, Cass, Castro, Chambers, Cherokee, Childress, Clay, Cochran, Coke, Coleman, Collin, Collingsworth, Colorado, Comal, Comanche, Concho, Cooke, Coryell, Cottle, Crane, Crockett, Crosby, Culberson, Dallam, Dallas, Dawson, Dewitt, Deaf Smith, Delta, Denton, Dickens, Dimmit, Donley, Duval, Eastland, Ector, Edwards, El Paso, Ellis, Erath, Falls, Fannin, Fayette, Fisher, Floyd, Foard, Fort Bend, Franklin, Freestone, Frio, Gaines, Galveston, Garza, Gillespie, Glasscock, Goliad, Gonzales, Gray, Grayson, Gregg, Grimes, Guadalupe, Hale, Hall, Hamilton, Hansford, Hardeman, Hardin, Harris, Harrison, Hartley, Haskell, Hays, Hemphill, Henderson, Hidalgo, Hill, Hockley, Hood, Hopkins, Houston, Howard, Hudspeth, Hunt, Hutchinson, Irion, Jack, Jackson, Jasper, Jeff Davis, Jefferson, Jim Hogg, Jim Wells, Johnson, Jones, Karnes, Kaufman, Kendall, Kenedy, Kent, Kerr, Kimble, King, Kinney,

STATE LAWS

		Kleberg, Knox, La Salle, Lamar, Lamb, Lampasas, Lavaca, Lee, Leon, Liberty, Limestone, Lipscomb, Live Oak, Llano, Loving, Lubbock, Lynn, Madison, Marion, Martin, Mason, Matagorda, Maverick, McCulloch, McLennan, McMullen, Medina, Menard, Midland, Milam, Mills, Mitchell, Montague, Montgomery, Moore, Morris, Motley, Nacogdoches, Navarro, Newton, Nolan, Nueces, Ochiltree, Oldham, Orange, Palo Pinto, Panola, Parker, Parmer, Pecos, Polk, Potter, Presidio, Rains, Randall, Reagan, Real, Red River, Reeves, Refugio, Roberts, Robertson, Rockwall, Runnels, Rusk, Sabine, San Augustine, San Jacinto, San Patricio, San Saba, Schleicher, Scurry, Shackelford, Shelby, Sherman, Smith, Somervell, Starr, Stephens, Sterling, Stonewall, Sutton, Swisher, Tarrant, Taylor, Terrell, Terry, Throckmorton, Titus, Tom Green, Travis, Trinity, Tyler, Upshur, Upton, Uvalde, Val Verde, Van Zandt, Victoria, Walker, Waller, Ward, Washington
Statute	Texas tax code	Section 34.21
Utah		
Type of Sale	Tax deed	
Sale Date	May, last Wednesday	The tax sale is a public oral-bid foreclosure sale of real estate.
Bid Method	Premium bid	
Payment Method		
Interest Rate	N/A	
Redemption Period	N/A	
Over-the-Counter	No	
Municipalities	29	Beaver, Box Elder, Cache, Carbon, Daggett, Davis, Duchesne, Emery, Garfield, Grand, Iron, Juab, Kane, Millard, Morgan, Piute, Rich, Salt Lake, San Juan, Sanpete, Sevier, Summit, Tooele, Uintah, Utah, Wasatch, Washington, Wayne, Weber
Statute	Utah code	Title 59

STATE LAWS

Vermont

Type of Sale	Tax lien	
Sale Date	Varies by municipality	The tax sale is a public oral-bid foreclosure sale of real estate.
Bid Method	Premium bid	
Payment Method		
Interest Rate	12% per annum	
Redemption Period	1 year	
Over-the-Counter	No	
Municipalities	14	Addison, Bennington, Caledonia, Chittenden, Essex, Franklin, Grand Isle, Lamoille, Orange, Orleans, Rutland, Washington, Windham, Windsor
Statute	Vermont statutes	Title 32, Section 5260

Virginia

Type of Sale	Tax deed	The tax sale is a public oral-bid foreclosure sale of real estate.
Sale Date	Varies by municipality	The county of Arlington does not hold a sale every year.
Bid Method	Premium bid	
Payment Method		
Interest Rate	N/A	
Redemption Period	N/A	
Over-the-Counter	No	
Municipalities	95	Accomack, Albemarle, Alleghany, Amelia, Amherst, Appomattox, Arlington, Augusta, Bath, Bedford, Bland, Botetourt, Brunswick, Buchanan, Buckingham, Campbell, Caroline, Charles City, Charlotte, Chesterfield, Clarke, Craig, Culpeper, Cumberland, Dickenson, Dinwiddie, Essex, Fairfax, Fauquier, Floyd, Fluvanna, Franklin, Frederick, Giles, Gloucester, Goochland, Grayson, Greene, Greensville, Halifax, Hanover, Henrico, Henry,

	STATE LAWS	
		Highland, Isle of Wight, James City, King and Queen, King George, King William, Lancaster, Lee, Loudoun, Louisa, Lunenburg, Madison, Mathews, Mecklenburg, Middlesex, Montgomery, Nelson, New Kent, Northampton, Northumberland, Nottoway, Orange, Page, Patrick, Pittsylvania, Powhatan, Prince Edward, Prince George, Prince William, Pulaski, Rappahannock, Richmond, Roanoke, Rockbridge, Rockingham, Russell, Scott, Shenandoah, Smyth, Southampton, Spotsylvania, Stafford, Surry, Sussex, Tazewell, Warren, Washington, Westmorland, Wise, Wythe, York
Statute	Code of Virginia	Title 58, Chapter 32
Washington		
Type of Sale	Tax deed	
Sale Date	Varies by municipality	The tax sale is a public oral-bid foreclosure sale of real estate.
Bid Method	Premium bid	
Payment Method		
Interest Rate	N/A	
Redemption Period	N/A	
Over-the-Counter	No	
Municipalities	39	Adams, Asotin, Benton, Chelan, Clallam, Clark, Columbia, Cowlitz, Douglas, Ferry, Franklin, Garfield, Grant, Grays Harbor, Island, Jefferson, King, Kitsap, Kittitas, Klickitat, Lewis, Lincoln, Mason, Okanogan, Pacific, Pend Oreille, Pierce, San Juan, Skagit, Skamania, Snohomish, Spokane, Stevens, Thurston, Wahkiakum, Walla Walla, Whatcom, Whitman, Yakima
Statute	Revised code of Washington	Chapters 36, 60
West Virginia		
Type of Sale	Tax lien	Certificate of sale, certificate of purchase, tax certificate of sale, or tax certificate.

STATE LAWS

Sale Date	Varies by municipality	
Bid Method	Premium bid	Upon redemption, the premium amount is not returned; nor is interest applied to the amount.
Payment Method		
Interest Rate	12% per annum	
Redemption Period	18 months	
Over-the-Counter	Yes - liens No - deeds	
Municipalities	55	Barbour, Berkeley, Boone, Braxton, Brooke, Cabell, Calhoun, Clay, Doddridge, Fayette, Gilmer, Grant, Greenbrier, Hampshire, Hancock, Hardy, Harrison, Jackson, Jefferson, Kanawha, Lewis, Lincoln, Logan, Marion, Marshall, Mason, McDowell, Mercer, Mineral, Mingo, Monongalia, Monroe, Morgan, Nicholas, Ohio, Pendleton, Pleasants, Pocahontas, Preston, Putnam, Raleigh, Randolph, Ritchie, Roane, Summers, Taylor, Tucker, Tyler, Upshur, Wayne, Webster, Wetzel, Wirt, Wood, Wyoming
Statute	West Virginia code	Section 11A-3-23

Wisconsin

Type of Sale	Tax deed	
Sale Date	Varies by municipality	
Bid Method	Premium bid	The opening bid for deed sales is set equal to the appraised value of the property, which may be significantly less than the fair market value of the property.
Payment Method		
Interest Rate	18%	
Redemption Period	2 years	
Over-the-Counter	No	

STATE LAWS		
Municipalities	72	Adams, Ashland, Barren, Bayfleld, Brown, Buffalo, Burnett, Calumet, Chippewa, Clark, Crawford, Columbia, Dane, Dodge, Door, Douglas, Dunn, Eau Claire, Florence, Fond du, Lac, Forest, Grant, Green, Green Lake, Iowa, Iron, Jackson, Jefferson, Juneau, Kenosha, Kewaunee, La Crosse, Lafayette, Langlade, Lincoln, Manitowoc, Marathon, Marinette, Marquette, Menominee, Milwaukee, Monroe, Oconto, Oneida, Outagamie, Ozaukee, Pepin, Pierce, Polk, Portage, Price, Racine, Richland, Rock, Rusk, Sauk, Sawyer, Shawano, Sheboygan, St. Croix, Taylor, Trempealeau, Vernon, Vilas, Walworth, Washburn, Washington, Waukesha, Waupaca, Waushara, Winnebago, Wood
Statute	Wisconsin statutes	Chapter 75
Wyoming		
Type of Sale	Tax lien	Certificate of purchase.
Sale Date	July- September	Notice of the tax sale is published once each week for 3 weeks in a local newspaper. The first notice must be published 4 weeks before the sale and end before the first week of September.
Bid Method	Random selection or bid down ownership	
Payment Method		Payment is required immediately upon purchase.
Interest Rate	18% per annum plus 3% penalty	
Redemption Period	4 years	The property owner, mortgage holders, and other individuals with a recorded interest in the property must be served notice of the redemption. Notice must be served by certified or registered mail. Service by publication is once a week for 3 weeks. The first notice must be published no more than 5 months before the application of tax deed is made. The investor must apply for a tax deed before 4

STATE LAWS

		years have expired, but not more than 6 years after the tax sale. Once notification is served and 3 months have passed, the investor may apply for a tax deed that entitles the holder to right of possession of the property. If a tax lien certificate or tax deed is issued in error and the municipality causes the error, the municipality pays the investor an amount equal to the redemption amount. If the error was due to some other factor, the investor receives a first lien with an 8% interest rate. The lien is superior to all liens, except tax liens sold for subsequent taxes and the payment of taxes by another individual.
Subsequent Taxes	Optional	If subsequent taxes are not paid by the original tax lien holder, the subsequent delinquent taxes become cause for the sale of subsequent tax lien certificates.
Foreclosure	Within 10 years	The tax line certificate holder must foreclose the right of redemption between 4 and 10 years of the tax sale.
Over-the-Counter	Yes	Unsold tax lien certificates may be offered for sale at either public or private auctions at any time determined by the municipality.
Municipalities	23	Albany, Big Horn, Campbell, Carbon, Converse, Crook, Fremont, Goshen, Hot Springs, Johnson, Laramie, Lincoln, Natrona, Niobrara, Park, Platte, Sheridan, Sublette, Sweetwater, Teton, Uinta, Washakie, Weston
Statute	Wyoming statutes	Section 39-3-108, 39-4-102
District of Columbia		
Type of Sale	Lien	Certificate of sale or tax lien.
Sale Date	July	
Bid Method	Premium bid	Any action to foreclose must be preceded by a title search from a qualified title company. The title search may be ordered after expiration of 4 months of the redemption period. However, actions to foreclose may not be initiated until the 6-month redemption period has expired.

STATE LAWS		
Payment Method		
Interest Rate	12% per annum	
Redemption Period	6 months	
Over-the-Counter	No	
Municipalities		
Statute	D.C. code	Section 47-1304
Guam		
Type of Sale	Hybrid deed	Tax sold property or deed.
Sale Date		
Bid Method	Premium bid	
Payment Method		
Interest Rate	12% per annum	
Redemption Period	1 year	
Over-the-Counter	No	
Municipalities		
Statute	11 Guam law	Section 24812
Puerto Rico		
Type of Sale	Tax lien	Certificate of purchase.
Sale Date		
Bid Method		
Payment Method		
Interest Rate	20% penalty	
Redemption Period	1 year	
Over-the-Counter		
Municipalities		
Statute		

Bibliography

Allen, C. W.; Hill, C.; Kennedy, D.; Sutton, G. *Inc. & Grow Rich*, 2nd Ed., Sage International, 1999.

Ashby, D. *Make Money Trading Mortgages*, The Wellington Company, Inc., PDF File, 2004.

Bbyrd2100@centurytel.net (2005). *Real Estate Investing*, PDF File.

Carey, C. H., and Carey B. (2005). *Make Money in Real Estate Tax Liens*, John Wiley & Sons, Inc.

Loftis, L. B., Esq. (2005). *Profit by Investing in Real Estate Tax Liens*, Dearborn Trade Publishing.

Moskowitz, J., J.D. (1994). *The 16% Solution*, Andrews and McMeel.

Pellegrino, M, Esq. (2005). *Tax Lien$ - The Complete Guide to Investing in New Jersey Tax Liens*, Lake Neepaulin Publishing.

USA Properties, *Tax Lien Certificates*, PDF File.

USA Properties, *Tax Lien Sales*, PDF File.

Villanova, L. (2002). *The "You Can Do It" Guide to Success in Tax Lien and Tax Deed Investing*, Vol. 1., 1st Books Library.

Yocom, J. (2002). *Tax Lien Certificates - A Little Known Government Program That Can Make You Financially Independent*, 1st Books Library.

GLOSSARY

401(k)/403(b) An investment plan sponsored by an employer that enables individuals to set aside pre-tax income for retirement or emergency purposes. 401(k) plans are provided by private corporations. 403(b) plans are provided by non-profit organizations.

401(k)/403(b) Loan A type of financing using a loan against the money accumulated in a 401(k)/403(b) plan.

Abatement Sometimes referred to as free rent or early occupancy. A condition that could happen in addition to the primary term of the lease.

Above Building Standard Finishes and specialized designs that have been upgraded in order to accommodate a tenant's requirements.

Absorption Rate The speed and amount of time at which rentable space, in square feet, is filled.

Abstract or Title Search The process of reviewing all transactions that have been recorded publicly in order to determine whether any defects in the title exist that could interfere with a clear property ownership transfer.

Accelerated Cost Recovery System A calculation for taxes to provide more depreciation for the first few years of ownership.

Accelerated Depreciation A method of depreciation where the value of a property depreciates faster in the first few years after purchasing it.

Acceleration Clause A clause in a contract that gives the lender the right to demand immediate payment of the balance of the loan if the borrower defaults on the loan.

Acceptance The seller's written approval of a buyer's offer.

Ad Valorem A Latin phrase that translates as "according to value." Refers to a tax that is imposed on a property's value that is typically based on the local government's evaluation of the property.

Addendum An addition or update for an existing contract between parties.

Additional Principal Payment Additional money paid to the lender, apart from the scheduled loan payments, to pay more of the principal balance, shortening the length of the loan.

Adjustable-Rate Mortgage (ARM) A home loan with an interest rate that is adjusted periodically in order to reflect changes in a specific financial resource.

Adjusted Funds From Operations (AFFO) The rate of REIT performance or ability to pay dividends that is used by many analysts who have concerns about the quality of earnings as measured by Funds From Operations (FFO).

Adjustment Date The date at which the interest rate is adjusted for an adjustable-rate mortgage (ARM).

Adjustment Period The amount of time between adjustments for an interest rate in an ARM.

Administrative Fee A percentage of the value of the assets under management, or a fixed annual dollar amount charged to manage an account.

Advances The payments the servicer makes when the borrower fails to send a payment.

Adviser A broker or investment banker who represents an owner in a transaction and is paid a retainer and/or a performance fee once a financing or sales transaction has closed.

Agency Closing A type of closing in which a lender uses a title company or other firm as an agent to finish a loan.

Agency Disclosure A requirement in most states that agents who act for both buyers or sellers must disclose who they are working for in the transaction.

Aggregation Risk The risk that is associated with warehousing mortgages during the process of pooling them for future security.

Agreement of Sale A legal document the buyer and seller must approve and sign that details the price and terms in the transaction.

Alienation Clause The provision in a loan that requires the borrower to pay the total balance of the loan at once if the property is sold or the ownership transferred.

Alternative Mortgage A home loan that does not match the standard terms of a fixed-rate mortgage.

Alternative or Specialty Investments Types of property that are not considered to be conventional real estate investments, such as self-storage facilities, mobile homes, timber, agriculture, or parking lots.

Amortization The usual process of paying a loan's interest and principal via scheduled monthly payments.

Amortization Schedule A chart or table that shows the percentage of each payment that will be applied toward principal and interest over the life of the mortgage and how the loan balance decreases until it reaches zero.

Amortization Tables The mathematical tables that are used to calculate what a borrower's monthly payment will be.

Amortization Term The number of months it will take to amortize the loan.

Anchor The business or individual who is serving as the primary draw to a commercial property.

Annual Mortgagor Statement A yearly statement to borrowers which details the remaining principal balance and amounts paid throughout the year for taxes and interest.

Annual Percentage Rate (APR) The interest rate that states the actual cost of borrowing money over the course of a year.

Annuity The regular payments of a fixed sum.

Application The form a borrower must complete in order to apply for a mortgage loan, including information such as income, savings, assets, and debts.

Application Fee A fee some lenders charge that may include charges for items such as property appraisal or a credit report unless those fees are included elsewhere.

Appraisal The estimate of the value of a property on a particular date given by a professional appraiser, usually presented in a written document.

Appraisal Fee The fee charged by a professional appraiser for his estimate of the market value of a property.

Appraisal Report The written report presented by an appraiser regarding the value of a property.

Appraised Value The dollar amount a professional appraiser assigned to the value of a property in his report.

Appraiser A certified individual who is qualified by education, training, and experience to estimate the value of real and personal property.

Appreciation An increase in the home's or property's value.

Appreciation Return The amount gained when the value of the real estate assets increases during the current quarter.

Arbitrage The act of buying securities in one market and selling them immediately in another market in order to profit from the difference in price.

ARM Index A number that is publicly published and used as the basis for interest rate adjustments on an ARM.

As-Is Condition A phrase in a purchase or lease contract in which the new tenant accepts the existing condition of the premises as well as any physical defects.

Assessed Value The value placed on a home that is determined by a tax assessor in order to calculate a tax base.

Assessment (1) The approximate value of a property. (2) A fee charged in addition to taxes in order to help pay for items such as water, sewer, street improvements, etc.

Assessor A public officer who estimates the value of a property for the purpose of taxation.

Asset A property or item of value owned by an individual or company.

Asset Management Fee A fee that is charged to investors based on the amount of money they have invested into real estate assets for the particular fund or account.

Asset Management The various tasks and areas around managing real estate assets from the initial investment until the time it is sold.

Asset Turnover The rate of total revenues for the previous 12 months divided by the average total assets.

Assets Under Management The amount of the current market value of real estate assets that a manager is responsible to manage and invest.

Assignee Name The individual or business to whom the lease, mortgage, or other contract has been re-assigned.

Assignment The transfer of rights and responsibilities from one party to another for paying a debt. The original party remains liable for the debt should the second party default.

Assignor The person who transfers the rights and interests of a property to another.

Assumable Mortgage A mortgage that is capable of being transferred to a different borrower.

Assumption The act of assuming the mortgage of the seller.

Assumption Clause A contractual provision that enables the buyer to take responsibility for the mortgage loan from the seller.

Assumption Fee A fee charged to the buyer for processing new records when they are assuming an existing loan.

Attorn To agree to recognize a new owner of a property and to pay rent to the new landlord.

Average Common Equity The sum of the common equity for the last five quarters divided by five.

Average Downtime The number of months that are expected between a lease's expiration and the beginning of a replacement lease under the current market conditions.

Average Free Rent The number of months the rent abatement concession is expected to be granted to a tenant as part of an incentive to lease under current market conditions.

Average Occupancy The average rate of each of the previous 12 months that a property was occupied.

Average Total Assets The sum of the total assets of a company for the previous five quarters divided by five.

Back Title Letter A letter that an attorney receives from a title insurance company before examining the title for insurance purposes.

Back-End Ratio The calculation lenders use to compare a borrower's gross monthly income to their total debt.

Balance Sheet A statement that lists an individual's assets, liabilities, and net worth.

Balloon Loan A type of mortgage in which the monthly payments are not large enough to repay the loan by the end of the term, and the final payment is one large payment of the remaining balance.

Balloon Payment The final huge payment due at the end of a balloon mortgage.

Balloon Risk The risk that a borrower may not be able to come up with the funds for the balloon payment at maturity.

Bankrupt The state an individual or business is in if they are unable to repay their debt when it is due.

Bankruptcy A legal proceeding where a debtor can obtain relief from payment of certain obligations through restructuring their finances.

Base Loan Amount The amount that forms the basis for the loan payments.

Base Principal Balance The original loan amount once

adjustments for subsequent fundings and principal payments have been made without including accrued interest or other unpaid debts.

Base Rent A certain amount that is used as a minimum rent, providing for rent increases over the term of the lease agreement.

Base Year The sum of actual taxes and operating expenses during a given year, often that in which a lease begins.

Basis Point A term for 1/100 of one percentage point.

Before-Tax Income An individual's income before taxes have been deducted.

Below-Grade Any structure or part of a structure that is below the surface of the ground that surrounds it.

Beneficiary An employee who is covered by the benefit plan his or her company provides.

Beta The measurement of common stock price volatility for a company in comparison to the market.

Bid The price or range an investor is willing to spend on whole loans or securities.

Bill of Sale A written legal

document that transfers the ownership of personal property to another party.

Binder (1) A report describing the conditions of a property's title. (2) An early agreement between seller and buyer.

Biweekly Mortgage A mortgage repayment plan that requires payments every two weeks to help repay the loan over a shorter amount of time.

Blanket Mortgage A rare type of mortgage that covers more than one of the borrower's properties.

Blind Pool A mixed fund that accepts capital from investors without specifying property assets.

Bond Market The daily buying and selling of thirty-year treasury bonds that also affects fixed rate mortgages.

Book Value The value of a property based on its purchase amount plus upgrades or other additions with depreciation subtracted.

Break-Even Point The point at which a landlord's income from rent matches expenses and debt.

Bridge Loan A short-term loan for individuals or companies that are still seeking more permanent financing.

Broker A person who serves as a go-between for a buyer and seller.

Brokerage The process of bringing two or more parties together in exchange for a fee, commission, or other compensation.

Buildable Acres The portion of land that can be built on after allowances for roads, setbacks, anticipated open spaces, and unsuitable areas have been made.

Building Code The laws set forth by the local government regarding end use of a given piece of property. These law codes may dictate the design, materials used, and/or types of improvements that will be allowed.

Building Standard Plus Allowance A detailed list provided by the landlord stating the standard building materials and costs necessary to make the premises inhabitable.

Build-Out Improvements to a property's space that have been implemented according to the tenant's specifications.

Build-to-Suit A way of leasing property, usually for commercial purposes, in which the developer or landlord builds to a tenant's specifications.

Buydown A term that usually refers to a fixed-rate mortgage for which additional payments can be applied to the interest rate for a temporary period, lowering payments for a period of one to three years.

Buydown Mortgage A style of home loan in which the lender receives a higher payment in order to convince them to reduce the interest rate during the initial years of the mortgage.

Buyer's Remorse A nervousness that first-time homebuyers tend to feel after signing a sales contract or closing the purchase of a house.

Call Date The periodic or continuous right a lender has to call for payment of the total remaining balance prior to the date of maturity.

Call Option A clause in a loan agreement that allows a lender to demand repayment of the entire principal balance at any time.

Cap A limit on how much the monthly payment or interest rate is allowed to increase in an adjustable-rate mortgage.

Capital Appreciation The change in a property's or

portfolio's market value after it has been adjusted for capital improvements and partial sales.

Capital Expenditures The purchase of long-term assets, or the expansion of existing ones, that prolongs the life or efficiency of those assets.

Capital Gain The amount of excess when the net proceeds from the sale of an asset are higher than its book value.

Capital Improvements Expenses that prolong the life of a property or add new improvements to it.

Capital Markets Public and private markets where individuals or businesses can raise or borrow capital.

Capitalization The mathematical process that investors use to derive the value of a property using the rate of return on investments.

Capitalization Rate The percentage of return as it is estimated from the net income of a property.

Carryback Financing A type of funding in which a seller agrees to hold back a note for a specified portion of the sales price.

Carrying Charges Costs incurred to the landlord when initially leasing out a property and then during the periods of vacancy.

Cash Flow The amount of income an investor receives on a rental property after operating expenses and loan payments have been deducted.

Cashier's Check A check the bank draws on its own resources instead of a depositor's account.

Cash-on-Cash Yield The percentage of a property's net cash flow and the average amount of invested capital during the specified operating year.

Cash-Out Refinance The act of refinancing a mortgage for an amount that is higher than the original amount for the purpose of using the leftover cash for personal use.

Certificate of Deposit A type of deposit that is held in a bank for a limited time and pays a certain amount of interest to the depositor.

Certificate of Deposit Index (CODI) A rate that is based on interest rates of six-month CDs and is often used to determine interest rates for some ARMs.

Certificate of Eligibility A type of document that the Department of Veterans Affairs issues to

verify the eligibility of a veteran for a VA loan.

Certificate of Occupancy (CO) A written document issued by a local government or building agency that states that a home or other building is inhabitable after meeting all building codes.

Certificate of Reasonable Value (CRV) An appraisal presented by the Department of Veterans Affairs that shows the current market value of a property.

Certificate of Veteran Status A document veterans or reservists receive if they have served 90 days of continuous active duty (including training time).

Chain of Title The official record of all transfers of ownership over the history of a piece of property.

Chapter 11 The part of the federal bankruptcy code that deals with reorganizations of businesses.

Chapter 7 The part of the federal bankruptcy code that deals with liquidations of businesses.

Circulation Factor The interior space that is required for internal office circulation and is not included in the net square footage.

Class A A property rating that

is usually assigned to those that will generate the maximum rent per square foot, due to superior quality and/or location.

Class B A good property that most potential tenants would find desirable but lacks certain attributes that would bring in the top dollar.

Class C A building that is physically acceptable but offers few amenities, thereby becoming cost-effective space for tenants who are seeking a particular image.

Clear Title A property title that is free of liens, defects, or other legal encumbrances.

Clear-Span Facility A type of building, usually a warehouse or parking garage, consisting of vertical columns on the outer edges of the structure and clear spaces between the columns.

Closed-End Fund A mixed fund with a planned range of investor capital and a limited life.

Closing The final act of procuring a loan and title in which documents are signed between the buyer and seller and/or their respective representation and all money concerned in the contract changes hands.

Closing Costs The expenses that are related to the sale of real estate including loan, title, and appraisal fees and are beyond the price of the property itself.

Closing Statement See: Settlement Statement.

Cloud on Title Certain conditions uncovered in a title search that present a negative impact to the title for the property.

Commercial Mortgage-Backed Securities (CMBS) A type of securities that is backed by loans on commercial real estate.

Collateralized Mortgage Obligation (CMO) Debt that is fully based on a pool of mortgages.

Co-Borrower Another individual who is jointly responsible for the loan and is on the title to the property.

Cost of Funds Index (COFI) An index used to determine changes in the interest rates for certain ARMs.

Co-Investment Program A separate account for an insurance company or investment partnership in which two or more pension funds may co-invest their capital in an individual property or a portfolio of properties.

Co-Investment The condition that occurs when two or more pension funds or groups of funds are sharing ownership of a real estate investment.

Collateral The property for which a borrower has obtained a loan, thereby assuming the risk of losing the property if the loan is not repaid according to the terms of the loan agreement.

Collection The effort on the part of a lender, due to a borrower defaulting on a loan, which involves mailing and recording certain documents in the event that the foreclosure procedure must be implemented.

Commercial Mortgage A loan used to purchase a piece of commercial property or building.

Commercial Mortgage Broker A broker specialized in commercial mortgage applications.

Commercial Mortgage Lender A lender specialized in funding commercial mortgage loans.

Commingled Fund A pooled fund that enables qualified employee benefit plans to mix their capital in order to achieve professional management, greater diversification, or investment

positions in larger properties.

Commission A compensation to salespeople that is paid out of the total amount of the purchase transaction.

Commitment The agreement of a lender to make a loan with given terms for a specific period.

Commitment Fee The fee a lender charges for the guarantee of specified loan terms, to be honored at some point in the future.

Common Area Assessments Sometimes called Homeowners' Association Fees. Charges paid to the homeowners' association by the individual unit owners, in a condominium or planned unit development (PUD), that are usually used to maintain the property and common areas.

Common Area Maintenance The additional charges the tenant must pay in addition to the base rent to pay for the maintenance of common areas.

Common Areas The portions of a building, land, and amenities, owned or managed by a planned unit development (PUD) or condominium's homeowners' association, that are used by all of the unit owners who share in the common expense of operation and maintenance.

Common Law A set of unofficial laws that were originally based on English customs and used to some extent in several states.

Community Property Property that is acquired by a married couple during the course of their marriage and is considered in many states to be owned jointly, unless certain circumstances are in play.

Comparable Sales Also called Comps or Comparables. The recent selling prices of similar properties in the area that are used to help determine the market value of a property.

Compound Interest The amount of interest paid on the principal balance of a mortgage in addition to accrued interest.

Concessions Cash, or the equivalent, that the landlord pays or allows in the form of rental abatement, additional tenant finish allowance, moving expenses, or other costs expended in order to persuade a tenant to sign a lease.

Condemnation A government agency's act of taking private property, without the owner's consent, for public use through the power of eminent domain.

Conditional Commitment A lender's agreement to make a loan providing the borrower meets certain conditions.

Conditional Sale A contract to sell a property that states that the seller will retain the title until all contractual conditions have been fulfilled.

Condominium A type of ownership in which all of the unit owners own the property, common areas, and buildings jointly, and have sole ownership in the unit to which they hold the title.

Condominium Conversion Changing an existing rental property's ownership to the condominium form of ownership.

Condominium Hotel A condominium project that involves registration desks, short-term occupancy, food and telephone services, and daily cleaning services, and is generally operated as a commercial hotel even though the units are individually owned.

Conduit A strategic alliance between lenders and unaffiliated organizations that acts as a source of funding by regularly purchasing loans, usually with a goal of pooling and securitizing them.

Conforming Loan A type of mortgage that meets the

conditions to be purchased by Fannie Mae or Freddie Mac.

Construction Documents The drawings and specifications an architect and/or engineer provides to describe construction requirements for a project.

Construction Loan A short-term loan to finance the cost of construction, usually dispensed in stages throughout the construction project.

Construction Management The process of ensuring that the stages of the construction project are completed in a timely and seamless manner.

Construction-to-Permanent Loan A construction loan that can be converted to a longer-term traditional mortgage after construction is complete.

Consultant Any individual or company that provides the services to institutional investors, such as defining real estate investment policies, making recommendations to advisers or managers, analyzing existing real estate portfolios, monitoring and reporting on portfolio performance, and/or reviewing specified investment opportunities.

Consumer Price Index (CPI) A measurement of inflation, relating to the change in the prices of goods and services that are regularly purchased by a specific population during a certain period of time.

Contiguous Space Refers to several suites or spaces on a floor (or connected floors) in a given building that can be combined and rented to a single tenant.

Contingency A specific condition that must be met before either party in a contract can be legally bound.

Contract An agreement, either verbal or written, to perform or not to perform a certain thing.

Contract Documents See: Construction Documents.

Contract Rent Also known as Face Rent. The dollar amount of the rental obligation specified in a lease.

Conventional Loan A long-term loan from a non-governmental lender that a borrower obtains for the purchase of a home.

Convertible Adjustable-Rate Mortgage A type of mortgage that begins as a traditional ARM but contains a provision to enable the borrower to change to a fixed-rate mortgage during a certain period of time.

Convertible Debt The point in a mortgage at which the lender has the option to convert to a partially or fully owned property within a certain period of time.

Convertible Preferred Stock Preferred stock that can be converted to common stock under certain conditions that have been specified by the issuer.

Conveyance The act of transferring a property title between parties by deed.

Cooperative Also called a Co-op. A type of ownership by multiple residents of a multi-unit housing complex in which they all own shares in the cooperative corporation that owns the property, thereby having the right to occupy a particular apartment or unit.

Cooperative Mortgage Any loan that is related to a cooperative residential project.

Core Properties The main types of property, specifically office, retail, industrial, and multi-family.

Co-Signer A second individual or party who also signs a promissory note or loan agreement, thereby taking responsibility for the debt in the event that the primary borrower cannot pay.

Cost-Approach Improvement Value The current expenses for constructing a copy or replacement for an existing structure, but subtracting an estimate of the accrued depreciation.

Cost-Approach Land Value The estimated value of the basic interest in the land, as if it were available for development to its highest and best use.

Cost-of-Sale Percentage An estimate of the expenses of selling an investment that represents brokerage commissions, closing costs, fees, and other necessary sales costs.

Coupon The token or expected interest rate the borrower is charged on a promissory note or mortgage.

Courier Fee The fee that is charged at closing for the delivery of documents between all parties concerned in a real estate transaction.

Covenant A written agreement, included in deeds or other legal documents, that defines the requirements for certain acts or use of a property.

Credit An agreement in which a borrower promises to repay the lender at a later date and receives something of value in exchange.

Credit Enhancement The necessary credit support, in addition to mortgage collateral, in order to achieve the desired credit rating on mortgage-backed securities.

Credit History An individual's record which details his current and past financial obligations and performance.

Credit Life Insurance A type of insurance that pays the balance of a mortgage if the borrower dies.

Credit Rating The degree of creditworthiness a person is assigned based on his credit history and current financial status.

Credit Report A record detailing an individual's credit, employment, and residence history used to determine the individual's creditworthiness.

Credit Repository A company that records and updates credit applicants' financial and credit information from various sources.

Credit Score Sometimes called a Credit Risk Score. The number contained in a consumer's credit report that represents a statistical summary of the information.

Creditor A party to whom other parties owe money.

Cross-Collateralization A group of mortgages or properties that jointly secures one debt obligation.

Cross-Defaulting A provision that allows a trustee or lender to require full payment on all loans in a group, if any single loan in the group is in default.

Cumulative Discount Rate A percentage of the current value of base rent with all landlord lease concessions taken into account.

Current Occupancy The current percentage of units in a building or property that is leased.

Current Yield The annual rate of return on an investment, expressed as a percentage.

Deal Structure The type of agreement in financing an acquisition. The deal can be un-leveraged, leveraged, traditional debt, participating debt, participating/convertible debt, or joint ventures.

Debt Any amount one party owes to another party.

Debt Service Coverage Ratio (DSCR) A property's yearly net operating income divided by the yearly cost of debt service.

Debt Service The amount of money that is necessary to

meet all interest and principal payments during a specific period.

Debt-to-Income Ratio The percentage of a borrower's monthly payment on long-term debts divided by his gross monthly income.

Dedicate To change a private property to public ownership for a particular public use.

Deed A legal document that conveys property ownership to the buyer.

Deed in Lieu of Foreclosure A situation in which a deed is given to a lender in order to satisfy a mortgage debt and to avoid the foreclosure process.

Deed of Trust A provision that allows a lender to foreclose on a property in the event that the borrower defaults on the loan.

Default The state that occurs when a borrow fails to fulfill a duty or take care of an obligation, such as making monthly mortgage payments.

Deferred Maintenance Account A type of account that a borrower must fund to provide for maintenance of a property.

Deficiency Judgment The legal assignment of personal liability to a borrower for the unpaid balance of a mortgage, after foreclosing on the property has failed to yield the full amount of the debt.

Defined-Benefit Plan A type of benefit provided by an employer that defines an employee's benefits either as a fixed amount or a percentage of the beneficiary's salary when he retires.

Defined-Contribution Plan A type of benefit plan provided by an employer in which an employee's retirement benefits are determined by the amount that has been contributed by the employer and/or employee during the time of employment, and by the actual investment earnings on those contributions over the life of the fund.

Delinquency A state that occurs when the borrower fails to make mortgage payments on time, eventually resulting in foreclosure, if severe enough.

Delinquent Mortgage A mortgage in which the borrower is behind on payments.

Demising Wall The physical partition between the spaces of two tenants or from the building's common areas.

Deposit Also referred to as

Earnest Money. The funds that the buyer provides when offering to purchase property.

Depreciation A decline in the value of property or an asset, often used as a tax-deductible item.

Derivative Securities A type of securities that has been created from other financial instruments.

Design/Build An approach in which a single individual or business is responsible for both the design and construction.

Disclosure A written statement, presented to a potential buyer, that lists information relevant to a piece of property, whether positive or negative.

Discount Points Fees that a lender charges in order to provide a lower interest rate.

Discount Rate A figure used to translate present value from future payments or receipts.

Discretion The amount of authority an adviser or manager is granted for investing and managing a client's capital.

Distraint The act of seizing a tenant's personal property when the tenant is in default, based on the right the landlord has in satisfying the debt.

Diversification The act of spreading individual investments out to insulate a portfolio against the risk of reduced yield or capital loss.

Dividend Yield The percentage of a security's market price that represents the annual dividend rate.

Dividend Distributions of cash or stock that stockholders receive.

Dividend-Ex Date The initial date on which a person purchasing the stock can no longer receive the most recently announced dividend.

Document Needs List The list of documents a lender requires from a potential borrower who is submitting a loan application.

Documentation Preparation Fee A fee that lenders, brokers, and/ or settlement agents charge for the preparation of the necessary closing documents.

Dollar Stop An agreed amount of taxes and operating expenses each tenant must pay out on a prorated basis.

Down Payment The variance between the purchase price and the portion that the mortgage lender financed.

DOWNREIT A structure of organization that makes it possible for REITs to purchase properties using partnership units.

Draw A payment from the construction loan proceeds made to contractors, subcontractors, home builders, or suppliers.

Due Diligence The activities of a prospective purchaser or mortgager of real property for the purpose of confirming that the property is as represented by the seller and is not subject to environmental or other problems.

Due on Sale Clause The standard mortgage language that states the loan must still be repaid if the property is resold.

Earnest Money See: Deposit.

Earthquake Insurance A type of insurance policy that provides coverage against earthquake damage to a home.

Easement The right given to a non-ownership party to use a certain part of the property for specified purposes, such as servicing power lines or cable lines.

Economic Feasibility The viability of a building or project in terms of costs and revenue where the degree of viability is established by extra revenue.

Economic Rent The market rental value of a property at a particular point in time.

Effective Age An estimate of the physical condition of a building presented by an appraiser.

Effective Date The date on which the sale of securities can commence once a registration statement becomes effective.

Effective Gross Income (EGI) The total property income that rents and other sources generate after subtracting a vacancy factor estimated to be appropriate for the property.

Effective Gross Rent (EGR) The net rent that is generated after adjusting for tenant improvements and other capital costs, lease commissions, and other sales expenses.

Effective Rent The actual rental rate that the landlord achieves after deducting the concession value from the base rental rate a tenant pays.

Electronic Authentication A way of providing proof that a particular electronic document is genuine, has arrived unaltered, and came from the indicated source.

Eminent Domain The power of the government to pay the fair market value for a property, appropriating it for public use.

Encroachment Any improvement or upgrade that illegally intrudes onto another party's property.

Encumbrance Any right or interest in a property that interferes with using it or transferring ownership.

End Loan The result of converting to permanent financing from a construction loan.

Entitlement A benefit of a VA home loan. Often referred to as eligibility.

Environmental Impact Statement Legally required documents that must accompany major project proposals where there will likely be an impact on the surrounding environment.

Equal Credit Opportunity Act (ECOA) A federal law that requires a lender or other creditor to make credit available for applicants regardless of sex, marital status, race, religion, or age.

Equifax One of the three primary credit-reporting bureaus.

Equity The value of a property after existing liabilities have been deducted.

Employee Retirement Income Security Act (ERISA) A legislation that controls the investment activities, mainly of corporate and union pension plans.

Errors and Omissions Insurance A type of policy that insures against the mistakes of a builder or architect.

Escalation Clause The clause in a lease that provides for the rent to be increased to account for increases in the expenses the landlord must pay.

Escrow A valuable item, money, or documents deposited with a third party for delivery upon the fulfillment of a condition.

Escrow Account Also referred to as an Impound Account. An account established by a mortgage lender or servicing company for the purpose of holding funds for the payment of items, such as homeowner's insurance and property taxes.

Escrow Agent A neutral third party who makes sure that all conditions of a real estate transaction have been met before any funds are transferred or property is recorded.

Escrow Agreement A written agreement between an escrow agent and the contractual parties that defines the basic obligations of each party, the money (or other valuables) to be deposited in escrow, and how the escrow agent is to dispose of the money on deposit.

Escrow Analysis An annual investigation a lender performs to make sure they are collecting the appropriate amount of money for anticipated expenditures.

Escrow Closing The event in which all conditions of a real estate transaction have been met, and the property title is transferred to the buyer.

Escrow Company A neutral company that serves as a third party to ensure that all conditions of a real estate transaction are met.

Escrow Disbursements The dispensing of escrow funds for the payment of real estate taxes, hazard insurance, mortgage insurance, and other property expenses as they are due.

Escrow Payment The funds that are withdrawn by a mortgage servicer from a borrower's escrow account to pay property taxes and insurance.

Estate The total assets, including property, of an individual after he has died.

Estimated Closing Costs An estimation of the expenses relating to the sale of real estate.

Estimated Hazard Insurance An estimation of hazard insurance, or homeowner's insurance, that will cover physical risks.

Estimated Property Taxes An estimation of the property taxes that must be paid on the property, according to state and county tax rates.

Estoppel Certificate A signed statement that certifies that certain factual statements are correct as of the date of the statement and can be relied upon by a third party, such as a prospective lender or purchaser.

Eviction The legal removal of an occupant from a piece of property.

Examination of Title A title company's inspection and report of public records and other documents for the purpose of determining the chain of ownership of a property.

Exclusive Agency Listing A written agreement between a property owner and a real estate broker in which the owner promises to pay the broker a commission if certain property is leased during the listing period.

Exclusive Listing A contract that allows a licensed real estate agent to be the only agent who can sell a property for a given time.

Executed Contract An agreement in which all parties involved have fulfilled their duties.

Executor The individual who is named in a will to administer an estate. Executrix is the feminine form.

Exit Strategy An approach investors may use when they wish to liquidate all or part of their investment.

Experian One of the three primary credit-reporting bureaus.

Face Rental Rate The rental rate that the landlord publishes.

Facility Space The floor area in a hospitality property that is dedicated to activities, such as restaurants, health clubs, and gift shops, that interactively service multiple people and is not directly related to room occupancy.

Funds Available for Distribution (FAD) The income from operations, with cash expenditures subtracted, that may be used for leasing commissions and tenant improvement costs.

FAD Multiple The price per share of a REIT divided by its funds available for distribution.

Fair Credit Reporting Act (FCRA) The federal legislation that governs the processes credit reporting agencies must follow.

Fair Housing Act The federal legislation that prohibits the refusal to rent or sell to anyone based on race, color, religion, sex, family status, or disability.

Fair Market Value The highest price that a buyer would be willing to pay, and the lowest a seller would be willing to accept.

Fannie Mae See: Federal National Mortgage Association.

Fannie Mae's Community Home Buyer's Program A community lending model based on borrower income in which mortgage insurers and Fannie Mae offer flexible underwriting guidelines in order to increase the buying power for a low- or moderate-income family and to decrease the total amount of cash needed to purchase a home.

Farmer's Home Administration (FMHA) An agency within the U.S. Department of Agriculture that provides credit to farmers and other rural residents.

Federal Home Loan Mortgage Corporation (FHLMC) Also known as Freddie Mac. The company that buys mortgages from lending institutions, combines them with other loans, and sells shares to investors.

Federal Housing Administration (FHA) A government agency that provides low-rate mortgages to buyers who are able to make a down payment as low as 3 percent.

Federal National Mortgage Association (FNMA) Also known as Fannie Mae. A congressionally chartered, shareholder-owned company that is the nation's largest supplier of home mortgage funds. The company buys mortgages from lenders and resells them as securities on the secondary mortgage market.

Fee Simple The highest possible interest a person can have in a piece of real estate.

Fee Simple Estate An unconditional, unlimited inheritance estate in which the owner may dispose of or use the property as desired.

Fee Simple Interest Owning all the rights in a real estate parcel.

Funds From Operations (FFO) A ratio that is meant to highlight the amount of cash a company's real estate portfolio generates relative to its total operating cash flow.

FFO Multiple The price of a REIT share divided by its funds from operations.

FHA Loans Mortgages that the Federal Housing Administration (FHA) insures.

FHA Mortgage Insurance A type of insurance that requires a fee to be paid at closing in order to insure the loan with the Federal Housing Administration (FHA).

Fiduciary Any individual who holds authority over a plan's asset management, administration or disposition, or renders paid investment advice regarding a plan's assets.

Finance Charge The amount of interest to be paid on a loan or credit card balance.

Firm Commitment A written agreement a lender makes to loan money for the purchase of property.

First Mortgage The main mortgage on a property.

First Refusal Right/ Right of First Refusal A lease clause that gives a tenant the first opportunity to buy a property or to lease additional space in a property at the same price and terms as those contained in an offer from a third party that the owner has expressed a willingness to accept.

First-Generation Space A new space that has never before been occupied by a tenant and is currently available for lease.

First-Loss Position A security's position that will suffer the first economic loss if the assets below it lose value or are foreclosed on.

Fixed Costs Expenses that remain the same despite the level of sales or production.

Fixed Rate An interest rate that does not change over the life of the loan.

Fixed Time The particular weeks of a year that the owner of a timeshare arrangement can access his or her accommodations.

Fixed-Rate Mortgage A loan with an unchanging interest rate over the life of the loan.

Fixture Items that become a part of the property when they are permanently attached to the property.

Flat Fee An amount of money

that an adviser or manager receives for managing a portfolio of real estate assets.

Flex Space A building that provides a flexible configuration of office or showroom space combined with manufacturing, laboratory, warehouse, distribution, etc.

Float The number of freely traded shares owned by the public.

Flood Certification The process of analyzing whether a property is located in a known flood zone.

Flood Insurance A policy that is required in designated flood zones to protect against loss due to flood damage.

Floor Area Ratio (FAR) A measurement of a building's gross square footage compared to the square footage of the land on which it is located.

For Sale By Owner (FSBO) A method of selling property in which the property owner serves as the selling agent and directly handles the sales process with the buyer or buyer's agent.

Force Majeure An external force that is not controlled by the contractual parties and prevents them from complying with the provisions of the contract.

Foreclosure The legal process in which a lender takes over ownership of a property once the borrower is in default in a mortgage arrangement.

Forward Commitments Contractual agreements to perform certain financing duties according to any stated conditions.

Four Quadrants of the Real Estate Capital Markets The four market types that consist of Private Equity, Public Equity, Private Debt, and Public Debt.

Freddie Mac See: Federal Home Loan Mortgage Corporation.

Front-End Ratio The measurement a lender uses to compare a borrower's monthly housing expense to gross monthly income.

Full Recourse A loan on which the responsibility of a loan is transferred to an endorser or guarantor in the event of default by the borrower.

Full-Service Rent A rental rate that includes all operating expenses and real estate taxes for the first year.

Fully Amortized ARM An ARM with a monthly payment that is sufficient to amortize the remaining balance at the current interest accrual rate over the amortization term.

Fully Diluted Shares The number of outstanding common stock shares if all convertible securities were converted to common shares.

Future Proposed Space The space in a commercial development that has been proposed but is not yet under construction, or the future phases of a multi-phase project that has not yet been built.

General Contractor The main person or business that contracts for the construction of an entire building or project, rather than individual duties.

General Partner The member in a partnership who holds the authority to bind the partnership and shares in its profits and losses.

Gift Money a buyer has received from a relative or other source that will not have to be repaid.

Ginnie Mae See: Government National Mortgage Association.

Going-In Capitalization Rate The rate that is computed by dividing the expected net operating income for the first year by the value of the property.

Good Faith Estimate A lender's or broker's estimate that shows all costs associated with obtaining a home loan including loan processing, title, and inspection fees.

Government Loan A mortgage that is insured or guaranteed by the FHA, the Department of Veterans Affairs (VA), or the Rural Housing Service (RHS).

Government National Mortgage Association (GNMA) Also known as Ginnie Mae. A government-owned corporation under the U.S. Department of Housing and Urban Development (HUD) that performs the same role as Fannie Mae and Freddie Mac in providing funds to lenders for making home loans, but only purchases loans that are backed by the federal government.

Grace Period A defined time period in which a borrower may make a loan payment after its due date without incurring a penalty.

Graduated Lease A lease, usually long-term, in which rent payments vary in accordance with future contingencies.

Graduated Payment Mortgage A mortgage that requires low payments during the first years of the loan, but eventually requires larger monthly payments over the term of the loan that become fixed later in the term.

Grant To give or transfer an interest in a property by deed or other documented method.

Grantee The party to whom an interest in a property is given.

Grantor The party who is transferring an interest in a property.

Gross Building Area The sum of areas at all floor levels, including the basement, mezzanine, and penthouses included in the principal outside faces of the exterior walls without allowing for architectural setbacks or projections.

Gross Income The total income of a household before taxes or expenses have been subtracted.

Gross Investment in Real Estate (Historic Cost) The total amount of equity and debt that is invested in a piece of real estate minus proceeds from sales or partial sales.

Gross Leasable Area The amount of floor space that is designed for tenants' occupancy and exclusive use.

Gross Lease A rental

arrangement in which the tenant pays a flat sum for rent, and the landlord must pay all building expenses out of that amount.

Gross Real Estate Asset Value The total market value of the real estate investments under management in a fund or individual accounts, usually including the total value of all equity positions, debt positions, and joint venture ownership positions.

Gross Real Estate Investment Value The market value of real estate investments that are held in a portfolio without including debt.

Gross Returns The investment returns generated from operating a property without adjusting for adviser or manager fees.

Ground Lease Land being leased to an individual that has absolutely no residential dwelling on the property; or if it does, the ground (or land) is the only portion of the property being leased.

Ground Rent A long-term lease in which rent is paid to the land owner, normally to build something on that land.

Growing-Equity Mortgage A fixed-rate mortgage in which payments increase over a

specified amount of time with the extra funds being applied to the principal.

Guarantor The part who makes a guaranty.

Guaranty An agreement in which the guarantor promises to satisfy the debt or obligations of another, if and when the debtor fails to do so.

Hard Cost The expenses attributed to actually constructing property improvements.

Hazard Insurance Also known as Homeowner's Insurance or Fire Insurance. A policy that provides coverage for damage from forces such as fire and wind.

Highest and Best Use The most reasonable, expected, legal use of a piece of vacant land or improved property that is physically possible, supported appropriately, financially feasible, and that results in the highest value.

High-Rise In a suburban district, any building taller than six stories. In a business district, any building taller than 25 stories.

Holdbacks A portion of a loan funding that is not dispersed until an additional condition is met, such as the completion of construction.

Holding Period The expected length of time, from purchase to sale, that an investor will own a property.

Hold-Over Tenant A tenant who retains possession of the leased premises after the lease has expired.

Home Equity Conversion Mortgage (HECM) Also referred to as a Reverse Annuity Mortgage. A type of mortgage in which the lender makes payments to the owner, thereby enabling older homeowners to convert equity in their homes into cash in the form of monthly payments.

Home Equity Line An open-ended amount of credit based on the equity a homeowner has accumulated.

Home Equity Loan A type of loan that allows owners to borrow against the equity in their homes up to a limited amount.

Home Inspection A pre-purchase examination of the condition a home is in by a certified inspector.

Home Inspector A certified professional who determines the structural soundness and operating systems of a property.

Home Price The price that a buyer and seller agree upon, generally based on the home's appraised market value.

Homeowners' Association (HOA) A group that governs a community, condominium building, or neighborhood and enforces the covenants, conditions, and restrictions set by the developer.

Homeowners' Association Dues The monthly payments that are paid to the homeowners' association for maintenance and communal expenses.

Homeowner's Insurance A policy that includes coverage for all damages that may affect the value of a house as defined in the terms of the insurance policy.

Homeowner's Warranty A type of policy homebuyers often purchase to cover repairs, such as heating or air-conditioning, should they stop working within the coverage period.

Homestead The property an owner uses as his primary residence.

Housing Expense Ratio The percentage of gross income that is devoted to housing costs each month.

HUD (Housing and Urban Development) A federal agency

that oversees a variety of housing and community development programs, including the FHA.

HUD Median Income The average income for families in a particular area, which is estimated by HUD.

HUD-1 Settlement Statement Also known as the Closing Statement or Settlement Sheet. An itemized listing of the funds paid at closing.

HUD-1 Uniform Settlement Statement A closing statement for the buyer and seller that describes all closing costs for a real estate transaction or refinancing.

HVAC Heating, ventilating, and air-conditioning.

Hybrid Debt A position in a mortgage that has equity-like features of participation in both cash flow and the appreciation of the property at the point of sale or refinance.

Implied Cap Rate The net operating income divided by the sum of a REIT's equity market capitalization and its total outstanding debt.

Impounds The part of the monthly mortgage payment that is reserved in an account in order to pay for hazard insurance, property taxes, and private mortgage insurance.

Improvements The upgrades or changes made to a building to improve its value or usefulness.

Incentive Fee A structure in which the fee amount charged is based on the performance of the real estate assets under management.

Income Capitalization Value The figure derived for an income-producing property by converting its expected benefits into property value.

Income Property A particular property that is used to generate income but is not occupied by the owner.

Income Return The percentage of the total return generated by the income from property, fund, or account operations.

Index A financial table that lenders use for calculating interest rates on ARMs.

Indexed Rate The sum of the published index with a margin added.

Indirect Costs Expenses of development other than the costs of direct material and labor that are related directly to the construction of improvements.

Individual Account Management The process of maintaining accounts that have been established for individual plan sponsors or other investors for investment in real estate, where a firm acts as an adviser in obtaining and/or managing a real estate portfolio.

Inflation Hedge An investment whose value tends to increase at a greater rate than inflation, contributing to the preservation of the purchasing power of a portfolio.

Inflation The rate at which consumer prices increase each year.

Initial Interest Rate The original interest rate on an ARM which is sometimes subject to a variety of adjustments throughout the mortgage.

Initial Public Offering (IPO) The first time a previously private company offers securities for public sale.

Initial Rate Cap The limit specified by some ARMs as the maximum amount the interest rate may increase when the initial interest rate expires.

Initial Rate Duration The date specified by most ARMs at which the initial rate expires.

Inspection Fee The fee that a licensed property inspector charges for determining the current physical condition of the property.

Inspection Report A written report of the property's condition presented by a licensed inspection professional.

Institutional-Grade Property A variety of types of real estate properties usually owned or financed by tax-exempt institutional investors.

Insurance Binder A temporary insurance policy that is implemented while a permanent policy is drawn up or obtained.

Insurance Company Separate Account A real estate investment vehicle only offered by life insurance companies, which enables an ERISA-governed fund to avoid creating unrelated taxable income for certain types of property investments and investment structures.

Insured Mortgage A mortgage that is guaranteed by the FHA or by private mortgage insurance (PMI).

Interest Accrual Rate The rate at which a mortgage accrues interest.

Interest-Only Loan A mortgage

for which the borrower pays only the interest that accrues on the loan balance each month.

Interest Paid over Life of Loan The total amount that has been paid to the lender during the time the money was borrowed.

Interest Rate The percentage that is charged for a loan.

Interest Rate Buy-Down Plans A plan in which a seller uses funds from the sale of the home to buy down the interest rate and reduce the buyer's monthly payments.

Interest Rate Cap The highest interest rate charge allowed on the monthly payment of an ARM during an adjustment period.

Interest Rate Ceiling The maximum interest rate a lender can charge for an ARM.

Interest Rate Floor The minimum possible interest rate a lender can charge for an ARM.

Interest The price that is paid for the use of capital.

Interest-Only Strip A derivative security that consists of all or part of the portion of interest in the underlying loan or security.

Interim Financing Also known as Bridge or Swing Loans. Short-term financing a seller uses to bridge the gap between the sale of one house and the purchase of another.

Internal Rate of Return (IRR) The calculation of a discounted cash flow analysis that is used to determine the potential total return of a real estate asset during a particular holding period.

Inventory The entire space of a certain proscribed market without concern for its availability or condition.

Investment Committee The governing body that is charged with overseeing corporate pension investments and developing investment policies for board approval.

Investment Manager An individual or company that assumes authority over a specified amount of real estate capital, invests that capital in assets using a separate account, and provides asset management.

Investment Policy A document that formalizes an institution's goals, objectives, and guidelines for asset management, investment advisory contracting, fees, and utilization of consultants and other outside professionals.

Investment Property A piece of real estate that generates some form of income.

Investment Strategy The methods used by a manager in structuring a portfolio and selecting the real estate assets for a fund or an account.

Investment Structures Approaches to investing that include un-leveraged acquisitions, leveraged acquisitions, traditional debt, participating debt, convertible debt, triple-net leases, and joint ventures.

Investment-Grade CMBS Commercial mortgage-backed securities that have ratings of AAA, AA, A, or BBB.

Investor Status The position an investor is in, either taxable or tax-exempt.

Joint Liability The condition in which responsibility rests with two or more people for fulfilling the terms of a home loan or other financial debt.

Joint Tenancy A form of ownership in which two or more people have equal shares in a piece of property, and rights pass to the surviving owner(s) in the event of death.

Joint Venture An investment business formed by more than one party for the purpose of

acquiring or developing and managing property and/or other assets.

Judgment The decision a court of law makes.

Judicial Foreclosure The usual foreclosure proceeding some states use, which is handled in a civil lawsuit.

Jumbo Loan A type of mortgage that exceeds the required limits set by Fannie Mae and Freddie Mac each year.

Junior Mortgage A loan that is a lower priority behind the primary loan.

Just Compensation The amount that is fair to both the owner and the government when property is appropriated for public use through eminent domain.

Landlord's Warrant The warrant a landlord obtains to take a tenant's personal property to sell at a public sale to compel payment of the rent or other stipulation in the lease.

Late Charge The fee that is imposed by a lender when the borrower has not made a payment when it was due.

Late Payment The payment made to the lender after the due date has passed.

Lead Manager The investment banking firm that has primary responsibility for coordinating the new issuance of securities.

Lease A contract between a property owner and tenant that defines payments and conditions under which the tenant may occupy the real estate for a given period of time.

Lease Commencement Date The date at which the terms of the lease are implemented.

Lease Expiration Exposure Schedule A chart of the total square footage of all current leases that expire in each of the next five years, without taking renewal options into account.

Lease Option A financing option that provides for homebuyers to lease a home with an option to buy, with part of the rental payments being applied toward the down payment.

Leasehold The limited right to inhabit a piece of real estate held by a tenant.

Leasehold State A way of holding a property title in which the mortgagor does not actually own the property but has a long-term lease on it.

Leasehold Interest The right to hold or use property for a specific period of time at a given price without transferring ownership.

Lease-Purchase A contract that defines the closing date and solutions for the seller in the event that the buyer defaults.

Legal Blemish A negative count against a piece of property such as a zoning violation or fraudulent title claim.

Legal Description A way of describing and locating a piece of real estate that is recognized by law.

Legal Owner The party who holds the title to the property, although the title may carry no actual rights to the property other than as a lien.

Lender A bank or other financial institution that offers home loans.

Letter of Credit A promise from a bank or other party that the issuer will honor drafts or other requests for payment upon complying with the requirements specified in the letter of credit.

Letter of Intent An initial agreement defining the proposed terms for the end contract.

Leverage The process of increasing the return on an investment by borrowing some of the funds at an interest rate less than the return on the project.

Liabilities A borrower's debts and financial obligations, whether long- or short-term.

Liability Insurance A type of policy that protects owners against negligence, personal injury, or property damage claims.

London InterBank Offered Rate (LIBOR) The interest rate offered on Eurodollar deposits traded between banks and used to determine changes in interest rate for ARMs.

Lien A claim put by one party on the property of another as collateral for money owed.

Lien Waiver A waiver of a mechanic's lien rights that is sometimes required before the general contractor can receive money under the payment provisions of a construction loan and contract.

Life Cap A limit on the amount an ARM's interest rate can increase during the mortgage term.

Lifecycle The stages of development for a property: pre-development, development, leasing, operating, and rehabilitation.

Lifetime Payment Cap A limit on the amount that payments can increase or decrease over the life of an ARM.

Lifetime Rate Cap The highest possible interest rate that may be charged, under any circumstances, over the entire life of an ARM.

Like-Kind Property A term that refers to real estate that is held for productive use in a trade or business or for investment.

Limited Partnership A type of partnership in which some partners manage the business and are personally liable for partnership debts, but some partners contribute capital and share in profits without the responsibility of management.

Line of Credit An amount of credit granted by a financial institution up to a specified amount for a certain period of time to a borrower.

Liquid Asset A type of asset that can be easily converted into cash.

Liquidity The ease with which an individual's or company's assets can be converted to cash without losing their value.

Listing Agreement An agreement between a property owner and a real estate broker that authorizes the broker to attempt to sell or lease the property at a specified price and terms in return for a commission or other compensation.

Loan An amount of money that is borrowed and usually repaid with interest.

Loan Application A document that presents a borrower's income, debt, and other obligations to determine credit worthiness, as well as some basic information on the target property.

Loan Application Fee A fee lenders charge to cover expenses relating to reviewing a loan application.

Loan Commitment An agreement by a lender or other financial institution to make or ensure a loan for the specified amount and terms.

Loan Officer An official representative of a lending institution who is authorized to act on behalf of the lender within specified limits.

Loan Origination The process of obtaining and arranging new loans.

Loan Origination Fee A fee lenders charge to cover the costs related to arranging the loan.

Loan Servicing The process a lending institution goes through for all loans it manages. This involves processing payments, sending statements, managing the escrow/impound account, providing collection services on delinquent loans, ensuring that insurance and property taxes are made on the property, handling pay-offs and assumptions, as well as various other services.

Loan Term The time, usually expressed in years, that a lender sets in which a buyer must pay a mortgage.

Loan-to-Value (LTV) The ratio of the amount of the loan compared to the appraised value or sales price.

Lock-Box Structure An arrangement in which the payments are sent directly from the tenant or borrower to the trustee.

Lock-In A commitment from a lender to a borrower to guarantee a given interest rate for a limited amount of time.

Lock-In Period The period of time during which the borrower is guaranteed a specified interest rate.

Lockout The period of time during which a loan may not be paid off early.

Long-Term Lease A rental agreement that will last at least three years from initial signing to the date of expiration or renewal.

Loss Severity The percentage of lost principal when a loan is foreclosed.

Lot One of several contiguous parcels of a larger piece of land.

Low-Documentation Loan A mortgage that requires only a basic verification of income and assets.

Low-Rise A building that involves fewer than four stories above the ground level.

Lump-Sum Contract A type of construction contract that requires the general contractor to complete a building project for a fixed cost that is usually established beforehand by competitive bidding.

Magic Page A story of projected growth that describes how a new REIT will achieve its future plans for funds from operations or funds available for distribution.

Maintenance Fee The charge to homeowners' association members each month for the repair and maintenance of common areas.

Maker One who issues a promissory note and commits to paying the note when it is due.

Margin A percentage that is added to the index and fixed for the mortgage term.

Mark to Market The act of changing the original investment cost or value of a property or portfolio to the level of the current estimated market value.

Market Capitalization A measurement of a company's value that is calculated by multiplying the current share price by the current number of shares outstanding.

Market Rental Rates The rental income that a landlord could most likely ask for a property in the open market, indicated by the current rents for comparable spaces.

Market Study A forecast of the demand for a certain type of real estate project in the future that includes an estimate of the square footage that could be absorbed and the rents that could be charged.

Market Value The price a property would sell for at a particular point in time in a competitive market.

Marketable Title A title that is free of encumbrances and can be marketed immediately to a willing purchaser.

Master Lease The primary lease that controls other subsequent leases and may cover more property than all subsequent leases combined.

Master Servicer An entity that acts on behalf of a trustee for security holders' benefit in collecting funds from a borrower, advancing funds in the event of delinquencies and, in the event of default, taking a property through foreclosure.

Maturity Date The date at which the total principal balance of a loan is due.

Mechanic's Lien A claim created for securing payment priority for the price and value of work performed and materials furnished in constructing, repairing, or improving a building or other structure.

Meeting Space The space in hotels that is made available to the public to rent for meetings, conferences, or banquets.

Merged Credit Report A report that combines information from the three primary credit-reporting agencies including: Equifax, Experian, and TransUnion.

Metes and Bounds The surveyed boundary lines of a piece of land described by listing the compass directions (bounds) and distances (metes) of the boundaries.

Mezzanine Financing A financing position somewhere between equity and debt, meaning that there are higher-priority debts above and equity below.

Mid-Rise Usually, a building which shows four to eight stories above ground level. In a business district, buildings up to 25 stories may also be included.

Mixed-Use A term referring to space within a building or project which can be used for more than one activity.

Modern Portfolio Theory (MPT) An approach of quantifying risk and return in an asset portfolio which emphasizes the portfolio rather than the individual assets and how the assets perform in relation to each other.

Modification An adjustment in the terms of a loan agreement.

Modified Annual Percentage Rate (APR) An index of the cost of a loan based on the standard APR but adjusted for the amount of time the borrower expects to hold the loan.

Monthly Association Dues A

payment due each month to a homeowners' association for expenses relating to maintenance and community operations.

Mortgage An amount of money that is borrowed to purchase a property using that property as collateral.

Mortgage Acceleration Clause A provision enabling a lender to require that the rest of the loan balance is paid in a lump sum under certain circumstances.

Mortgage Banker A financial institution that provides home loans using its own resources, often selling them to investors such as insurance companies or Fannie Mae.

Mortgage Broker An individual who matches prospective borrowers with lenders that the broker is approved to deal with.

Mortgage Broker Business A company that matches prospective borrowers with lenders that the broker is approved to deal with.

Mortgage Constant A figure comparing an amortizing mortgage payment to the outstanding mortgage balance.

Mortgage Insurance (MI) A policy, required by lenders on some loans, that covers the lender against certain losses that are incurred as a result of a default on a home loan.

Mortgage Insurance Premium (MIP) The amount charged for mortgage insurance, either to a government agency or to a private MI company.

Mortgage Interest Deduction The tax write-off that the IRS allows most homeowners to deduct for annual interest payments made on real estate loans.

Mortgage Life and Disability Insurance A type of term life insurance borrowers often purchase to cover debt that is left when the borrower dies or becomes too disabled to make the mortgage payments.

Mortgagee The financial institution that lends money to the borrower.

Mortgagor The person who requests to borrow money to purchase a property.

Multi-Dwelling Units A set of properties that provide separate housing areas for more than one family but only require a single mortgage.

Multiple Listing Service A service that lists real estate offered for sale by a particular real estate agent that can be shown or sold by other real estate agents within a certain area.

National Association of Real Estate Investment Trusts (NAREIT) The national, non-profit trade organization that represents the real estate investment trust industry.

National Council of Real Estate Investment Fiduciaries (NCREIF) A group of real estate professionals who serve on committees; sponsor research articles, seminars and symposiums; and produce the NCREIF Property Index.

NCREIF Property Index (NPI) A quarterly and yearly report presenting income and appreciation components.

Negative Amortization An event that occurs when the deferred interest on an ARM is added, and the balance increases instead of decreases.

Net Asset Value (NAV) The total value of an asset or property minus leveraging or joint venture interests.

Net Asset Value Per Share The total value of a REIT's current assets divided by outstanding shares.

Net Assets The total value of assets minus total liabilities based on market value.

Net Cash Flow The total income generated by an investment property after expenses have been subtracted.

Net Investment in Real Estate Gross investment in properties minus the outstanding balance of debt.

Net Investment Income The income or loss of a portfolio or business minus all expenses, including portfolio and asset management fees, but before gains and losses on investments are considered.

Net Operating Income (NOI) The pre-tax figure of gross revenue minus operating expenses and an allowance for expected vacancy.

Net Present Value (NPV) The sum of the total current value of incremental future cash flows plus the current value of estimated sales proceeds.

Net Purchase Price The gross purchase price minus any associated financed debt.

Net Real Estate Investment Value The total market value of all real estate minus property-level debt.

Net Returns The returns paid to investors minus fees to advisers or managers.

Net Sales Proceeds The income from the sale of an asset, or part of an asset, minus brokerage commissions, closing costs, and market expenses.

Net Square Footage The total space required for a task or staff position.

Net Worth The worth of an individual or company figured on the basis of a difference between all assets and liabilities.

No-Cash-Out Refinance Sometimes referred to as a Rate and Term Refinance. A refinancing transaction that is intended only to cover the balance due on the current loan and any costs associated with obtaining the new mortgage.

No-Cost Loan A loan for which there are no costs associated with the loan that are charged by the lender, but with a slightly higher interest rate.

No-Documentation Loan A type of loan application that requires no income or asset verification, usually granted based on strong credit with a large down payment.

Nominal Yield The yield investors receive before it is adjusted for fees, inflation, or risk.

Non-Assumption Clause A provision in a loan agreement that prohibits transferring a mortgage to another borrower without approval from the lender.

Non-Compete Clause A provision in a lease agreement that specifies that the tenant's business is the only one that may operate in the property in question, thereby preventing a competitor moving in next door.

Non-Conforming Loan Any loan that is too large or does not meet certain qualifications to be purchased by Fannie Mae or Freddie Mac.

Non-Discretionary Funds The funds that are allocated to an investment manager who must have approval from the investor for each transaction.

Non-Investment-Grade CMBS Also referred to as High-Yield CMBS. Commercial mortgage-backed securities that have ratings of BB or B.

Non-Liquid Asset A type of asset that is not turned into cash very easily.

Non-Performing Loan A loan agreement that cannot meet its contractual principal and interest payments.

Non-Recourse Debt A loan that limits the lender's options to collect on the value of the real estate in the event of a default by the borrower.

Nonrecurring Closing Costs Fees that are only paid one time in a given transaction.

Note A legal document requiring a borrower to repay a mortgage at a specified interest rate over a certain period of time.

Note Rate The interest rate that is defined in a mortgage note.

Notice of Default A formal written notification a borrower receives once the borrower is in default stating that legal action may be taken.

Offer A term that describes a specified price or spread to sell whole loans or securities.

One-Year Adjustable-Rate Mortgage An ARM for which the interest rate changes annually, generally based on movements of a published index plus a specified margin.

Open Space A section of land or water that has been dedicated for public or private use or enjoyment.

Open-End Fund A type of commingled fund with an infinite life, always accepting new investor capital and making new investments in property.

Operating Cost Escalation A clause that is intended to adjust rents to account for external standards such as published indexes, negotiated wage levels, or building-related expenses.

Operating Expense The regular costs associated with operating and managing a property.

Opportunistic A phrase that generally describes a strategy of holding investments in underperforming and/or under-managed assets with the expectation of increases in cash flow and/or value.

Option A condition in which the buyer pays for the right to purchase a property within a certain period of time without the obligation to buy.

Option ARM Loan A type of mortgage in which the borrower has a variety of payment options each month.

Original Principal Balance The total principal owed on a mortgage before a borrower has made a payment.

Origination Fee A fee that most

lenders charge for the purpose of covering the costs associated with arranging the loan.

Originator A company that underwrites loans for commercial and/or multi-family properties.

Out-Parcel The individual retail sites located within a shopping center.

Overallotment A practice in which the underwriters offer and sell a higher number of shares than they had planned to purchase from the issuer.

Owner Financing A transaction in which the property seller agrees to finance all or part of the amount of the purchase.

Parking Ratio A figure, generally expressed as square footage, that compares a building's total rentable square footage to its total number of parking spaces.

Partial Payment An amount paid that is not large enough to cover the normal monthly payment on a mortgage loan.

Partial Sales The act of selling a real estate interest that is smaller than the whole property.

Partial Taking The appropriating of a portion of an owner's property under the laws of Eminent Domain.

Participating Debt Financing that allows the lender to have participatory rights to equity through increased income and/or residual value over the balance of the loan or original value at the time the loan is funded.

Party in Interest Any party that may hold an interest, including employers, unions, and, sometimes, fiduciaries.

Pass-Through Certificate A document that allows the holder to receive payments of principal and interest from the underlying pool of mortgages.

Payment Cap The maximum amount a monthly payment may increase on an ARM.

Payment Change Date The date on which a new payment amount takes effect on an ARM or GPM, usually in the month directly after the adjustment date.

Payout Ratio The percentage of the primary earnings per share, excluding unusual items, that are paid to common stockholders as cash dividends during the next 12 months.

Pension Liability The full amount of capital that is required to finance vested pension fund benefits.

Percentage Rent The amount

of rent that is adjusted based on the percentage of gross sales or revenues the tenant receives.

Per-Diem Interest The interest that is charged or accrued daily.

Performance Bond A bond that a contractor posts to guarantee full performance of a contract in which the proceeds will be used for completing the contract or compensating the owner for loss in the event of nonperformance.

Performance Measurement The process of measuring how well an investor's real estate has performed regarding individual assets, advisers/managers, and portfolios.

Performance The changes each quarter in fund or account values that can be explained by investment income, realized or unrealized appreciation, and the total return to the investors before and after investment management fees.

Performance-Based Fees The fees that advisers or managers receive that are based on returns to investors.

Periodic Payment Cap The highest amount that payments can increase or decrease during a given adjustment period on an ARM.

Periodic Rate Cap The maximum amount that the interest rate can increase or decrease during a given adjustment period on an ARM.

Permanent Loan A long-term property mortgage.

Personal Property Any items belonging to a person that is not real estate.

PITI Principal, Interest, Taxes, Insurance. The items that are included in the monthly payment to the lender for an impounded loan, as well as mortgage insurance.

PITI Reserves The amount in cash that a borrower must readily have after the down payment and all closing costs are paid when purchasing a home.

Plan Assets The assets included in a pension plan.

Plan Sponsor The party that is responsible for administering an employee benefit plan.

Planned Unit Development (PUD) A type of ownership where individuals actually own the building or unit they live in, but common areas are owned jointly with the other members of the development or association. Contrast with condominium, where an individual actually owns the airspace of his unit, but the buildings and common areas are owned jointly with the others in the development or association.

Plat A chart or map of a certain area showing the boundaries of individual lots, streets, and easements.

Pledged Account Mortgage (PAM) A loan tied to a pledged savings account for which the fund and earned interest are used to gradually reduce mortgage payments.

Point Also referred to as a Discount Point. A fee a lender charges to provide a lower interest rate, equal to 1 percent of the amount of the loan.

Portfolio Management A process that involves formulating, modifying, and implementing a real estate investment strategy according to an investor's investment objectives.

Portfolio Turnover The amount of time averaged from the time an investment is funded until it is repaid or sold.

Power of Attorney A legal document that gives someone the authority to act on behalf of another party.

Power of Sale The clause included in a mortgage or deed of trust that provides the mortgagee (or trustee) with the right and power to advertise and sell the property at public auction if the borrower is in default.

Pre-Approval The complete analysis a lender makes regarding a potential borrower's ability to pay for a home as well as a confirmation of the proposed amount to be borrowed.

Pre-Approval Letter The letter a lender presents that states the amount of money they are willing to lend a potential buyer.

Preferred Shares Certain stocks that have a prior distributions claim up to a defined amount before the common shareholders may receive anything.

Pre-Leased A certain amount of space in a proposed building that must be leased before construction may begin or a certificate of occupancy may be issued.

Prepaid Expenses The amount of money that is paid before it is due, including taxes, insurance, and/or assessments.

Prepaid Fees The charges that a borrower must pay in advance regarding certain recurring items, such as interest, property taxes, hazard insurance, and PMI, if applicable.

Prepaid Interest The amount of interest that is paid before its due date.

Prepayment The money that is paid to reduce the principal balance of a loan before the date it is due.

Prepayment Penalty A penalty that may be charged to the borrower when he pays off a loan before the planned maturity date.

Prepayment Rights The right a borrower is given to pay the total principal balance before the maturity date free of penalty.

Prequalification The initial assessment by a lender of a potential borrower's ability to pay for a home as well as an estimate of how much the lender is willing to supply to the buyer.

Price-to-Earnings Ratio The comparison that is derived by dividing the current share price by the sum of the primary earnings per share from continuing operations over the past year.

Primary Issuance The preliminary financing of an issuer.

Prime Rate The best interest rate reserved for a bank's preferred customers.

Prime Space The first-generation space that is available for lease.

Prime Tenant The largest or highest-earning tenant in a building or shopping center.

Principal The amount of money originally borrowed in a mortgage, before interest is included and with any payments subtracted.

Principal Balance The total current balance of mortgage principal not including interest.

Principal Paid over Life of Loan The final total of scheduled payments to the principal that the lender calculates to equal the face amount of the loan.

Principal Payments The lender's return of invested capital.

Principle of Conformity The concept that a property will probably increase in value if its size, age, condition, and style are similar to other properties in the immediate area.

Private Debt Mortgages or other liabilities for which an individual is responsible.

Private Equity A real estate

investment that has been acquired by a noncommercial entity.

Private Mortgage Insurance (PMI) A type of policy that a lender requires when the borrower's down payment or home equity percentage is under 20 percent of the value of the property.

Private Placement The sale of a security in a way that renders it exempt from the registration rules and requirements of the SEC.

Private REIT A real estate investment company that is structured as a real estate investment trust that places and holds shares privately rather than publicly.

Pro Rata The proportionate amount of expenses per tenant for the property's maintenance and operation.

Processing Fee A fee some lenders charge for gathering the information necessary to process the loan.

Production Acres The portion of land that can be used directly in agriculture or timber activities to generate income, but not areas used for such things as machinery storage or support.

Prohibited Transaction Certain transactions that may not be performed between a pension plan and a party in interest, such as the following: the sale, exchange or lease of any property; a loan or other grant of credit; and furnishing goods or services.

Promissory Note A written agreement to repay the specific amount over a certain period of time.

Property Tax The tax that must be paid on private property.

Prudent Man Rule The standard to which ERISA holds a fiduciary accountable.

Public Auction An announced public meeting held at a specified location for the purpose of selling property to repay a mortgage in default.

Public Debt Mortgages or other liabilities for which a commercial entity is responsible.

Public Equity A real estate investment that has been acquired by REITs and other publicly traded real estate operating companies.

Punch List An itemized list that documents incomplete or unsatisfactory items after the contractor has declared the space to be mostly complete.

Purchase Agreement The written contract the buyer and seller both sign defining the terms and conditions under which a property is sold.

Purchase Money Transaction A transaction in which property is acquired through the exchange of money or something of equivalent value.

Purchase-Money Mortgage (PMM) A mortgage obtained by a borrower that serves as partial payment for a property.

Qualified Plan Any employee benefit plan that the IRS has approved as a tax-exempt plan.

Qualifying Ratio The measurement a lender uses to determine how much they are willing to lend to a potential buyer.

Quitclaim Deed A written document that releases a party from any interest they may have in a property.

Rate Cap The highest interest rate allowed on a monthly payment during an adjustment period of an ARM.

Rate Lock The commitment of a lender to a borrower that guarantees a certain interest rate

for a specific amount of time.

Rate-Improvement Mortgage A loan that includes a clause that entitles a borrower to a one-time-only cut in the interest rate without having to refinance.

Rating Agencies Independent firms that are engaged to rate securities' creditworthiness on behalf of investors.

Rating A figure that represents the credit quality or creditworthiness of securities.

Raw Land A piece of property that has not been developed and remains in its natural state.

Raw Space Shell space in a building that has not yet been developed.

Real Estate Agent An individual who is licensed to negotiate and transact the real estate sales.

Real Estate Fundamentals The factors that drive the value of property.

Real Estate Settlement Procedures Act (RESPA) A legislation for consumer protection that requires lenders to notify borrowers regarding closing costs in advance.

Real Property Land and anything else of a permanent

nature that is affixed to the land.

Real Rate of Return The yield given to investors minus an inflationary factor.

Realtor A real estate agent or broker who is an active member of a local real estate board affiliated with the National Association of Realtors.

Recapture The act of the IRS recovering the tax benefit of a deduction or a credit that a taxpayer has previously taken in error.

Recorder A public official who records transactions that affect real estate in the area.

Recording The documentation that the registrar's office keeps of the details of properly executed legal documents.

Recording Fee A fee real estate agents charge for moving the sale of a piece of property into the public record.

Recourse The option a lender has for recovering losses against the personal assets of a secondary party who is also liable for a debt that is in default.

Red Herring An early prospectus that is distributed to prospective investors that includes a note in red ink on the cover stating that

the SEC-approved registration statement is not yet in effect.

Refinance Transaction The act of paying off an existing loan using the funding gained from a new loan that uses the same property as security.

Regional Diversification Boundaries that are defined based on geography or economic lines.

Registration Statement The set of forms that are filed with the SEC (or the appropriate state agency) regarding a proposed offering of new securities or the listing of outstanding securities on a national exchange.

Regulation Z A federal legislation under the Truth in Lending Act that requires lenders to advise the borrower in writing of all costs that are associated with the credit portion of a financial transaction.

Rehab Short for Rehabilitation. Refers to an extensive renovation intended to extend the life of a building or project.

Rehabilitation Mortgage A loan meant to fund the repairing and improving of a resale home or building.

Real Estate Investment Trust (REIT) A trust corporation that combines the capital of several investors for the purpose of acquiring or providing funding for real estate.

Remaining Balance The amount of the principal on a home loan that has not yet been paid.

Remaining Term The original term of the loan after the number of payments made has been subtracted.

Real Estate Mortgage Investment Conduit (REMIC) An investment vehicle that is designed to hold a pool of mortgages solely to issue multiple classes of mortgage-backed securities in a way that avoids doubled corporate tax.

Renewal Option A clause in a lease agreement that allows a tenant to extend the term of a lease.

Renewal Probability The average percentage of a building's tenants who are expected to renew terms at market rental rates upon the lease expiration.

Rent Commencement Date The date at which a tenant is to begin paying rent.

Rent Loss Insurance A policy that covers loss of rent or rental value for a landlord due to any condition that renders the leased premises inhabitable, thereby excusing the tenant from paying rent.

Rent The fee paid for the occupancy and/or use of any rental property or equipment.

Rentable/Usable Ratio A total rentable area in a building divided by the area available for use.

Rental Concession See: Concessions.

Rental Growth Rate The projected trend of market rental rates over a particular period of analysis.

Rent-Up Period The period of time following completion of a new building when tenants are actively being sought and the project is stabilizing.

Real Estate Owned (REO) The real estate that a savings institution owns as a result of foreclosure on borrowers in default.

Repayment Plan An agreement made to repay late installments or advances.

Replacement Cost The projected cost by current standards of constructing a building that is equivalent to the building being appraised.

Replacement Reserve Fund
Money that is set aside for replacing of common property in a condominium, PUD, or cooperative project.

Request for Proposal (RFP)
A formal request that invites investment managers to submit information regarding investment strategies, historical investment performance, current investment opportunities, investment management fees, and other pension fund client relationships used by their firm.

Rescission The legal withdrawing of a contract or consent from the parties involved.

Reserve Account An account that must be funded by the borrower to protect the lender.

Resolution Trust Corp. (RTC)
The congressional corporation established for the purpose of containing, managing, and selling failed financial institutions, thereby recovering taxpayer funds.

Retail Investor An investor who sells interests directly to consumers.

Retention Rate The percentage

of trailing year's earnings that have been dispersed into the company again. It is calculated as 100 minus the trailing 12-month payout ratio.

Return on Assets The measurement of the ability to produce net profits efficiently by making use of assets.

Return on Equity The measurement of the return on the investment in a business or property.

Return on Investments The percentage of money that has been gained as a result of certain investments.

Reverse Mortgage See: Home Equity Conversion Mortgage.

Reversion Capitalization Rate
The capitalization rate that is used to derive reversion value.

Reversion Value A benefit that an investor expects to receive as a lump sum at the end of an investment.

Revolving Debt A credit arrangement that enables a customer to borrow against a predetermined line of credit when purchasing goods and services.

Revenue per Available Room (RevPAR) The total room

revenue for a particular period divided by the average number of rooms available in a hospitality facility.

Right of Ingress or Egress The option to enter or to leave the premises in question.

Right of Survivorship The option that survivors have to take on the interest of a deceased joint tenant.

Right to Rescission A legal provision that enables borrowers to cancel certain loan types within three days after they sign.

Risk Management A logical approach to analyzing and defining insurable and non-insurable risks while evaluating the availability and costs of purchasing third-party insurance.

Risk-Adjusted Rate of Return A percentage that is used to identify investment options that are expected to deliver a positive premium despite their volatility.

Road Show A tour of the executives of a company that is planning to go public, during which the executives travel to a variety of cities to make presentations to underwriters and analysts regarding their company and IPO.

Roll-Over Risk The possibility that tenants will not renew their lease.

Sale-Leaseback An arrangement in which a seller deeds a property, or part of it, to a buyer in exchange for money or the equivalent, then leases the property from the new owner.

Sales Comparison Value A value that is calculated by comparing the appraised property to similar properties in the area that have been recently sold.

Sales Contract An agreement that both the buyer and seller sign defining the terms of a property sale.

Second Mortgage A secondary loan obtained on a piece of property.

Secondary Market A market in which existing mortgages are bought and sold as part of a mortgages pool.

Secondary (Follow-On) Offering An offering of stock made by a company that is already public.

Second-Generation or Secondary Space Space that has been occupied before and becomes available for lease again, either by the landlord or as a sublease.

Secured Loan A loan that is secured by some sort of collateral.

Securities and Exchange Commission (SEC) The federal agency that oversees the issuing and exchanging of public securities.

Securitization The act of converting a non-liquid asset into a tradable form.

Security The property or other asset that will serve as a loan's collateral.

Security Deposit An amount of money a tenant gives to a landlord to secure the performance of terms in a lease agreement.

Seisen (Seizen) The ownership of real property under a claim of freehold estate.

Self-Administered REIT A REIT in which the management are employees of the REIT or similar entity.

Self-Managed REIT See: Self-Administered REIT.

Seller Carry-Back An arrangement in which the seller provides the financing to purchase a home.

Seller Financing A type of funding in which the borrower

may use part of the equity in the property to finance the purchase.

Senior Classes The security classes who have the highest priority for receiving payments from the underlying mortgage loans.

Separate Account A relationship in which a single pension plan sponsor is used to retain an investment manager or adviser under a stated investment policy exclusively for that sponsor.

Servicer An organization that collects principal and interest payments from borrowers and manages borrowers' escrow accounts on behalf of a trustee.

Servicing The process of collecting mortgage payments from borrowers as well as related responsibilities.

Setback The distance required from a given reference point before a structure can be built.

Settlement or Closing Fees Fees that the escrow agent receives for carrying out the written instructions in the agreement between borrower and lender and/or buyer and seller.

Settlement Statement See: HUD-1 Settlement Statement.

Shared-Appreciation Mortgage

A loan that enables a lender or other party to share in the profits of the borrower when the borrower sells the home.

Shared-Equity Transaction A transaction in which two people purchase a property, one as a residence and the other as an investment.

Shares Outstanding The number of shares of outstanding common stock minus the treasury shares.

Site Analysis A determination of how suitable a specific parcel of land is for a particular use.

Site Development The implementation of all improvements that are needed for a site before construction may begin.

Site Plan A detailed description and map of the location of improvements to a parcel.

Slab The flat, exposed surface that is laid over the structural support beams to form the building's floor(s).

Social Investing A strategy in which investments are driven in partially or completely by social or non-real estate objectives.

Soft Cost The part of an equity investment, aside from the literal cost of the improvements, that could be tax-deductible in the first year.

Space Plan A chart or map of space requirements for a tenant that includes wall/door locations, room sizes, and even furniture layouts.

Special Assessment Certain charges that are levied against real estates for public improvements to benefit the property in question.

Special Servicer A company that is hired to collect on mortgages that are either delinquent or in default.

Specified Investing A strategy of investment in individually specified properties, portfolios, or commingled funds are fully or partially detailed prior to the commitment of investor capital.

Speculative Space Any space in a rental property that has not been leased prior to construction on a new building begins.

Stabilized Net Operating Income Expected income minus expenses that reflect relatively stable operations.

Stabilized Occupancy The best projected range of long-term occupancy that a piece of rental property will achieve after existing in the open market for a reasonable period of time with terms and conditions that are comparable to similar offerings.

Step-Rate Mortgage A loan that allows for a gradual interest rate increase during the first few years of the loan.

Step-Up Lease (Graded Lease) A lease agreement that specifies certain increases in rent at certain intervals during the complete term of the lease.

Straight Lease (Flat Lease) A lease agreement that specifies an amount of rent that should be paid regularly during the complete term of the lease.

Strip Center Any shopping area that is made up of a row of stores but is not large enough to be anchored by a grocery store.

Subcontractor A contractor who has been hired by the general contractor, often specializing in a certain required task for the construction project.

Subdivision The most common type of housing development created by dividing a larger tract of land into individual lots for sale or lease.

Sublessee A person or business that holds the rights of use and occupancy under a lease contract with the original lessee, who still retains primary responsibility for the lease obligations.

Subordinate Financing Any loan with a priority lower than loans that were obtained beforehand.

Subordinate Loan A second or third mortgage obtained with the same property being used as collateral.

Subordinated Classes Classes that have the lowest priority of receiving payments from underlying mortgage loans.

Subordination The act of sharing credit loss risk at varying rates among two or more classes of securities.

Subsequent Rate Adjustments The interest rate for ARMs that adjusts at regular intervals, sometimes differing from the duration period of the initial interest rate.

Subsequent Rate Cap The maximum amount the interest rate may increase at each regularly scheduled interest rate adjustment date on an ARM.

Super Jumbo Mortgage A loan that is over $650,000 for some lenders or $1,000,000 for others.

Surety A person who willingly binds himself to the debt or obligation of another party.

Surface Rights A right or easement that is usually granted with mineral rights that enables the holder to drill through the surface.

Survey A document or analysis containing the precise measurements of a piece of property as performed by a licensed surveyor.

Sweat Equity The non-cash improvements in value that an owner adds to a piece of property.

Synthetic Lease A transaction that is considered to be a lease by accounting standards but a loan by tax standards.

Taking Similar to condemning, or any other interference with rights to private property, but a physical seizure or appropriation is not required.

Tax Base The determined value of all property that lies within the jurisdiction of the taxing authority.

Tax Lien A type of lien placed against a property if the owner has not paid property or personal taxes.

Tax Roll A record that contains the descriptions of all land parcels and their owners that is located within the county.

Tax Service Fee A fee that is charged for the purpose of setting up monitoring of the borrower's property tax payments by a third party.

Teaser Rate A small, short-term interest rate offered on a mortgage in order to convince the potential borrower to apply.

Tenancy by the Entirety A form of ownership held by spouses in which they both hold title to the entire property with right of survivorship.

Tenancy in Common A type of ownership held by two or more owners in an undivided interest in the property with no right of survivorship.

Tenant (Lessee) A party who rents a piece of real estate from another by way of a lease agreement.

Tenant at Will A person who possesses a piece of real estate with the owner's permission.

Tenant Improvement (TI) Allowance The specified amount of money that the landlord contributes toward tenant improvements.

Tenant Improvement (TI) The upgrades or repairs that are made to the leased premises by or for a tenant.

Tenant Mix The quality of the income stream for a property.

Term The length that a loan lasts or is expected to last before it is repaid.

Third-Party Origination A process in which another party is used by the lender to originate, process, underwrite, close, fund, or package the mortgages it expects to deliver to the secondary mortgage market.

Timeshare A form of ownership involving purchasing a specific period of time or percentage of interest in a vacation property.

Time-Weighted Average Annual Rate of Return The regular yearly return over several years that would have the same return value as combining the actual annual returns for each year in the series.

Title The legal written document that provides someone ownership in a piece of real estate.

Title Company A business that determines that a property title is clear and that provides title insurance.

Title Exam An analysis of the public records in order to confirm that the seller is the legal owner, and there are no encumbrances on the property.

Title Insurance A type of policy that is issued to both lenders and buyers to cover loss due to property ownership disputes that may arise at a later date.

Title Insurance Binder A written promise from the title insurance company to insure the title to the property, based on the conditions and exclusions shown in the binder.

Title Risk The potential impediments in transferring a title from one party to another.

Title Search The process of analyzing all transactions existing in the public record in order to determine whether any title defects could interfere with the clear transfer of property ownership.

Total Acres The complete amount of land area that is contained within a real estate investment.

Total Assets The final amount of all gross investments, cash and equivalents, receivables, and other assets as they are presented on the balance sheet.

Total Commitment The complete funding amount that is promised once all specified conditions have been met.

Total Expense Ratio The comparison of monthly debt obligations to gross monthly income.

Total Inventory The total amount of square footage commanded by property within a geographical area.

Total Lender Fees Charges that the lender requires for obtaining the loan, aside from other fees associated with the transfer of a property.

Total Loan Amount The basic amount of the loan plus any additional financed closing costs.

Total Monthly Housing Costs The amount that must be paid each month to cover principal, interest, property taxes, PMI, and/or either hazard insurance or homeowners' association dues.

Total of All Payments The total cost of the loan after figuring the sum of all monthly interest payments.

Total Principal Balance The sum of all debt, including the original loan amount adjusted for subsequent payments and any unpaid items that may be included in the principal balance by the mortgage note or by law.

Total Retail Area The total floor area of a retail center that is currently leased or available for lease.

Total Return The final amount of income and appreciation returns per quarter.

Townhouse An attached home that is not considered to be a condominium.

Trade Fixtures Any personal property that is attached to a structure and used in the business but is removable once the lease is terminated.

Trading Down The act of purchasing a property that is less expensive than the one currently owned.

Trading Up The act of purchasing a property that is more expensive than the one currently owned.

Tranche A class of securities that may or may not be rated.

TransUnion Corporation One of the primary credit-reporting bureaus.

Transfer of Ownership Any process in which a property changes hands from one owner to another.

Transfer Tax An amount specified by state or local authorities when ownership in a piece of property changes hands.

Treasury Index A measurement that is used to derive interest rate changes for ARMs.

Triple Net Lease A lease that requires the tenant to pay all property expenses on top of the rental payments.

Trustee A fiduciary who oversees property or funds on behalf of another party.

Truth-in-Lending The federal legislation requiring lenders to fully disclose the terms and conditions of a mortgage in writing.

TurnKey Project A project in which all components are within a single supplier's responsibility.

Two- to Four-Family Property A structure that provides living space for two to four families while ownership is held in a single deed.

Two-Step Mortgage An ARM with two different interest rates: one for the loan's first five or seven years and another for the remainder of the loan term.

Under Construction The time period that exists after a building's construction has started but before a certificate of occupancy has been presented.

Under Contract The period of time during which a buyer's offer to purchase a property has been accepted, and the buyer is able to finalize financing arrangements without the concern of the seller making a deal with another buyer.

Underwriter A company, usually an investment banking firm, that is involved in a guarantee that an entire issue of stocks or bonds will be purchased.

Underwriters' Knot An approved knot according to code that may be tied at the end of an electrical cord to prevent the wires from being pulled away from their connection to each other or to electrical terminals.

Underwriting The process during which lenders analyze the risks a particular borrower presents and set appropriate conditions for the loan.

Underwriting Fee A fee that mortgage lenders charge for verifying the information on the loan application and making a final decision on approving the loan.

Unencumbered A term that refers to property free of liens or other encumbrances.

Unimproved Land See: Raw Land.

Unrated Classes Usually the lowest classes of securities.

Unrecorded Deed A deed that transfers right of ownership from one owner to another without being officially documented.

Umbrella Partnership Real Estate Investment Trust (UPREIT) An organizational structure in which a REIT's assets are owned by a holding company for tax reasons.

Usable Square Footage The total area that is included within the exterior walls of the tenant's space.

Use The particular purpose for which a property is intended to be employed.

VA Loan A mortgage through the VA program in which a down payment is not necessarily required.

Vacancy Factor The percentage of gross revenue that pro-forma income statements expect to be lost due to vacancies.

Vacancy Rate The percentage of space that is available to rent.

Vacant Space Existing rental space that is presently being marketed for lease minus space that is available for sublease.

Value-Added A phrase advisers and managers generally use to describe investments in underperforming and/or under-managed assets.

Variable Rate Mortgage (VRM) A loan in which the interest rate changes according to fluctuations in particular indexes.

Variable Rate Also called adjustable rate. The interest rate on a loan that varies over the term of the loan according to a predetermined index.

Variance A permission that enables a property owner to work around a zoning ordinance's literal requirements which cause a unique hardship due to special circumstances.

Verification of Deposit (VOD) The confirmation statement a borrower's bank may be asked to sign in order to verify the borrower's account balances and history.

Verification of Employment (VOE) The confirmation statement a borrower's employer may be asked to sign in order to verify the borrower's position and salary.

Vested Having the right to draw on a portion or on all of a pension or other retirement fund.

Veterans Affairs (VA) A federal government agency that assists veterans in purchasing a home without a down payment.

Virtual Storefront A retail business presence on the Internet.

Waiting Period The period of time between initially filing a registration statement and the date it becomes effective.

Warehouse Fee A closing cost fee that represents the lender's expense of temporarily holding a borrower's loan before it is sold on the secondary mortgage market.

Weighted-Average Coupon The average, using the balance of each mortgage as the weighting factor, of the gross interest rates of the mortgages underlying a pool as of the date of issue.

Weighted-Average Equity The part of the equation that is used to calculate investment-level income, appreciation, and total returns on a quarter-by-quarter basis.

Weighted-Average Rental Rates The average ratio of unequal rental rates across two or more buildings in a market.

Working Drawings The detailed blueprints for a construction project that comprise the contractual documents which describe the exact manner in which a project is to be built.

Workout The strategy in which a borrower negotiates with a lender to attempt to restructure the borrower's debt rather than go through the foreclosure proceedings.

Wraparound Mortgage A loan obtained by a buyer to use for the remaining balance on the seller's first mortgage, as well as an additional amount requested by the seller.

Write-Down A procedure used in accounting when an asset's book value is adjusted downward to reflect current market value more accurately.

Write-Off A procedure used in accounting when an asset is determined to be uncollectible and is therefore considered to be a loss.

Yield Maintenance Premium A penalty the borrower must pay in order to make investors whole in the event of early repayment of principal.

Yield Spread The difference in income derived from a commercial mortgage and from a benchmark value.

Yield The actual return on an

investment, usually paid in dividends or interest.

Zoning Ordinance The regulations and laws that control the use or improvement of land in a particular area or zone.

Zoning The act of dividing a city or town into particular areas and applying laws and regulations regarding the architectural design, structure, and intended uses of buildings within those areas.

Index

About the Author

J amaine is a freelance writer who spent more than 16 years as an Operations Research Systems Analyst for the U.S. Army. Her research skills, combined with knowledge acquired from a good friend who personally acquired, held, and managed more than 80 properties at any given time, were used to research and document the material presented in this book.